eBay®

YOUR
business

MAXIMIZE PROFITS
AND GET RESULTS

Janelle Elms,

Michael Bellomo,

Joel Elad

McGraw-Hill/Osborne

New York   Chicago   San Francisco   Lisbon
London   Madrid   Mexico City   Milan   New Delhi
San Juan   Seoul   Singapore   Sydney   Toronto

The *McGraw·Hill* Companies

McGraw-Hill/Osborne
2100 Powell Street, 10th Floor
Emeryville, California 94608
U.S.A.

To arrange bulk purchase discounts for sales promotions, premiums, or fund-raisers, please contact
McGraw-Hill/Osborne at the above address. For information on translations or book distributors
outside the U.S.A., please see the International Contact Information page immediately following
the index of this book.

eBay® Your Business: Maximize Profits and Get Results

1234567890 CUS CUS 01987654

ISBN 0-07-225711-3

Vice President & Group Publisher	Philip Ruppel
Vice President & Publisher	Jeffrey Krames
Acquisitions Editor	Marjorie McAneny
Project Editors	Lisa Theobald, Madhu Prasher
Acquisitions Coordinator	Agatha Kim
Copy Editor	Lisa Theobald
Proofreader	Paul Tyler
Indexer	Claire Splan
Computer Designer	International Typesetting & Composition
Illustrator	International Typesetting & Composition
Cover Design	Pattie Lee

This book was composed with Corel VENTURA™ Publisher.

Dedication

To my biggest cheerleader
Who is now an angel.
Thank you, Dad.

And Ed.

—Janelle

This book is dedicated to my friends Philip M. Wislar, Scott Craycraft, Tracy Buzcek, Robert Runnells, and Stephen Jordan. I especially want to thank my fellow connoisseur of the online auction, Joel Elad. Together, we've written a fine book.

—Michael

My thanks go out to my friends Anthony Choi, Eric Thompson, Phil Smith, Roger Mincheff, and Tom Chelle, who asked for help with eBay and constantly challenged me to stay current with the site. I would like to thank my mother for the gift of life and the inspiration to press on and keep dreaming. I especially want to thank Michael Bellomo for his motivation, organizational skills, and wacky sense of humor to help create the book we were born to write.

—Joel

About the Authors

Janelle Elms is a lead instructor touring nationwide with eBay University. A Silver PowerSeller on eBay (http://www.stores.ebay.com/AuctionProfitEducationConsulting), Janelle has recently wrapped production on a new training video for eBay called *Beyond the Basics*. Janelle's work with eBay has extended to teaching pilot training programs, including a leading-edge program initiated by Senator Hillary Rodham Clinton and designed to help small towns understand how to sell globally instead of just to local communities. Creator of the exclusive eBay 101 and 102 classes taught throughout the United States, Janelle has helped numerous individuals build successful businesses on eBay. To date, she has trained more than 10,000 people in eBay sales, marketing, customer service, and customer retention strategies. Janelle specializes in corporate consulting designed to teach companies how to develop or maximize an eBay sales channel. She is the author of two other eBay how-to books (now in their fifth printing): *Don't Throw It Away Sell It On eBay! A beginner's guide to selling and buying on eBay,* and *No Seriously What Do You Really Do For A Living? How to run a part-time to full-time business successfully on eBay.* Janelle has also started several eBay community groups in the Pacific Northwest, including the eBay for Beginners and eBay PowerSellers groups in her hometown of Seattle. As a national and corporate speaker and educator, Janelle believes that the eBay opportunity is available for all who seek to become a part of this global community.

Michael Bellomo holds an MBA from the University of California, Irvine, with an emphasis in IT Management and Consulting. He has also received a Juris Doctor in Law from the University of California, Hastings College of the Law, in San Francisco. Prior to his most recent academic work, he spent six years of the dot-com boom days as a network manager and consultant serving with financial and e-commerce technology companies in Silicon Valley. During his MBA tenure, he worked with The Knowledge Labs, a technology-based "think tank" in Mission Viejo, California, that specializes in knowledge management using broadband video. Michael has written 10 books on technology, including *Linux Blueprints* and *Windows 2000 Administration For Dummies*. His latest book, *Itanium Rising,* is a business-technology book ghostwritten with Jim Carlson, the former VP of marketing at Hewlett Packard. His books have been published worldwide in languages as varied as Italian, Portuguese, French, Dutch, German, Russian, and Chinese.

Joel Elad holds an MBA from the University of California, Irvine, with an emphasis in Entrepreneurship and Information Technology. He also received a BS in Computer Science and Engineering from the University of California, Los Angeles. In 1996, Joel officially joined eBay as user ID elad@best.com. Since then, he has completed thousands of successful auctions, and has more than 1350 unique positive recommendations from fellow eBay users. He is a Bronze level PowerSeller, an eBay Trading Assistant, and an eBay Store owner. In late 1998, Joel started a company called NewComix.Com that focuses on selling new comic books over the Internet, which he integrates into his eBay sales. He participated in eBay's initial focus group in 1997 and continues to contribute to various studies and focus groups for different eBay divisions. Joel is an education specialist trained by eBay and has authored several workshops on eBay usage and small business startups for the University of California, Irvine, and other institutions.

Contents

Acknowledgments

Endless thank you's must first go out to Marjorie McAneny—our wonderfully patient, wise, and decisive editor, coach, and hand-holder; Agatha Kim, our amazingly organized scheduler; and Lisa Theobald, who magically turns the common word into a fabulous book. A very special thank you to Lisa Suttora, of WhatDoISell.com fame, for her endless wisdom, eBay expertise, and friendship; Mary and Ray Melton, very dear friends, who take such good care of Winston (my rabbit) while I am on tour with eBay; to my Mom, sisters Jamie and Jonie, brother Jason, and their families—without their support and cheerleading I could not be who I am today. And Ed, for everything, always. Personally, I want to thank the eBay community and their stories full of insight, excitement, and enthusiasm; I feel blessed to be able to offer the building blocks to take you wherever you want to go on eBay. You are truly an inspiration to me. From such humble beginnings, a single web site that has changed so many lives forever—thank you, Pierre, for that vision and to Meg for her awe-inspiring ride at the helm.

—Janelle Elms

I'd like to acknowledge Marjorie McAneny's vision, Agatha Kim's timely assistance, and Lisa Theobald's attention to every detail. And thank you Pierre Omidyar and Jeff Skoll for taking us on this wild ride!

—Michael Bellomo

I'd like to acknowledge the help and resources provided by Ben Hanna and Dan Neary of eBay; Professor Mary Gilly of the UC Irvine Graduate School of Management; and Agatha Kim, Margie McAneny, and Lisa Theobald of McGraw-Hill.

—Joel Elad

Introduction

Welcome to the world of eBay! Whether you're watching movies or TV shows that refer to it, talking with friends who have used it, or listening to financial reports that cover it, eBay has become a national and global phenomenon.

When eBay began, very few people thought that consumers would buy and sell directly with people they've never met; however, today eBay is a global marketplace that's built on the community of these buyers and sellers, changing lives and the rules of commerce. eBay has been such a success, in fact, that its effect has ranged from being an arousing curiosity to a new type of sales technology that is so advanced, it's actually changed the way we do business. eBay has become such an important part of the market economy that no business should ignore it or its trading platform. If you're looking at this book, you're probably wondering how your business can adapt and profit from the eBay marketplace.

The answer is simple: you bring the power, experience, and professionalism of the products your business provides, and adapt them to the schedules, preferences, and pricing of millions of eager buyers around the world. By tapping into the excitement of online auctions, you can create a new mechanism for selling your products, while channeling that marketplace to find ways to save your company money.

eBay Is for Everyone

One of the most common misconceptions about the eBay marketplace is that it's most helpful to consumers, not businesses. However, although eBay started as a person-to-person trading site and maintains a vital community of individual buyers and sellers, the primary aspect of eBay is the sale of a product, from a seller to a buyer. And if there's one thing your company should know how to do, it's how to sell products.

eBay's ability to supercharge a company's sales has been nothing short of startling. One case in point is Sun Microsystems, which sold $10 million of its servers via eBay in 2003. Another case is IBM, which started selling used and refurbished computers on eBay in December 2000. By 2002, IBM had become one of eBay's top 10 sellers in the world. eBay today is a service that moves $50,000 of merchandise every *hour*.

The wave of the future is definitely favoring those who are shopping and selling with eBay; following in Sun and IBM's footsteps is Silicon Graphics, who sells graphics workstations via eBay. And for the future? Recently, Disney has set up a co-branded site with eBay called disneyauctions.com, and Ford is considering using eBay to sell vintage automobiles such as its stock of original Model-Ts. Don't think you have to be a big computer company to catch this trend. Not only are blue-chip giants benefiting from the eBay phenomenon, but smaller businesses are also enjoying great success on eBay.

Consider that an established business brings a lot of advantages to eBay over individual sellers. Your business brings a defined set of merchandise, the business know-how to manage the sales of those products, a reputation for the products you create, and experience in managing and running a business. These are all important qualities necessary for creating successful and profitable transactions. The most important issue that faces eBay is the trust involved in a transaction. As an established company, you can provide that trust before your first item is posted for sale.

It's relatively easy to adapt the way you operate your business to utilize eBay effectively. You can accomplish this by learning the needs and expectations of the eBay buyer, studying the marketplace, choosing the appropriate goods and frequency of sales, and automating the back-end so you're not overwhelmed with manual procedures. With a little work up front, you'll be able to enhance any size business so it can handle the one-on-one marketing and sales nature of eBay with the care and finesse that any other eBay seller can bring to the table.

The first step is to research, discuss, and try out new methods and business opportunities. For example, if you've ever looked at a storeroom of functional surplus equipment and felt that it was worth more than scrap metal, eBay can help. If your supply costs are getting out of hand but you don't know where to turn, eBay can help. If you've got good products that have regional or seasonal qualities preventing a high margin sale locally, eBay can help.

If you're in the category of people ready to try something new within your company, take a deep breath. You've opened the right book.

About this Book

eBay Your Business is designed to be an informative, comprehensive guide and "how-to" reference to help lead you through all the steps any business should begin to take advantage of eBay and the benefits it can offer an established company. In this book, we don't just jump into the site and push you through the process. Lots of books out there will teach you how to register and place a bid on an item. But an established business doesn't survive without some planning, and that's the important first step we walk through at the beginning of the book. By planning your auction in advance, you will be organized and able to take advantage of golden opportunities as they arise.

Selling your company wares on eBay isn't the only way to profit. Every business needs supplies, equipment, personnel, and money; with eBay, by saving on the first three, you get more of the fourth—money! Tapping into the vast network of eBay sellers and buyers helps you beyond the traditional auction—it opens you up to an audience who may not be familiar with your goods, an audience who can find out about all your products and services, an audience with whom you can build that golden one-on-one relationship.

The topics you'll find in this book include the following:

■ Evaluating your business to find goods or services to sell on eBay

■ Lowering procurement costs through an eBay business

■ Integrating eBay into your sales and marketing strategies

■ Creating your eBay account

■ Creating and launching auctions on eBay

■ Establishing methods and processes to handle these auctions

■ Integrating eBay sales back into your business

■ Using eBay to grow your business

Walk through the book at least once, talk with members of your company, and above all check out the eBay web site. As you progress, you'll mark lots of pages to use as references. In the end, the more time spent planning, the easier this project should be on you and your company.

Who Should Read This Book

Of course, this book is for those who want to take advantage of eBay. Whether you're working in a company the size of IBM or your local dry cleaner, this book can benefit you. You don't need to have a presence on the Internet. However, you'll find that you get the most out of this book if you are one (or more) of the following:

■ Marketing and sales managers interested in expanding their online marketing efforts, increasing sales, improving ROI on secondary goods, and creating new opportunities

■ Operations managers responsible for inventory management, asset liquidation and salvage, and/or supplies procurement

■ Executive managers responsible for expanding sales, adding sales channels, increasing ROI, and finding new avenues for the company

The key is that you are in a position within your business to have access to the merchandise for sale, the authority to represent your company when you list that merchandise on eBay, and the connections to work with other departments to help you achieve this. Because a company can use eBay to accomplish many different goals, you may have separate teams and separate strategies working on different goals. As long as each team is aware of the other and can help the other, your business can move forward with a strong eBay presence.

Incidentally, if you find that you want to learn more about eBay for yourself or a small business outside work, check out another great book from McGraw-Hill/Osborne: *How to Do Everything with Your eBay Business* by Greg Holden.

How This Book Is Organized

This book will walk you through how to integrate an eBay strategy into the existing operations of your company. Maybe you've already used eBay for personal purchases or sales, a friend told you about it, and you picked up some long-lost toy from your childhood. Perhaps you've been in a meeting where management has prioritized the improvement of raising the salvage amount received for old equipment. Maybe you've already got an eBay account to auction off the company skybox seats to the next game. In any case, you're ready to move forward.

Careful planning can make the difference between a successful operation and unhappy customers and losses. We walk through the eBay site, give you a close look at what products fit this strategy the best, and help you think about how to preserve the important contacts while expanding your sales to a new avenue. After that, we'll walk through everything you need to know for setting up an auction, systemizing your auctions to fit with company policies, and making it all bigger and better.

You'll figure out how to harness the power of eBay to do great things for your business. You can start small or start big; just make sure you start right. *eBay Your Business* will be along for the ride as your helpful guide.

Part I: How Your Company Can Benefit from eBay

In Part I, you'll get a quick summary and breakdown of the options and categories available on eBay. You'll be asked to think about the different ways your company can take advantage of eBay. You'll examine the goods and equipment within your business and choose the best ones for this strategy. You'll use eBay and other methods to figure out potential prices for these goods, and you'll see if you can lower your supply costs through various eBay categories.

Then you'll look at how you currently do business and come up with a method to add eBay into that picture without rocking the boat. You'll choose target areas and zero-in on the opportunities with the best return for your particular situation.

Part II: Bring Your Business to eBay

In Part II, you'll move from planning to execution. In the beginning, you'll go through the necessary steps to get started, some of the different web pages you'll want to visit, and the accounts you'll need to create. You'll finalize initial plans with actual products, launch dates, and more details. You'll decide how you're going to support these new sales. (When your auctions start appearing on eBay, that's just the beginning!)

Once you've posted the first few auctions, you'll learn from that experience to refine your next set of auctions. You'll go through all the important after-sales steps necessary for an eBay sale, keeping in mind that these new eBay customers can become new business customers as well.

Part III: Integrate Your eBay Business into Your Infrastructure

In Part III, it's time to get serious. By now, you may have some auctions generating revenue for the company. You've got to fold these sales back into your company so this data will be treated equally and you won't spend an exorbitant amount of time trying to reconcile eBay sales come the end of a quarter or a tax audit.

You'll take a look at the most commonly affected parts of a business that need to be updated—mainly accounting, marketing, inventory management, and finance. You'll see an overview and detailed information on options that can assist your company. Depending on the complexity of your infrastructure, and the amount of eBay auctions the company will run, you'll need to take an extensive look at particular programs. But we'll point you in the right direction, so you can get the help you and your business will need.

Part IV: Grow Your eBay Business

In Part IV you add it all up and learn about the next step. You're presented with different advanced options for your company to experiment with regarding eBay sales. You'll learn how to open a storefront on eBay and learn all the steps needed to create and manage that store. You'll be introduced to powerful software programs that can ease the burden of auction management, and you'll share in ideas and opportunities that can affect the rest of your business.

Most importantly, you'll discover ways you can take advantage of your eBay product listings to assist in the promotion and branding of your current business—the hidden benefits, online exposure, and brand new avenues of doing business that eBay can provide. And to prove it can be done, you'll learn about the companies that have already enjoyed these benefits and see examples that may surprise you.

Appendixes

In the appendixes, you'll find a series of lists you can skim through to find useful nuggets of information. Appendix A provides a list of important web links you can use when you're supplementing your knowledge of eBay or are looking for someone to help. Appendix B offers a glossary of eBay terms that you can turn to when you're exploring the site. It also includes eBay-specific terms that you should find useful, especially if you're new to the eBay world.

Appendix C gives a full listing of the eBay Business categories available to you, as well as the full eBay site listing of the various categories created to sell products.

Conventions Used in This Book

What would an Internet-related book be without conventions? The conventions you'll find here are a shorthand form of conveying specific information. These are kept constant throughout the book, so you won't be spending valuable time flipping back and forth through the book or scratching your head figuring out which web page to go to, or what to type, click, or press.

Working with Your Web Browser

You'll be working mostly with your web browser to access the world of eBay—and many of you are using Microsoft Internet Explorer. This program comes with many functions designed to make your experience easier, such as the ability to bookmark sites and add toolbars to your browser window.

Throughout this book, we'll talk about specific web pages that are "home pages" for different eBay functions. Internet Explorer allows you to bookmark that page so you can come back to it later without typing a long, complicated address. Simply ask Internet Explorer to add it to favorites so it'll appear on your list of favorite sites.

eBay Success Stories and Did You Know? Sidebars

We'll call attention to success stories on eBay that we think you'll find inspiring, uplifting, or amusing in the eBay Success Stories sidebars. And if there's something that's useful in a business, or at least a business cocktail party sort of meeting, we'll put it in a Did You Know? sidebar.

Special Section Headings

This book is structured to convey the information you need in a way that is direct and simple, while remaining complete. This book is for the hands-on user who will go out and put the methods in here to the test. To call your attention to special bits of information that you'll find useful, we'll occasionally list the information under special headings.

The Note section will call your attention to a tidbit of information that you might not have known but could find useful to your eBay operation.

A Tip is an item of information that will usually save you time, allow you to complete an action with a minimum of sweat equity, or impress your boss.

A Caution provides you with a heads-up in case you're about to do something that could have negative consequences. Pay attention when you see this heading—it could save the day when you're about to act.

Where to Go from Here

Unless you have a burning issue—and we mean burning, as in smoke coming out of one of your business's servers—start by going to the eBay web site and clicking around. Look at how auctions are designed, and think about what things catch your attention as you're going through the thousands of auctions available.

Find the categories you'll be using and see if you can identify some trends. We'll go through the research methods and tricks to build the right auctions for your products, but the more familiar you are with the eBay environment, the less time you'll spend spinning your wheels, trying to figure out which way is up, and the more time you'll get to hone your strategy for success on eBay.

Ready? *Then step right up to the greatest marketplace on Earth!*

Part I

How Your Company Can Benefit from eBay

Chapter 1

Welcome to the World of eBay

In this chapter...

■ Learn the basics of the eBay marketplace

■ Study the history and background of eBay

■ Navigate an eBay site

■ Consider the types of auctions

■ Create Categories on eBay

Its multicolored, four-letter logo has swept through our culture in a few short years since its simple beginnings in 1995, and the eBay phenomenon has transformed itself into an Internet giant and household word. Today, eBay moves merchandise at a rate of almost $65,000 per minute. Any organization not utilizing eBay as part of its business and marketing plans is missing out on an incredible stream of available revenue, not to mention an untapped 125 million customer channel.

If you're reading this book, you probably already have a general idea of what eBay is and what it can do for businesses. eBay is a raging success and you can make the most of this by taking advantage of its benefits: it can offer your business a way to save vast amounts on the equipment you regularly buy and ramp up the level of your selling platform. The eBay web site's home page, at http://www.eBay.com, is shown in Figure 1-1.

You may also know of eBay as a place where the most eccentric collector can find that rare missing item for his collection. But eBay is now becoming the shopping destination for consumers for collectible and noncollectible items alike, such as consumer electronics, apparel, and jewelry. Millions of people are familiar with how eBay operates, and they have learned that everyday purchases can now be made on eBay. For many, eBay has changed their way of living by enabling them to operate full-time businesses from the comfort of their own home or expand their existing brick-and-mortar business. eBay reports that more than 430,000 people make a living selling items on eBay. One of the unexpected benefits of this trend is that full-time eBay sellers also buy many of their supplies and equipment they need off the site, which creates a bonus market for some suppliers. eBay's reach continues to grow at a pace that is nothing short of breathtaking.

In less than a decade, eBay has evolved from a simple web site to a cultural phenomenon. eBay now serves a worldwide community of more than 20 different country-specific web sites, and more sites are coming on board all the time, as shown in Figure 1-2. eBay offers a slice of the market that is actively growing; as eBay expands its services, firms such as PayPal, MasterCard, and Visa make electronic payment transactions easier and more secure, and broadband Internet continues to make inroads into suburban and rural America, encouraging more and more people to surf over to eBay before they go out the door to the local mall. If you can gain the business of those people as new or returning customers, you've outflanked your competition without spending an arm and a leg on advertising.

FIGURE 1-1   The eBay home page

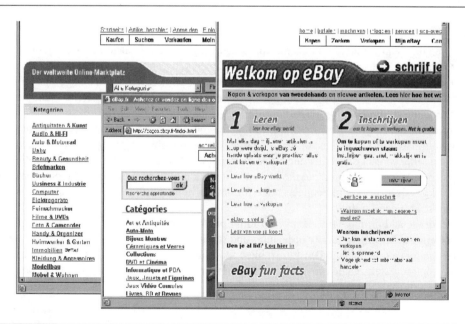

FIGURE 1-2   Examples of international eBay sites

Studies have shown that shoppers spend more using the eBay site than any other shopping destination on the Internet. For many people, eBay is the Number 1 place for buying and selling practically anything. In this chapter, we go through the basics of the eBay system and give you an idea of the types of items that are bought and sold every day.

Basics of the eBay Marketplace

It's easy to describe eBay as a giant flea market or swap meet, but that's not the full picture. Technically, eBay is a trading platform that allows buyers and sellers to negotiate and agree on a price for a given good or service. eBay never takes possession or verifies the product for sale, and unlike every retail store, it never asks you to pay to hold the goods in storage. eBay is focused on the marketplace, on creating a safe haven, where sellers "set up shop" and describe and post their items for sale, and where buyers can browse through an extensive selection, make offers, and purchase these items.

eBay relies on the basic honesty of people to honor their word and fulfill the deal between buyer and seller. Many systems are in place to encourage an honest marketplace, and eBay partners with other companies to help their sellers and buyers complete sales in a satisfactory manner. Whether it's connecting sellers with shipping companies, providing payment collection services, appraising sites, or providing insurance and fraud protection for buyers, eBay strives to enable a complete and safe shopping experience from its site.

It's that model of providing a platform for trading goods and letting the buyers and sellers negotiate the details that has allowed eBay to grow by leaps and bounds into the Number 1 global marketplace it is today.

Overview

On any given day, you'll find almost 30 million of items available for sale on eBay, organized into 50,000 categories (discussed a little later in this chapter) ranging from furniture to automobiles to consumer electronics. Over 125 million registered eBay users browse these categories, looking at the items for sale and making spending decisions about which products to purchase and how much money they are willing to spend.

Offers are made, and using either an auction-style bidding process or a fixed-price system, an item is sold based on the highest or desired price received. Unlike traditional sales methods, the buyer and seller contact each other directly to work out the details of completing the transaction, from payment method to shipping out the goods, without a middleman handling the payment and verifying the goods. eBay simply collects a fee for having items posted on its site and another fee if goods are sold successfully.

To encourage and promote the use of its trading platform, eBay facilitates the sale of these items by offering an extensive variety of features and services to make the sale safe and convenient. eBay offers sellers a complete and customizable opportunity to describe and portray the items they are selling accurately, while providing buyers with services such as escrow (for higher priced or valuable goods) and Buyer Protection.

Most important, beyond the commerce of eBay is a human element that cannot be overlooked—eBay's community. Figure 1-3 shows how eBay fosters a sense of community among its users, encouraging communication, dialogue, and learning through message boards, chat sessions, and online workshops. It's this sense of community that encourages eBay users to participate so actively in the sales process and become loyal to the company, ensuring a large and vibrant audience of consumers to whomever uses their trading platform properly to reach out and convert tens of millions of participants into paying repeat customers.

eBay History

The service we know as eBay was founded in 1995 by Pierre Omidyar, a software engineer living in the famed Silicon Valley of northern California. Omidyar mulled over the concept of an ideal trading environment and decided to create the software code that would allow for a "perfect marketplace," where buyers and sellers determine the market price for a given good.

Though Omidyar had been working on the idea for some time, the famous first eBay code was created over a Labor Day weekend. Considering what's happened since then, it was arguably a weekend very, very well spent. Omidyar posted the results on Labor Day 1995 and began advertising it quietly on free Internet user groups called Usenet. Slowly, users started finding the site and posting items they wanted to sell. Omidyar himself decided to sell a broken laser pointer he had, thinking maybe a tinkerer would want the spare parts for a buck. In the end, that broken laser pointer had a final bid of $14, and Omidyar began to realize what he had created.

FIGURE 1-3   Examples of eBay's community efforts

What's in a Name?

eBay was not Omidyar's first choice for a business name. He first called the service AuctionWeb and hosted it on his own web site that contained other freelance and personal interest web pages. His original site was called Echo Bay Technology Group, or ebay for short. This site contained information about the Ebola virus, a bio-tech startup, and more. When AuctionWeb took off, people were confused by the ebay name in the Internet web address, and the company promoted AuctionWeb to be the only focus of ebay.com, renaming the service eBay.

He partnered with Jeff Skoll, a Stanford MBA graduate and friend, to get the business up and running. Before Skoll came on board, the auction site was a free service, since Omidyar was hosting it on his personal web site. However, as more costs were incurred due to the high traffic this site generated, Omidyar began to charge small fees for using the service. This did not deter the flood of new users as Omidyar has originally hypothesized it would, as envelopes filled with auction fee payments piled up. Omidyar and Skoll hired employees and looked for office space. They also began to think about a long-term strategy. Critical features, such as the Feedback Forum, were born and continue to drive eBay's success today.

As eBay became a success, Omidyar and Skoll sought out venture funding—not particularly for the cash, much of which stayed in the bank, but for the connections and resources a well-funded venture capital firm could bring. One important aspect was CEO recruitment. While eBay was managed in a relaxed, loose environment, a multi-million-dollar (and now multi-billion-dollar) company required procedures, methods, and seasoned management.

They hired Meg Whitman, a consumer marketing leader who enjoyed success while managing and redefining companies such as Stride Ride, FTD florists, and the Playskool division of Hasbro, among others. Whitman became convinced of eBay's potential and saw how she could bring her expertise in global marketing and her business acumen (honed at the Harvard Business School) to navigate this new company through the choppy waters of expansion and formalization, while preserving the core elements of eBay's success. Shortly thereafter, she signed up to be CEO. Together, Whitman and the new management team put together an IPO plan, and eBay became a publicly traded stock on the NASDAQ market in 1998. The stock rose by 168 percent in its first open day of trading, and over the years, it has provided a handsome return on investment. Whitman has used her skills to reassure everybody—from the investment banks to the passionate full-time sellers—that eBay can succeed as a global trading platform while retaining its charm and culture. She's had to deftly negotiate through eBay's more publicized problems—from computer outages to policy changes to earnings projections—while keeping the day-to-day transactions running as seamlessly as possible.

eBay has grown to more than 5200 employees (and counting), and the company occupies a campus of office buildings in its original location in San Jose, California. Just as important as the employees are the users of eBay, who come in regularly each quarter to share opinions, test new functions, and provide input for short- and long-term direction.

Statistics

One of the most important distinctions of eBay is that it was profitable from the very first month, a virtual rarity in the Internet world. In 2003, eBay generated $2.17 billion in consolidated net revenues, a 78 percent increase over its 2002 revenue of $1.21 billion. It also hosted more than 970 million listings on its site in 2003, representing a 52 percent growth from 2002's numbers. If you take the gross merchandise sales (GMS) of all the successful eBay auctions in 2003, it would add up to $24 billion, 60 percent higher than in 2002. That's $2.8 million worth of goods sold per hour, or $761 of items sold per second!

eBay enjoys a growing membership that, at last count, surpassed 125 million users. Of that group, 51.7 million are active bidders and sellers. Hundreds of millions of "page views," or unique web pages, are generated from eBay's web site, and the average person will spend tens of minutes on a given eBay visit, one of the highest amounts for any Internet web site.

eBay has more than 29 million items listed at any given time. 3.6 million new listings are put up each and every day, which eBay organizes into one of 30-plus main categories. Figure 1-4 shows an example of the category layout. (See Appendix C for more categories.)

eBay's strong community is apparent in its wide variety of support resources. Users looking for help can consult one of eBay's 24 community help boards, 37 category-specific boards, or one of the dozen or so general discussion boards, as shown in Figure 1-5. Millions of users participate in these forums, sharing advice with fellow users, connecting over a similar hobby, or answering questions for new users.

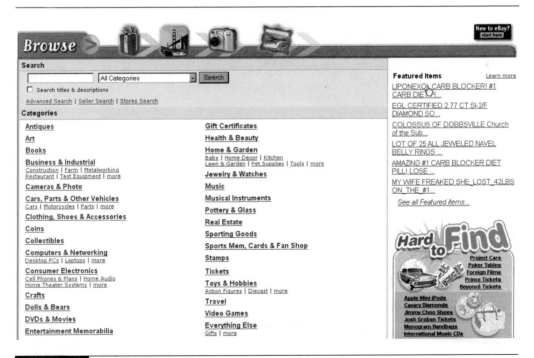

FIGURE 1-4   Browse through eBay's many categories

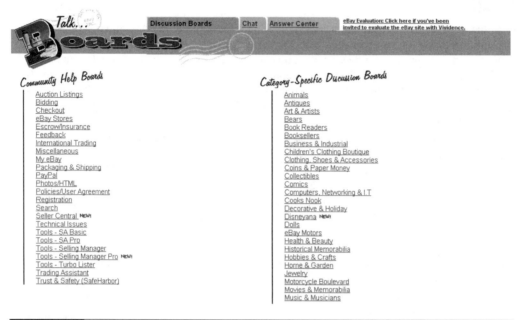

Community Help Boards

Auction Listings
Bidding
Checkout
eBay Stores
Escrow/Insurance
Feedback
International Trading
Miscellaneous
My eBay
Packaging & Shipping
PayPal
Photos/HTML
Policies/User Agreement
Registration
Search
Seller Central NEW!
Technical Issues
Tools - SA Basic
Tools - SA Pro
Tools - Selling Manager
Tools - Selling Manager Pro NEW!
Tools - Turbo Lister
Trading Assistant
Trust & Safety (SafeHarbor)

Category-Specific Discussion Boards

Animals
Antiques
Art & Artists
Bears
Book Readers
Booksellers
Business & Industrial
Children's Clothing Boutique
Clothing, Shoes & Accessories
Coins & Paper Money
Collectibles
Comics
Computers, Networking & I.T
Cooks Nook
Decorative & Holiday
Disneyana NEW!
Dolls
eBay Motors
Health & Beauty
Historical Memorabilia
Hobbies & Crafts
Home & Garden
Jewelry
Motorcycle Boulevard
Movies & Memorabilia
Music & Musicians

FIGURE 1-5   Help is but a click away

According to a recent eBay press release, small businesses purchased $2 billion in GMS of equipment and supplies on eBay, compared with $1 billion in 2002. The activity has grown to the point that in January 2003, eBay created a special portal site, http://www.ebaybusiness.com, to promote and aggregate most of the main business-specific categories for easier navigation and procurement purposes.

Site Navigation

eBay organized its web site to allow users to get to the important functions quickly while maintaining some consistency as the company updated its look. To this end, it provides two main areas to access vital subfunctions within the site. For our purposes, we'll call them the *text navigation bar* and the *button navigation bar,* since the first set of links is only in text, and the second set looks like a row of buttons.

These navigation bars are at the top of every single page within the eBay site. Whether you're looking at an individual auction page or using a seller function, you will find these links and shortcuts at the top of the page, ready to guide you when needed.

Text Navigation Bar

The text navigation bar gives you shortcuts to essential eBay functions that are primarily meant for day-to-day use.

Home   This link will take you back to the eBay home page. If you ever get lost while learning more about a given area, this link will always appear at the top of the page to "take you home" so you can continue with anything else you might be researching.

Pay   To give the eBay buyer an easy, convenient, one-stop screen to pay for purchases, like most e-commerce shopping carts, eBay created the Pay area, where all the buyer's completed auctions are available from one list. The user can arrange payment for purchases and find out answers to commonly asked questions about how to complete purchases.

Register   This option takes the user to the beginning of eBay's registration process. From here, anybody can sign up for free to bid on items on eBay. In addition, by providing payment and other information, that same user can sell items on eBay; fees are charged only for products they put up for sale on eBay.

Sign In   This link helps users keep track of whether or not they are signed into the eBay service (the link toggles between Sign In and Sign Out). The information that appears to users who are signed in differs from that shown to users who are not signed in. For example, if a user is signed in and looks at an auction which he or she won, the window will show pertinent information intended for that user. If the user is not signed in, that page will display other information. Because some computers are accessed by multiple people, or because some people access different accounts for work and personal use, a user can sign out of one ID and log in again with another ID, and using the Sign Out/Sign In link will help. This is a handy feature to use if you're concerned about the security of your account.

NOTE   *After you've signed in, never walk away from your computer unless you've clicked Sign Out to prevent unauthorized use of your eBay account.*

Services   eBay provides a lot of buyer and seller services to help users get through the auction process from start to finish. This link will take you to the main page for those services, so as buyers and sellers you can find the tools you need quickly.

Site Map   eBay provides a lot of functionality; sometimes, if you need a specific function, it's not readily available on the home page or some of the subcategory pages. If you know what you're looking for but can't find it, or if you want to see everything that eBay provides, click this link to see a long list of functions, all with hyperlinks to their specific web pages, grouped by main functions, such as Browse, Services, and Community.

Button Bar

The button bar contains the five main areas that buyers and sellers use as they create, maintain, and peruse their auction listings. These are the critical functions to know as your eBay experience expands and you become more comfortable with the site.

Buy   When you're ready to start shopping on eBay, clicking this link will take you to a Browse page with a text box to enter search words, a list of categories on eBay, and featured links and targeted advertising as you search for your favorite items. This page also features other ways to find things, such as searching by a particular theme (such as "office supplies"), or searching a particular region, which is a good idea if you want to buy heavy items and not have to pay exorbitant shipping costs.

Sell   This button takes you to eBay's main Sell Your Item form. Using this function will allow you to create auctions to be posted on the eBay web site. While many tools can assist you in posting items for sale, we'll be going through eBay's main selling functionality in Part II of the book, so you can have a better idea of all the necessary elements that go into building an ideal and profitable auction listing.

My eBay   This button takes you to the "hub" of your eBay activities. This collection of web pages, marked with tabs, will show you all the eBay activity, both buying and selling, going on with your eBay account. In addition, you can manage your feedback record, check on your account status, and set preferences for easier navigation of the site and easier tracking of your favorite auctions. This feature is discussed in detail in Chapter 10.

Community   Clicking this button takes you to the home page for all of eBay's community-building efforts. Everything from message boards, to online tutorials on eBay functionality, to the latest news and announcements can be accessed from the Community home page. It's a great place to go to find answers to questions as your eBay experience develops, and it's vital in helping you and your company understand the types of customers you'll be attracting to your eBay auctions. Fact-filled newsletters and special events are announced through this gateway, so it's something you should visit often while building your company's web strategy.

Help   This link takes you to eBay's main help page, where you can search for answers, see commonly asked questions and their responses, and learn how to contact customer support.

Types of Auctions

eBay offers a variety of online auction types that go way beyond the typical auction that comes to mind for most of us—such as an art dealer auction like Sotheby's or an auction of an estate.

Proxy Bidding Auction

In this most typical type of auction platform provided by eBay, a seller will determine the particular item's starting price. The first buyer can place a bid for the highest amount of money he or she is willing to spend for that item. Since no other bidders are on the scene yet, eBay will simply start the auction with the established starting price and say the first bidder is the highest bidder at that starting price. When another bidder enters the scene, eBay remembers the first person's high bid and will "proxy" bid for that user by going up in increments until the high bid is reached.

For example, let's say someone listed a clock with a starting price at $100. The first bidder, user A, bids $300 for the clock. eBay will set the High Bid Price at $100 and wait for more bidders. User B sees that the High Bid Price is still $100, with only one bidder, and he bids $200 for the clock. eBay will let bidders increment their offers by a fixed amount until one bidder remains. In a sense, once user B enters his $200 bid, eBay will respond like so: User B bids $120, user A bids $140, user B bids $160, user A bids $180, user B bids $200, user A bids $220. (In actuality, eBay's bidding increment for a $100 item is $2.50, but we used $20 for illustration purposes.) At this point, user B doesn't want to go higher, and the high price is set at $220. This way, user A can place his or her high bid without automatically having to pay that amount, and without worrying about having to come back later to bid on the item (unless he or she gets outbid). eBay doesn't automatically leap to user A's highest bid at the start. It goes through the back-and-forth process of bidding with all bidders, so the high bidder pays only as much as necessary to win the auction.

Dutch Auction

A Dutch auction, or *multiple item auction* according to eBay, is similar to a proxy bidding auction, except that this auction involves auctioning off multiple items in one listing. For example, let's say you have five copies of the same CD you want to sell, and you start the bidding at $10 each. A total of seven bidders put in high bids of $20, $15, $14, $13, $12, $11, and $10.01 for each CD. The highest five bidders will each win a CD, but each bidder will pay only the amount of the lowest winning bidder. In this case, all five high bidders people will pay only $12 for the CD (after the $11 and $10.01 bids are thrown out), regardless of the amount the highest bidder actually stated.

Reserve Auction

A reserve auction is similar to a regular auction with one key difference: the seller can set a starting price and add a second price, known as the *reserve* price. The auction must reach the level of the reserve price for the seller to be obligated to sell it. In other words, if you start an auction for a UNIX computer server at $1, but set a reserve price of $2500, the bidding must reach $2500 or the seller doesn't have to honor the high bid. eBay denotes whether the reserve is met by the words "Reserve met" or "Reserve not met" beside the high bidder price.

NOTE   *eBay charges an extra fee for using the reserve auction. However, if your auction successfully reaches or beats the reserve price, that fee is refunded to you.*

Fixed-Price Listing

A fixed-price listing is similar to a typical e-commerce sale and has very little to do with the actual auction process. In this type of listing, the seller sets a fixed price when the product is listed for sale. The first buyer who comes along and is willing to pay the fixed price will essentially buy the item and the sale closes, preventing other bidders from participating (unless, of course, you're selling multiple items, in which case, the quantity available is simply decreased by the amount the buyer wants to take). This selling format was added to encourage more quick sales, without the need to wait for an auction to close or the worry new users might have by bidding and outbidding other potential buyers to purchase the item. This format has helped encourage millions of new, easy transactions that continue to cement eBay as the Number 1 destination on the Internet when it's time to buy. You can bid and haggle or buy direct; eBay makes it that simple.

Business Categories Available on eBay

eBay is organized by category according to the item for sale. As eBay has grown in popularity, so has the number of dedicated categories used for various items—everything from animation art to the totally bizarre has its own category.

The eBay Business Marketplace (http://www.ebaybusiness.com), shown in Figure 1-6, is actually a subsection of the entire eBay offering.

eBay has picked the most common categories that benefit businesses and organized its subset of listings into four main areas: Industry Marketplaces, Office Technology, Wholesale Lots, and Other. Specifically, this collection includes the following subcategories:

FIGURE 1-6   The home page for the eBay Business Marketplace

Industry Marketplaces

Agriculture	Construction
Electronic components	Medical equipment
Industrial supplies	Laboratory & life science
Metalworking	Plastics equipment
Printing & graphic arts	Process equipment
Restaurant equipment	Retail equipment
Semiconductor manufacturing	Test equipment
Textile, apparel manufacturing	Woodworking equipment
Other industries	Forestry
Government & public safety	Mining
Oil & gas	Power & utilities
Specialty manufacturing	

Office Technology

Apple, Macintosh	Cell phones & plans
Computer monitors	Desktop PCs
Laptops, notebooks	Dell
HP, Compaq	IBM
Laptop accessories	Networking & telecom
Home networking	Phone systems, telecom
Routers	Servers
Wireless networking, wifi	Office products
Copiers & supplies	Office furniture
Office supplies	PDAs
Printers & accessories	Projectors
Software	

Wholesale Lots

All wholesale lots	Books
Clothing, shoes & accessories	Computers
Consumer electronics	Health and beauty supplies
Home	Jewelry & watches
Movies & entertainment	Sporting goods
Tools	Toys & hobbies

Other

Businesses for sale	eBay motors—commercial trucks
eBay motors—parts, car & truck	eBay motors—parts, motorcycle
Home improvement—tools	Pro audio equipment
Pro photography	Pro video equipment
Professional services	

Entire eBay Site of Categories

Your eBay experience shouldn't be limited to the Business Marketplace section of the eBay site. Based on the type of business you run and your access to different inventory—especially the unusual, one-of-a-kind, or experience-related inventory you could offer—your auctions could span multiple main categories.

Whether you're selling your company cars on eBay Motors, company-sponsored event tickets on the Tickets category, or excess uniforms on the Apparel category, eBay has a category for your business. If you explore Appendix C, you can see the maze of subcategories that eBay has to offer.

Summary

eBay is a trading platform that allows people to negotiate and agree on a price for a given good or service. eBay never takes possession or verifies the product for sale, and unlike at a retail store, you never pay to hold the good in storage. eBay focuses on the marketplace, on creating a safe haven where sellers come in to set up shop and describe and post items for sale and buyers can browse through an extensive selection, make offers, and buy these items. To do this, eBay relies on the basic honesty of people to honor their word and fulfill the deals between buyer and seller. eBay strives to enable a satisfying experience from its site.

In addition, eBay complements the sale of these items by offering an extensive variety of features and services to make the sale a safe and convenient one. It offers the seller a complete and customizable opportunity to describe and portray the item for sale, while providing the buyer with services such as escrow (for higher priced or valuable goods) and Buyer Protection.

The eBay Business Marketplace is a subsection of the entire eBay offering. eBay has chosen common categories to accommodate businesses' purchases and sales.

In Chapter 2, we'll talk about the types of products that your company can sell on eBay and help you figure out some hidden gems that can increase your revenue and explode your profits.

Chapter 2

Evaluating Your Business's Sales Potential

In this chapter...

- ■ Determine which of your company's products are the most suited for eBay
- ■ Identify potential goods, both obvious and non-obvious
- ■ Consider practicalities of shipping eBay items
- ■ Evaluate which divisions of your company will assist in the eBay strategy

Now that you've taken a look at the basics of eBay and what it has to offer, it's time to look to your company to see what it has to offer. Too often, sellers quickly toss up auctions for a pile of junked equipment and stop there, without considering what steps can be taken to make the auction a success. In this chapter, you'll learn how to take a complete look at the potential your company can realize by using eBay, even before listing your first auction.

Determine Products Most Suited for eBay

Deciding what articles to sell on eBay does require some serious thought. eBay presents a brand-new sales channel for your company with a huge and diverse customer base, and each potential customer has developed a particular set of characteristics regarding how and what he or she purchases online. In some cases, eBay buyers can be more exacting about what they want than a "normal" business customer.

Before you start brainstorming about what items your company might sell on eBay, you need to consider what kinds of eBay customers make up your base.

Profile of an eBay Buyer

While a business customer may be accustomed to lengthy shipping periods, such as four to six weeks, between order and delivery of their purchase, many eBay customers will inquire about the status of a shipment only minutes after the payment is sent. Customers may also ask many questions about the product before bidding. While you may be unaccustomed to answering such questions before closing a sale (chances are your main sales accounts have been working with you for some time and already know your products well), doing so helps to assure new eBay buyers that you are a responsible and responsive seller. Knowing that an eBay seller is helpful and responsive factors into most buyers' decisions on whether or not to bid for items. Most customers need to be assured of the level of customer service you as a seller would bring to the transaction. A quick and informative reply implies that you are professional, courteous, and will probably work after the sale to solve any problems that might occur. If the buyer's questions are ignored, that can imply that you won't provide a high level of service after the sale, which can discourage the buyer from investing time and money with your company.

Although eBay users may require more customer service than you might be accustomed to (given that eBay sales are direct to consumer), keep in mind that eBay buyers can bring some excellent cash-flow benefits to your company. For example, with your regular, non-eBay business customers, you may have to extend a temporary line of credit when they purchase from you, meaning that your company won't get paid for the goods until 7, 30, or 60 days after your customer has received the goods. To accommodate this, in your regular business you probably have to track accounts receivable pretty closely.

With eBay buyers, you get paid *before* the items ship, which means you should never have to worry about unpaid sales and you get your cash much more quickly to reinvest. eBay buyers usually understand without question that they pay up front before the item is shipped, they pay for shipping and sales tax (when applicable), and they decide whether to add special features such as insurance to a shipment. Because eBay transactions might be lower volume sales than those of a big distributor, for example, you don't have to offer as many perks in terms of discounts or credits to make the sale.

Throughout Part II of this book, as you construct auction listings for your company, we'll discuss other details about eBay buyers' behaviors that you can use to maximize your target audience and improve sales.

Identify Obvious and Non-obvious Goods

It's time to give some serious thought to what your company has to offer—both the regular products that your company manufactures, distributes, or retails and some other goods that might not be so obvious. The power of eBay means you have many more sales options than just your company's regular products. Ask yourself (and others in the company) the following questions to help determine some potential eBay sale opportunities:

- Do you have refurbished, returned, or recyclable items that you are not allowed to sell through your normal sales channels?

- Do you have an excess quantity of a supply that is rare or valuable on the market, and can you liquidate that inventory?

- Do you have any new product lines that are enjoying a demand that normal sales channels can't keep up with, perhaps due to long distribution times in the supply chain?

- Would you like to test out new products without having to buy up retail shelf space or train an entire sales force?

- Is inventory, such as off-season inventory, not moving through normal sales channels?

- Are you downsizing or disposing of goods that are functional, salable, or of potential interest to a buyer?

- If you've finished an equipment upgrade of some kind, is the older equipment still functional or operational?

- Are you upgrading and disposing of obsolete equipment that is functional, salable, or of interest to some buyer?

- Are you aware of any items—such as gifts, an overage of supplies, or a discovery of boxes of products in a storage closet—that are not being used in your daily business routine and might be of interest to a buyer?

IBM's Successful Adoption of eBay as a Sales Channel

"eBay is well-known as one of the really successful Internet companies," says Giga Information Group Vice President Mike Gilpin. "In PR terms, it's very desirable in these times of worldwide doubt about the value of e-business to just remind people that there really are some successful e-businesses out there."

Starting back in 2001, IBM began to use eBay's web site in what Gilpin calls "a key sales channel for reaching targeted buyers." The two companies began to work together on joint marketing programs both online and off. The result has been an unqualified success. According to Global Auction Sales Manager Billy Sturtevant, "Many of our eBay customers have never before owned IBM products, but they like the experience…. A high percentage of customers return to buy again."

Refurbished, Returned, Recyclable Items

Refurbished, returned, and recyclable items are perhaps the most popular items that businesses can list on eBay. Many of us work in companies that have merchandise that can't be placed back on retail shelves, such as returned merchandise, refurbished equipment, or used products that can't be sold as new—consider the scooters shown in Figure 2-1.

Your company may have recyclable items that still hold some value and shouldn't be discarded. These items are perfect for eBay, as "one person's trash is another person's treasure." Whether functional or not, refurbished and returned goods often hold value for someone, and the eBay system allows worldwide buyers to offer a bid price for their perceived value of your products.

TIP *Make sure that you note everything you know about a product's condition in the auction description, so you set your buyer's expectation prior to receiving the item.*

Inventory Liquidation

Before eBay, liquidating old equipment meant calling up a wholesale liquidator, who would show up at your business with a semi truck, fill it up with all the goods you couldn't sell anymore, and give you pennies on the dollar—on average from 5 to 15 percent of the fair market value. A liquidator can't afford to pay a lot for your old stuff—after all, the company has to come to you and haul off the equipment (a big bonus for you when the equipment is heavy or has to be discarded properly), and it has to turn around and sell the stuff to make a living.

With eBay, you can avoid the middleman and move some of this merchandise yourself, and a little effort on your end can mean higher monetary returns in the long run. By posting an eBay auction for old equipment, you can let surplus liquidators, resellers, and any other interested parties compete for your goods. Depending on the product, a bidding war could ensue and drive

FIGURE 2-1   Returned merchandise for sale on eBay

up the price beyond what you were expecting. Most of the time, the eBay auction competition should drive up the price beyond what you would receive from traditional liquidators, and because the buyer pays shipping or makes the shipping arrangements, you are saved from that additional burden.

For example, suppose that you recently had to shut down or move a division in your company and you're left with a number of PC desktop systems that you've paid for but cannot use anywhere else in the company. Instead of getting 10 cents on the dollar for the equipment, you can use eBay to find people who need these functioning computers and will pay anywhere from 40 to 50 percent of the current value, depending on how you position the computers on eBay.

If you do the math, you can see the positive returns from the sale of one type of item alone. Do it over and over again, with everything from Aeron chairs (like the one in Figure 2-2) to cubicle partitions to metal-cutting equipment, and the effort should be rewarding.

New Product Lines

The trading behavior in collectibles tells us that people like to buy unique items—one-of-a-kind items or those with limited availability—that let them "own a piece of history." Many companies, from toy makers to car makers, create prototypes or models of their products and usually do nothing with these models once the finished product goes to market. These valuable items can be used in eBay promotional campaigns to help sell the product and add some cash to the bottom line.

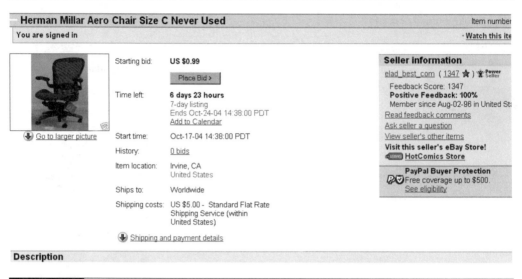

Herman Millar Aero Chair Size C Never Used   Item number

You are signed in   · Watch this ite

Starting bid:	**US $0.99**	
	Place Bid >	
Time left:	**6 days 23 hours**	
	7-day listing	
	Ends Oct-24-04 14:38:00 PDT	
	Add to Calendar	
Start time:	Oct-17-04 14:38:00 PDT	
History:	0 bids	
Item location:	Irvine, CA	
	United States	
Ships to:	Worldwide	
Shipping costs:	US $5.00 - Standard Flat Rate	
	Shipping Service (within	
	United States)	

Go to larger picture

Shipping and payment details

Seller information

elad_best_com (1347 ★) Power Seller

Feedback Score: 1347
Positive Feedback: 100%
Member since Aug-02-96 in United St

Read feedback comments
Ask seller a question
View seller's other items
Visit this seller's eBay Store!
HotComics Store

PayPal Buyer Protection
Free coverage up to $500.
See eligibility

Description

FIGURE 2-2   An Aeron chair, part of an inventory being liquidated on eBay

By working with your company's marketing department, you can create an eBay auction (or a series of auctions) timed around the release of a product. For example, if you're in the entertainment business, you could auction off the rare special effects model prototypes and behind-the-scenes documentation (production film scripts for a film that's about to be released and signed by the show stars, for example) to the public to remind them of the imminent product launch and allow them to be a part of the action. We will discuss more specifics of this technique in Part III of the book.

Slow-Moving/Off-Season Sales

Consider the "after Christmas" or "after inventory" sales at department stores. Retail stores need to get rid of extra inventory if it didn't sell at Christmas time and they need to make space for incoming inventory. You can use eBay as a channel to help you offer great deals to customers on seasonal merchandise. Seasonal merchandise, like the clothes shown in Figure 2-3, could sell even in the off-season, because even though it may be cold for some of us in January, shorts and t-shirts are appealing to the half of the globe enjoying summer weather—plus, if the prices are good, buyers don't mind stocking up on clothes for *next* summer.

In addition, if you're a regional business and you've saturated your market with a particular product, you can sell it on eBay and expand your reach to new regions. If the product appealed to buyers in your immediate region, it may appeal to those in other geographic regions as well. Because eBay reaches buyers worldwide, your market is virtually unlimited.

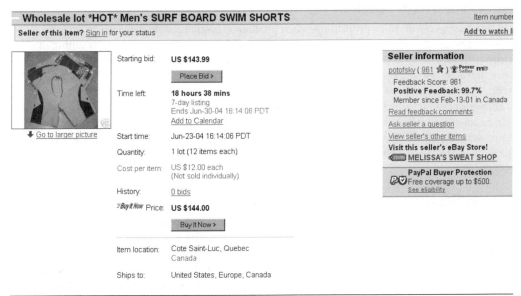

Wholesale lot *HOT* Men's SURF BOARD SWIM SHORTS — Item number
Seller of this item? Sign in for your status — Add to watch li

Starting bid:	**US $143.99**
	Place Bid >
Time left:	**18 hours 38 mins**
	7-day listing
	Ends Jun-30-04 16:14:06 PDT
	Add to Calendar
Start time:	Jun-23-04 16:14:06 PDT
Quantity:	1 lot (12 items each)
Cost per item:	US $12.00 each
	(Not sold individually)
History:	0 bids
Buy It Now Price:	**US $144.00**
	Buy It Now >
Item location:	Cote Saint-Luc, Quebec
	Canada
Ships to:	United States, Europe, Canada

Seller information
potofsky (961 ⭐) Power Seller me
Feedback Score: 961
Positive Feedback: 99.7%
Member since Feb-13-01 in Canada
Read feedback comments
Ask seller a question
View seller's other items
Visit this seller's eBay Store!
stores **MELISSA'S SWEAT SHOP**
PayPal Buyer Protection
Free coverage up to $500.
See eligibility

FIGURE 2-3 Off-season clothes can either sit in your storeroom in winter, or you can sell them on eBay to people in climates that differ from yours or to people who will wear them when the weather changes.

---

eBay Success Story

Sun Microsystems Uses eBay's Dynamic Pricing to Introduce Models

Starting in 2003, Sun has experimented with selling its newest products on eBay and has discovered that some customers are willing to pay a premium to get new products soon after general availability is announced. This lets Sun more accurately gauge the market's demand for products currently in development. More important, they receive customer input about the pricing and value of those systems.

"With pricing intelligence from our eBay efforts, we can provide timely adjustments to our global sales force. That allows them to be super competitive," said Jim Hill, director of dynamic pricing at Sun. "Over the course of about six months between January and June of 2003, we were able to sell about 40 Sun Enterprise 10000 systems and add something like $16 million to the bottom line over those two quarters. That was huge for Sun. With dynamic pricing, customers get great deals, and we're able to accomplish some key business objectives."

Downsizing Overproduction

Most companies rely on sales projections when producing goods for sale; because projections can be unrealized, a particular product may not sell as well as the company hoped, resulting in overproduction. The unsold material is not only unrealized profit, but it's costing the company money to warehouse it. Suppose you have a pallet or two of wigs that you just can't offload to anyone, as in the auction shown in Figure 2-4.

eBay allows you to auction these goods to buyers you currently do not have access to, who might be interested in buying a bundle of below-cost product. While you may have tapped out your personal business network when trying to solve these problems in the past, you can expand your network by using eBay to plug into a new international network of over 125 million registered users.

Obsolete Equipment/Computer Upgrading

The need to upgrade computers and/or mechanical equipment is a nightmare for every company executive and IT department head. With computers, it's especially maddening, as systems need to be upgraded every three years or so, and after the upgrade, perfectly functioning older computers may be of no use whatsoever in your company. With global competition, the declining prices for new systems, and the need for computer software that requires more resources, selectively upgrading pieces of your old system have now become almost as expensive—or sometimes more expensive—than a complete replacement of the system, and upgrades definitely add much more work and effort to the equation.

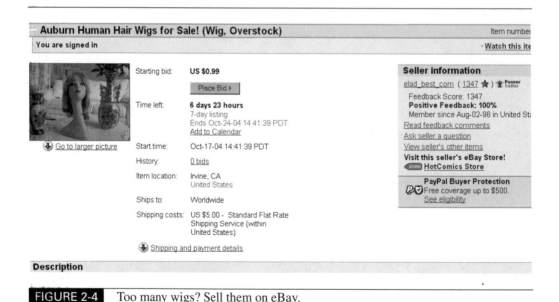

FIGURE 2-4   Too many wigs? Sell them on eBay.

However, using eBay, you can auction an entire network of computers to some eager entrepreneur who is starting up a new business, or you can sell computers individually or in smaller groups (Figure 2-5) to people or organizations who need a few computers that are newer than the systems they bought five or six years ago. The best part is that the sale of old equipment can help fund your company's upgrade and encourage the department to enjoy some extra benefits or add a few pieces of extra hardware without altering the company budget.

Unusual Items

Whether it's a vintage computer software documentation book on Windows 1.0, a full-scale prototype of a collectible your company produced, or sketches for clothing designs, many unusual items may be of interest to a buyer, and selling them on eBay could give your company a few more bucks in the bank.

Any historical or vintage items, prototypes, samples, signs, photographs, or other items could be considered collectibles today. If, for example, your company offered tie tacks for employees one year, it might become a collectible one day (Figure 2-6). Or some piece of vintage equipment might be just what a particular collector is looking for (Figure 2-7). If your company sponsors sporting teams, cultural institutions, or charities, the tickets you receive for your sponsorship can also be auctioned on eBay. Depending on consumer interest in your company, you could offer "experience" packages such as a VIP tour of your factory, lunch with a key person at your company, or tickets to a company-sponsored industry conference.

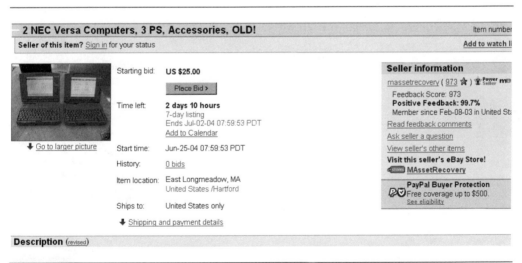

FIGURE 2-5   Old computers can be sold to help defray the cost of installing new systems.

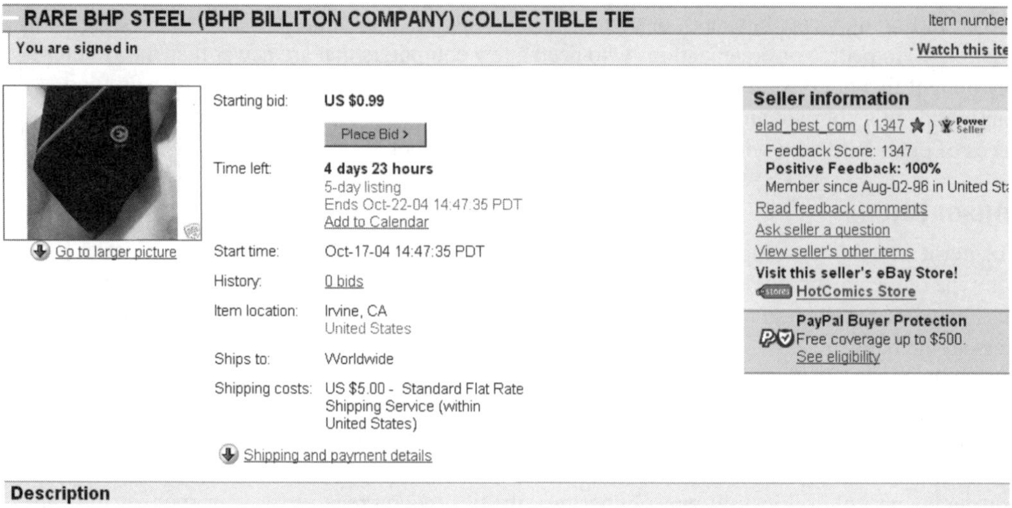

FIGURE 2-6   An unusual but collectible company item can be sold.

FIGURE 2-7   A vintage company product can be sold for a profit.

Outlawed Products

Of course, not everything is allowed to be sold on eBay. One of the most infamous auction listings in eBay's early days was a man attempting to sell one of his kidneys. While the auction was canceled, the publicity generated from the incident helped propel eBay into the mainstream in the United States and abroad. You cannot sell human parts, rights to human beings, Nazi items, or September 11 terrorist attack memorabilia, for example. Following is a list of items prohibited for sale on eBay:

Airline and transit related items	Alcohol
Animals and wildlife products	Catalog sales
Counterfeit currency and stamps	Counterfeit items
Credit cards	Drugs and drug paraphernalia
Embargoed goods from prohibited countries	Firearms
Fireworks	Government IDs and licenses
Human parts and remains	Links (you can't sell "information," like the link to a free report)
Lock-picking devices	Lottery tickets
Mailing lists and personal information	Plants and seeds
Postage meters	Prescription drugs and devices
Recalled items	Satellite and cable TV descramblers
Stocks and other securities	Stolen property
Surveillance equipment	Tobacco

Note that this is by no means a definitive list of products that eBay will not allow you to sell. This list is constantly evolving and changing, so if you're even remotely concerned about your item not being favorably looked upon by eBay management, check out the latest version of the list online at http://pages.ebay.com/help/sell/item_allowed.html.

Practical Considerations for eBay Sales

One of eBay's most powerful benefits is that it allows you to enjoy a global reach with your eBay listings and attract buyers from across the globe to participate and purchase items your business lists for sale, regardless of the size or location of your company. Naturally, because you're reaching out to more than your local market, most auctions are resolved with you shipping the product to the winning bidder.

Did you know?

You Can Control Shipping Costs

Although heavy items tend to appeal mostly to local customers because of the difficulty and cost of shipping, some firms, such as Reliable Tool, do ship heavy equipment across the United States. Therefore, don't let the weight or difficulty in shipping an item be an insurmountable barrier to listing your items on eBay.

Because you're depending on third-party shippers to handle fulfillment of these sales, you may need to consider that certain items may cause extra effort or incidental costs that will reduce your profit potential and affect your company's reputation. For instance, items that are extremely heavy, like the anvil shown in Figure 2-8, may appeal only to a local market.

Because buyers typically pay for shipping as well as the goods they purchase, they are going to factor their shipping cost into the total price for the auction. If they are paying too much for shipping, they could be reluctant to bid a fair price for the item itself. Conversely, if you pay for the shipping cost to encourage bidders to participate, make sure your potential profit is enough to cover these extra costs.

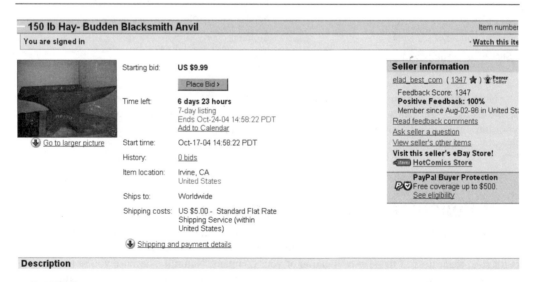

FIGURE 2-8   Heavy items in particular require that you factor in shipping costs based on weight.

It's important to note that sometimes if buyers are already accustomed to high markups because they have to import certain goods, the cost savings they realize on eBay greatly outweigh the shipping costs. If the item is of such a unique and collectible value that it warrants a high bid, you can still profit from posting the item. In other cases, you can just arrange for local pickup only, which tells the buyer that he or she must come to you and make all of the arrangements to transport the item from your location to the ship-to location.

TIP   *Thankfully, some companies have designed their businesses to fulfill this need. The folks at http://www.uship.com, for example, can help you ship unique, fragile, heavy, or difficult items at a reasonable cost.*

Evaluate Who Will Assist You in the eBay Strategy

Choosing items to sell and coming up with base prices at which to sell those items is important, of course, but a successful eBay strategy will involve cooperation and/or support from various divisions within your company. Because a variety of elements go into fulfilling a successful sale, the more support you have, the easier it will be to integrate an eBay strategy into your company's operations.

Table 2-1 offers a summary of the departments within your company and how they can help.

Inventory Management

You may have seen news clips near the holiday shopping season about yet another hot toy craze that has overwhelmed American consumers: hordes of frantic shoppers all grabbing for that last Furby or Tickle Me Elmo toy, for example. A similar scenario can happen in business because of poor inventory management—two (or more) people reaching for the last product as they both try to fulfill an order by shipping that particular item. In the end, you'll have at least one dissatisfied customer and a lost sale. If you're selling items using the same inventory from which other departments sell, poor planning could result in inadequate inventory and unsatisfied customers.

Department	Responsibilities
Inventory management	Keeps track of outgoing inventory
Marketing	Provides product descriptions
Sales	Sets pricing strategies
Information technology (IT)	Provides HTML for web product listings and troubleshoots technical problems
Accounting	Manages accounts receivable and accounts payable

TABLE 2-1   How Departments Can Assist an eBay Effort

Therefore, it's important to communicate with your company's inventory management personnel, advising them of your plans to start selling product X on eBay, and discussing ways to work together to best sell this product online. Perhaps if inventory is plentiful, and more products can be made or shipped in easily, you can grab items when needed and fill orders. But you may need to parcel off a piece of a pallet and sell only that portion until it's sold out, and then you can ask for more merchandise before posting future auctions. In some cases, you can integrate your sales with other departments, whether you're using real-time processing or daily batching of receipts, so you're removing items from inventory along with everyone else. The basic inventory level must be monitored and the items replenished whenever the company sees fit.

Marketing and Sales

The essence of an eBay auction is to accommodate the sale of a product from a seller to a buyer. The job of marketing is to promote the company and its goods to the consumer, and a sales force is responsible for projecting sales and assisting with transactions between the buyer and seller. If you're selling products that were sold before you started using eBay, involving the marketing and sales departments in the eBay equation could save you a lot of time and energy before you take it online—descriptions of items for sale, photos of those items, or specification listings can be provided by marketing and sales folks who can help you identify what to highlight and teach you how to present this item to the public to maximize interest. Sales people can also tell you how to accommodate the buyer to help him or her make a purchase in the most efficient way possible.

As your eBay strategy progresses, another important function of marketing is to use efforts to benefit the rest of the company. As explained in great detail in Chapter 13, a company's marketing efforts can be enhanced with several timed-event auctions on eBay to create greater awareness of your company's new product line, for example. The key is to demonstrate the value that an eBay strategy can bring to marketing and sales efforts and gain buy-in from the departments so they will coordinate events around one integrated timeline.

Information Technology/Computer Support

Since eBay is an Internet web site, and the only way to describe your item and post it for sale is by inputting information into a web page, computer involvement is a necessity. Whether creating an electronic version of your company's marketing materials, digitalizing pictures of your products, or formatting a manual containing specifications of your items, your IT department can help you locate, categorize, and upload electronic files for use in your eBay auctions. The IT folks may be able to upload an important report the sales department created for customers, and this information can save you time when posting information about new auctions—why reinvent the wheel if you don't have to?

Your company's IT department could be a great asset in several different ways. For example, many IT professionals know how to create Hypertext Markup Language (HTML) documents that are used for web pages. They could help by creating a template for you to use in all your listings—something that takes advantage of HTML and organizes and presents the information in a clean, readable, and professional format on the eBay page.

As you increase the number of items to be auctioned on eBay, you may find that acquiring auction software can help you automate and post many items, and the IT department can help you figure out how to install and use this software, especially if it requires integration with a variety of other systems, such as accounting and inventory management systems.

Finally, if IT resources handle storage of product photos—whether for the company web site, marketing brochures, or mail-order catalogs—they could coordinate hosting those images on the company's eBay site, so you don't have to pay some outside company to do this. In addition, part of the IT staff could be assigned the duty of digitally altering photos to make them easier to fit and load onto a listing.

Accounting/Finance

Some people say that the best headache a business can have is one caused by trying to handle a huge influx of money. When it comes to eBay sales, however, it's important that your company have a support system in place to track payments, since you are waiting on that payment to arrive before you ship an item to a buyer. You also need a system for tracking total revenue to help determine the future and success of your eBay strategy. While an eBay entrepreneur can invent a system to track cash flow, chances are your company has already created a system with rules, methods, and generally accepted accounting principles. Therefore, a discussion of the eBay strategy with the accounting department is vital. Your CFO (chief financial officer) or comptroller may present several options, which could depend on the company's current cash flow position, complexity of the systems being used, and the official's interests or beliefs in the future of this strategy.

In some cases, you or the accounting department may be required to keep separate books for this effort for a while, to prove to the company CFO or board of directors that the eBay business is successful before the company is willing to invest in the integration of eBay sales into the main company records. This strategy is also viable if the company sees this eBay strategy as a self-sustaining business. By keeping independent records, management can see whether the revenue generated from this operation can cover the expenses incurred. In other cases, however, each sale needs to be integrated into the company ledgers so management can measure profit and loss for a given product line—especially if you've decided to sell current products alongside other channels' current sales, as this information is important to estimate the life of the product, regardless of the sales channel used.

> **TIP**   *Don't worry about the technicalities of finances for now, because Chapters 4 and 11 will go into greater detail about how to separate sales channels and tie new sales records to the company books.*

The important thing to establish at the beginning of your eBay strategy is that the accounting department is on board and supports the project. Because the current accounting system may not be flexible enough to allow for quick sales to be easily assimilated, you and the accounting staff need to be aware of the challenges and changes that need to be made to accommodate eBay sales.

Summary

When working with your brand-new eBay sales channel, keep in mind that you've got a customer base that's very diverse and that each customer has developed his or her own set of buying characteristics. While eBay buyers come with their own sets of demands and requirements that can differ from a face-to-face business customer, they bring many benefits in areas such as up-front payments.

Many companies have returned merchandise that they can't place on retail shelves, refurbished equipment or products that they can't sell as new, recyclable items they don't want to throw away without receiving some salvage value, as well as off-season, slow-moving, or obsolete equipment that could be sold. Whether functional or not, refurbished, used, and returned goods will hold value for some buyer, and the eBay system allows worldwide buyers to offer a bid price for their perceived value of your products (not to mention your regular, everyday product lines).

A successful eBay strategy will involve cooperation and/or support from various divisions within your company. Because a variety of elements go into a sale, the more internal support you have, the easier it will be to integrate this strategy into the company operations for scalability and maximization of profit.

Chapter 3

Research Prices
for Your Products

In this chapter...

■ Research potential prices for products on eBay

■ Use the eBay search engine

■ Search completed items

■ View selling prices of previous items

■ Identify sellers in your field and analyze their listings

■ Consider the "willingness to pay" factor

Now that you've identified what you want to sell on eBay, your next step is to estimate at what price you will sell each product. Doing this will help you set your pricing strategy, decide what type of listing to use to sell the item, and gauge how much time you should spend researching and describing the item.

Buyers on eBay will eventually determine the final price your product earns, but it's important that you do research first. Without researching the current market of eBay, you may price your item too high, wasting your time and money on fees for listings that will never sell. Conversely, as we have seen time and time again, businesses that don't do sufficient research and price their items too low lose out on possible financial gains. Since you are selling on the eBay Marketplace, this is where your research and price determination will occur.

Research Potential Prices for Products on eBay

Thankfully, the best avenue for determining a price is right in front of you—eBay itself. With almost 4 million auctions occurring every day on eBay, the site collects incredible amounts of valuable data, such as individual bids, asking prices, and successful high bid amounts. By searching the vast records that eBay can offer, you can quickly determine at what price many given products will sell, based on the type of item and its particular characteristics.

The eBay Search Engine

One of the most critical tools available to you throughout your eBay experience is the eBay search engine. This tool is your ticket to navigating through the millions of transactions that eBay generates to find the information you need. On virtually every page within the eBay site, you'll see a text box in the upper-right corner with a Search button next to it. You'll also see a text box with a Search button at the top of the eBay home page, as shown in Figure 3-1, and Search fields and buttons are located near the top of auction category pages. Type in the name of an item in this field, and eBay will find it for you.

The true power of the eBay search engine comes with the options it provides to limit searches to various categories, keywords, and price ranges. This helps you cut down the volume of search data into a manageable chunk of information that can be parsed, interpreted, and averaged.

FIGURE 3-1   The eBay home page and Search features

Did you know?

What It's Worth

According to a recent article by a Houston, Texas, news source, eBay sellers report that their biggest hurdle is meeting customer expectations on what items should be worth and making sure the public understands how the auction process works. "Don't go into it blind; really educate yourself on what eBay has to offer," said eBay store owner Tina Quattlebaum. "eBay supports these types of endeavors very much; they've got a great support community and great resources."

Dean of eBay Education Jim Griffith goes on to say, "The cool thing about selling on eBay is you can do this because you set your own hours, you list when you want to list, you can sell from your own home, you store your items in the home, you can make it work for you so it's working on your schedule. Start with something you like and then see if you can market and promote it on eBay to get customers."

The potential reward is enormous. In 2003, eBay offered more than 971 million items for sale. Total value of items sold was a jaw-dropping *$24 billion.*

Search Page and Commands

Let's look at the eBay Search: Find Items page, shown in Figure 3-2, which is available by clicking the Advanced Search link at the upper-right of every eBay page. You'll notice a handy Search list along the left side, plus other search options throughout the page. We consider the following to be the five most important searches:

- Find Items (basic search)
- More Search Options (advanced search)
- Items By Seller
- Items By Bidder
- Items In Stores

Find Items

This basic search page lets you conduct a search on all the items posted on eBay at any given moment. Your primary search starts with specific keywords that represent the item you're looking for, or the actual item number of the auction. You type that information into the Enter Keyword Or Item Number text box. That's the only required field to complete for searching all of eBay's listings.

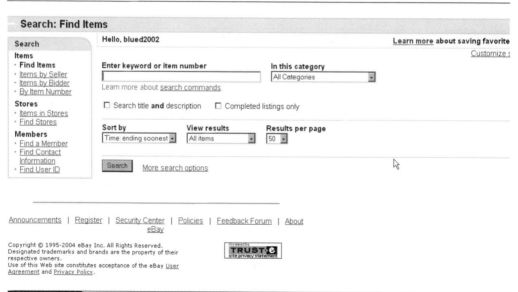

FIGURE 3-2   The eBay Search page, showing different types of searches

> **TIP**
>
> *By default, eBay searches only the titles of the auction listings, each of which has a maximum length of 55 characters. For more results, check the Search Title And Description checkbox, and eBay will search through every auction title* and *description. Be warned, however, that you will get* many *more listings using that search method, but it can help you find exactly what you're looking for.*

You can limit your search by entering more information based on the options presented by clicking the More Search Options link at the bottom of the page. For example, you can search for items within a price range, remove search results that have a specific word in the title, search in only one main category or one specific geographic region, and sort and customize how the results are shown.

When using the eBay search engine, keep in mind the commands you can use to generate more results. Table 3-1 shows some examples.

More Search Options

By clicking the More Search Options link, you can expand your search criteria. You can search by the region or zip code where an item is available for purchase as well as the item's actual location. You can search by different currencies or by different eBay features used in highlighting the auction, as shown in Figure 3-3.

For example, let's say that you're researching prices for a new Snap-on tool set from your company's machine room. It's a heavy set that you don't want to transport, so you want to limit your search to your local area. You can perform a search with the words *Snap-on, tool,* and *set;* search by your region only; and you find that sets are selling from $400 to $1000. While a few auctions ended in the $1000 range, you notice that most of the sets sold in the $600 to $800 range. This research gives you a more reliable target price for your tool set.

If You Type This in the Search Box	You'll Get These Results
Herman Miller Aeron	Items with the three words *Herman, Miller,* and *Aeron* in any order in the title
"IBM Thinkpad"	Items with the specific phrase *IBM Thinkpad* in the title
Deskjet 4**	Items with the word *Deskjet,* the number *4,* and a word or number following (such as Deskjet 4000, Deskjet 4300, Deskjet 4300c)
(HP, Compaq)	Items that have either the word *HP* or the word *Compaq* in the title
Workstation–(computer, desktop, PC)	Items that have the word *workstation* in the title and do not have the word *computer, desktop,* or *PC* in the title
(tractor, trailer)+Caterpillar	Items that have the word *Caterpillar* in the title and either the word *tractor* or *trailer* in the title

TABLE 3-1 Search Functions and Results

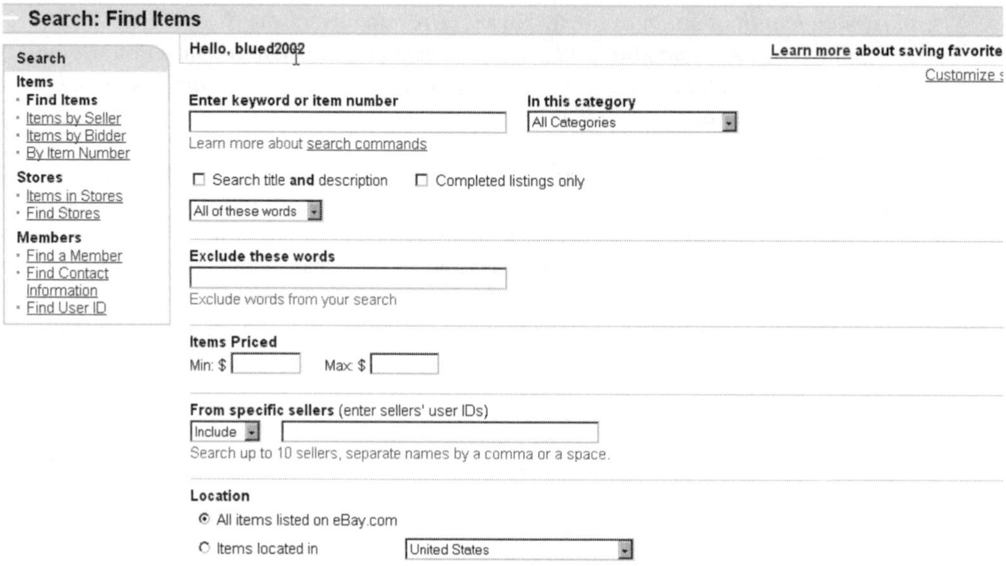

Search: Find Items

Search	Hello, blued2002		Learn more about saving favorite

Items
· **Find Items**
· Items by Seller
· Items by Bidder
· By Item Number

Stores
· Items in Stores
· Find Stores

Members
· Find a Member
· Find Contact Information
· Find User ID

Customize

Enter keyword or item number

Learn more about search commands

In this category
All Categories

☐ Search title **and** description   ☐ Completed listings only

All of these words

Exclude these words

Exclude words from your search

Items Priced
Min: $ ⬚   Max: $ ⬚

From specific sellers (enter sellers' user IDs)
Include
Search up to 10 sellers, separate names by a comma or a space.

Location
◉ All items listed on eBay.com
○ Items located in   United States

FIGURE 3-3   More search options

Items by Seller

Clicking Items By Seller lets you look at all the auctions a seller currently offers (as well as any completed auctions from the last 30 days), sort the results, and customize the results page, as shown in Figure 3-4. This is valuable marketing information about your competition.

Items by Bidder

Click Items By Bidder and you can learn about the shopping habits of a particular buyer. This search page will list all the auctions for which a bidder has placed *any* bid or auctions where the bidder currently has the *highest* bid. Like the Items By Seller search, you can research completed auctions for this bidder for the past 30 days. By searching a bidder's history, you can gain a sense of how that bidder uses eBay when shopping. If 90 percent of the user's bids focused on a niche market of comic books, for example, you could determine that this person probably uses eBay to complete a comic book collection.

More important, however, is the fact that you can see what bidders are looking to buy and whether they were successful. If you go further into the listing, you can find out exactly what the bidder's highest bid was for the item if the person didn't win, as shown in Figure 3-5. This gives you insight into potential demand if you post the same item on eBay, and a potential customer for that product since the bidder didn't win it earlier.

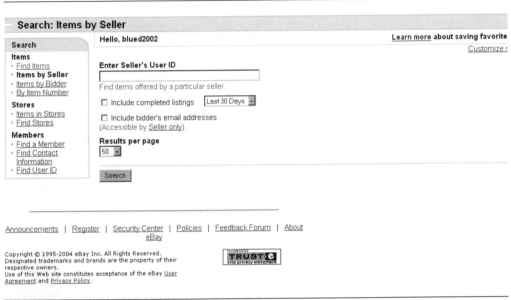

FIGURE 3-4   Search for items by seller

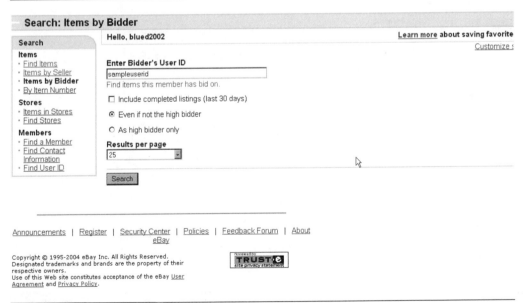

FIGURE 3-5   Searching for a bidder's history

If you begin to cultivate steady customers and want to do advanced research into their shopping behavior, you can search their bidding history and, perhaps, if they win one of your auctions, recommend other items you have for sale that they might purchase on eBay.

Items in Stores

Since most eBay searches search only auction listings (or fixed-price listings) and not eBay store items, clicking this link will allow you to create a search based either on store and auction listings or just store listings.

As shown in Figure 3-6, the screen looks just like the basic search page, with one exception: if you click the Search Store Inventory Items Only checkbox, the search will focus only on active eBay store listings. If you click the Find Stores link, you'll be able to search for actual stores that either contain listings with the keywords you provide or use the keywords as part of their name or description.

Completed Items Search

Because most items on eBay are sold via the auction process, and many bidders wait until the last hours to place their bids, an item's true value is not evident in current listings but rather in the completed listing. When the bidding process stops, you can see the final price of the item as well as a list of bids that led up to the final amount.

FIGURE 3-6   Searching through the eBay store listings

Only the seller and high bidder can see private information about each other, so they can communicate and seal the deal. However, anybody can see the eBay user ID and final bid amount.

> **NOTE** *You need to have a current eBay account to view completed listings. We will revisit this topic in Chapter 6, after you have created your eBay membership.*

When it comes to researching prices, some people say your best bet is to start with searching completed items only. Be aware, however, that to get the complete picture of supply and demand, not just pricing, you should search currently listed items to see the quantity of your product for sale and compare that to the number of completed items in your search, as shown in Figure 3-7.

If, for example, very few completed items are available but a growing amount of newly listed auctions appear, this would indicate that the market is getting flooded with an item and prices will probably shift lower because of that. Conversely, if a healthy and steady stream of completed auctions are shown but very few new listings appear, this would indicate a supply shortage, and it offers you a perfect opportunity to enter the market with your product.

Besides seeing what the top-priced item has sold for, utilize the completed item search to assist you in your pricing strategies and placement of the item. Additional considerations of these top completed listings should include:

1. Category—with over 50,000 categories on eBay, we don't want you to have to pick one out of the dark. Look at those top-selling listings—which category did the winning sellers choose?

2. Title—Did these listings include keywords in their title that you had not thought to use? Businesses, many times, are too close to the subject they are selling and leave out crucial keywords that drive buyers to the listings.

3. Pricing Strategy—Did the seller start the item low to create emotional bidding tension and end up with a high price? Or did they have to include a reserve option in their listing for protection in a fluctuating market? Perhaps the top-selling items are all selling for a static price, in which case, a fixed-priced listing platform would work well for your new listing.

4. Description—Did the top listing descriptions include anything beyond what your item description states? Perhaps the crucial "100% money back guarantee" statement, an 800 service number, or free gift wrap to help build credibility with your buyers.

5. Pictures—Are there additional close-up photos on the winning listings? These top sellers have realized that the buyers in their market want to see a certain detail of this item.

6. Date Ended—Very important information in determining the positioning of your item on eBay's platform. What day of the week, and time, did the most successful listings end? Although the most amount of people are on eBay Sunday evenings, that does not mean that *your* buyers are on at that time. Utilize this powerful marketing data to determine those potential customers' buying habits.

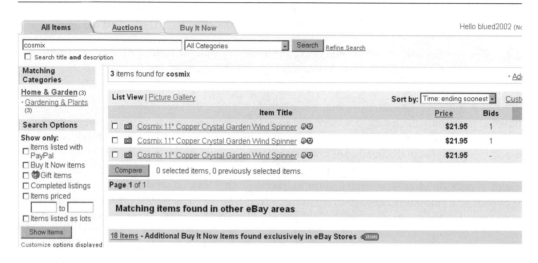

FIGURE 3-7   A search result you might find on eBay showing active auctions

How to ... **View Selling Prices of Items**

If you have an active eBay account, you can do more extensive research on final prices for items by looking beyond what is selling at present and viewing the prices for which items have actually sold after the auction is closed. To do this, search under the Completed Items area of the eBay web site.

1. Log into your eBay account.

2. Click the Advanced Search link in the upper-right corner of the page.

3. In the Enter Keyword field, type text indicating what you're looking for. For example, if you're checking to see what network printers have been selling for on eBay, type **network printers** in the field. But don't click the Search button yet.

4. Select the Completed Listings Only checkbox. The screen should look similar to the following:

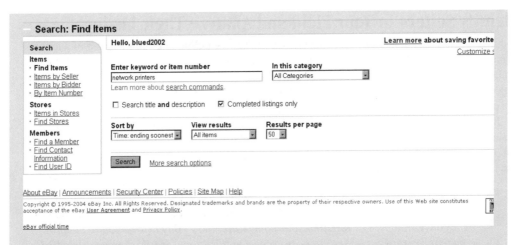

5. Now click the Search button. The completed listing page will appear.

6. To determine the range of sale prices, click the Sort By field, and you'll see a pop-up menu of choices for how to display the data, as shown next:

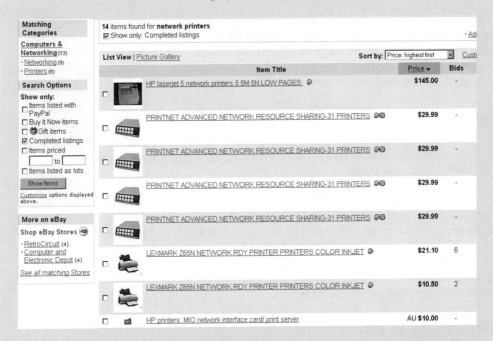

7. Re-order the auctions "Price: highest first." This will not only tell you what the high price points are for this item, but which top sellers are getting those prices. This way you'll see who is making the most money on this item, not the sellers who aren't listing their items correctly.

Identify Sellers in Your Field and Analyze Their Listings

You may begin to see a trend in the product area you're researching. Perhaps a group of auctions all have titles worded in the same way, in the same style, or use a unique keyword that binds them all. In that case, check to see whether those auctions are by the same seller. Hundreds of thousands of people use eBay sales as a full-time career, so you should begin to locate sellers who focus on that product area and offer multiple listings for similar items.

Keeping track of those sellers can be very valuable marketing information if you're going into a related field. You can watch the auctions of a particular seller very easily, and you can study the last 30 days of a particular seller's business (whereas the general search engine provides only the last 15 day's history of auctions).

> TIP
>
> *You can save a seller to your My Favorites Sellers list within My eBay. This way, you'll be able to track the seller's listings with a single click. Moreover, instead of hiring analysts or mystery shoppers to research your competition, My eBay allows you to monitor competitor strategies online. You can receive notification e-mails when a targeted seller adds new auctions, giving you real-time insight into dynamic pricing strategies, marketing offers, and product mix, which allows you to respond quickly and to compete at record speed to retain and get new customers.*

On the left side of the Search page, click the Items By Seller link. The next Search page prompts you for the seller's user ID and asks you questions such as how far back you want to see in terms of auctions (that is, only current auctions, last day, last two days, last week, last two weeks; and you can indicate how you want to sort the listings—by starting time, ending time, or price). Finally, you decide how many listings you want to review per page.

> TIP
>
> *If you're researching a seller with a lot of listings and you have a high-speed Internet connection, you should consider choosing All Items On One Page for Results Per Page. This way, you can see everything on one page without having to click multiple links. You can scroll up and down for quick comparisons, especially if the seller lists the same items week after week.*

This concept works in reverse as well. Suppose that after searching through countless listings, you see the same user ID over and over again buying the merchandise you want to sell. You can click the Items By Buyer link and search all the listings for which the buyer has placed a bid, or you can display only the listings for which the buyer placed the high bid, as shown in Figure 3-8.

By looking at all the auctions for which the user has placed a bid, you get a sense of the user's likes and dislikes regarding a particular product, and this could be helpful later on as you start cross-selling other products to your customers.

"Willingness to Pay" Factor

If you can't find the exact item that you want to post, and you can't find any sellers that sell something very similar to what you want to post, another factor could help you determine potential price—what we call the "willingness to pay" factor. Quite simply, this is a percentage you can determine based on somewhat similar listings and the ending prices they receive versus the retail value of that product.

Current auctions bid on by <u>blued2002</u> (2)

For auction items, bold price means at least one bid has been received.

In some cases, <u>blued2002</u> (<u>2</u>) may no longer be the high bidder.

1 - 3 of 3 total. Click on the column headers to sort

Item	Start	End	Price	Title	High Bidder	Se
<u>4907220066</u>	Jun-22-04	Jun-27-04 23:57:46	**US $39.49**	Stunning TOP SKY BLUE FIRE MOONSTONE Pendant	<u>blued2002</u>	clubge
<u>4907527688</u>	Jun-24-04	Jul-01-04 12:05:31	**US $38.00**	unusual OPAL & BLUE TOPAZ SLIDE Pendant Sterling	<u>blued2002</u>	jontin
<u>4907771635</u>	Jun-25-04	Jul-02-04 14:02:13	**US $19.99**	Sterling Large FANCY Gorgeous BALI UNAKITE Pendant	<u>blued2002</u>	jenndl

<u>Announcements</u> | <u>Register</u> | <u>Security Center</u> | <u>Policies</u> | <u>Feedback Forum</u> | <u>About</u>
eBay

Copyright © 1995-2004 eBay Inc. All Rights Reserved.
Designated trademarks and brands are the property of their respective owners.
Use of this Web site constitutes acceptance of the eBay <u>User Agreement</u> and

FIGURE 3-8   Results of clicking the Items By Buyer link

Look at other high-priced items in your field, match the items as closely as possible to your items, and see what they go for as a percentage of their retail value. For example, if a Sun server that retailed for $10,000 sells on eBay for anywhere from $2000 to $4000, you could assume that a heavy, expensive, computer server that's similar to a Sun server may go for 20 to 40 percent of the retail price. This is not an exact science, but it's a good rule of thumb to keep in mind.

In the end, use high-level category searches to determine a general price. If all else fails, consider the "let it go" price. Start your product at $1.00 or $9.99 with no reserve and monitor the bidding activity on that auction. If you don't require a particular return on an item, perhaps for equipment you've already written off on your company books, this can be a quick and effective way to realize that price point.

Summary

Once you've identified what you want to sell on eBay, the next step is estimating what you think the product will sell for. By searching the vast records using eBay's search engine, you can quickly determine what many products will sell for, based on the type of item and its particular characteristics. With millions of auctions posted every day on eBay, the auction site records tens of millions of bids, asking prices, and successful high bid amounts.

If you can't find the exact item that you want to post, and you can't find any sellers that sell something very similar to what you want to post, another factor could help you determine potential price—the "willingness to pay" factor. This is a percentage you can determine based on similar listings and the ending prices they receive versus the retail value of that product.

Chapter 4

Compare eBay with Existing Sales Channels

In this chapter...

- Pursue dual-channel strategies
- Develop strategies for shipping, timing, and pricing
- Decide which avenues are best suited for eBay
- Sell liquidated inventory and new product lines
- Consider the eBay Wholesale category

At first glance, you might be wondering why the title of this chapter is "*Compare* eBay with Existing Sales Channels" and not "*Use* eBay with Existing Sales Channels." You need to understand how eBay works compared to other methods, so you can best decide how to make your eBay channel effective. In this chapter, you will learn how to use eBay to open up new sales channels. As with any kind of new sales channel, remember that you want new channels to enhance your overall business and further your growth, so the extra effort makes sense in the grand scheme of your business's goals.

Structuring eBay to Enhance Sales

Minimizing conflict between new and existing sales channels is essential for businesses seeking an online presence, because above all you want to avoid the phenomenon called *product cannibalization,* or *line cannibalization*. The cannibalization of a product line occurs when a company tries to move into a new market area via a new product extension, or gain entry into a related market, and these sales end up negatively affecting existing sales. Instead of enticing new customers, some of the company's old buyers simply move from purchasing via normal channels to purchasing via the new area—in other words, the same customers buy the new product, except the sales are split between the two new sales channels, so no new sales are gained. This has the unhealthy effect of dissipating the energy spent establishing the new channel along with cutting sales of the original channel products—and the morale of your sales force—in half.

For example, let's say that you're in the business of selling color printers via local computer stores. To establish an online presence, you decide to start selling your color printers on eBay as well. Your ads look similar to the images shown in Figure 4-1.

Because you sell the same models in your stores and online, computer-savvy customers who might have bought the printer from the store end up purchasing the same product via eBay as they search for the printer at the lowest possible price. This auction could depress the printer sales you'd get in your retail store, especially if the printer offered on eBay is significantly lower in price than the same printer offered in your store.

The bottom line: Always remember to strive for a respectable profit margin, regardless of whether the product is on a real or virtual shelf. In most cases, when executed properly, your eBay sales should generate brand-new customers, and your products will thrive on both shelves.

FIGURE 4-1   At left, the color printer ad in the local paper; at right, your company's eBay auction page

Dual-Channel Strategies

You can avoid the channel sales cannibalization trap by creating at the outset a strategy that will take care of both channels without one channel stealing sales from the other. This is called the successful implementation of a *dual-channel* strategy, and you can pursue several methods to accomplish this, depending on the type of business you're in and the nature of the goods sold.

Shipping Strategies

A dual-channel shipping strategy is based on distribution agreements. By altering where you'll ship an item, you can avoid conflict between two or more sales channels and generate additional income.

For example, suppose that you've granted a distribution company the exclusive rights to sell your product in North America. However, that leaves six other continents in which to explore sales potential. You could set up auctions that are visible to and accept bids only from people not living in North America without violating the agreement you signed with your North American distributor. This allows you to relate directly with your international customers, without the need for a geographically local distributor. And you may find international distributors who are willing to buy large quantities of your product off eBay.

An eBay seller was in Finland visiting relatives when, quite by accident, he discovered a great product that protects you from slipping on the ice. He inquired into purchasing this item wholesale from the company. They agreed and he received an exclusive North American contract. He made sure that the contract stated that he could also sell this item on eBay while agreeing to only ship to the US and non-European countries.

Timing Strategies

Obviously, retail stores want to have the "latest and greatest" items to attract people to shop at their stores. After all, why should a customer get in the car, drive to the store, find a parking spot, navigate through the aisles, wait in line to pay for the item, and drive home, when he or she can simply click around on the computer and have the item delivered the next day via FedEx or UPS, for the same amount or less?

Retail stores are obsessed with making their shelf space valuable, and they stock items that will make them a decent profit. With thousands of products fighting to get shelf space, your company should protect any space it's already earned at retail stores by not cannibalizing your sales through an eBay channel. You can avoid cannibalizing by using a timing strategy.

A timing strategy involves giving an existing sales channel an exclusive "lead time" on selling new products. For example, you could decide that your hot new toy will be available for the first six months only on retail shelves. When that time period has expired, you can pursue other channels to sell your toy, such as through your eBay auctions. Toys make an excellent example for timing strategies, actually. After all, if you're going to fill demand for a toy via your eBay strategy, retail stores will be less willing to give up valuable shelf space during the holidays if they have no exclusivity to drive customers to their stores.

The key to this strategy is to reassure your existing channels that they have a guaranteed lead time so they can maximize their profits while the product is new and desired. While retail stores would love to have every item fly off their shelves constantly, they understand that at some point, sales will slow down and a competing channel, such as an eBay auction, won't affect their bottom line as much, if at all.

Pricing Strategies

Suppose you are a distributor for Chicago Silver car audio components and you sell these items in your brick-and-mortar store. You have just received the contract to be the components' exclusive dealer on eBay. However, your contract states that in order to keep the high-end car audio market intact, you are required to sell your Chicago Silver merchandise on eBay for manufacturer's standard retail price (MSRP).

You can execute several pricing strategies on eBay that can help avoid conflict and assist in higher sales. They involve altering the elements of product price markup and shipping costs.

Consider a listing for a Chicago Silver amplifier that has an MSRP of $1299. If you simply placed an auction on eBay for an opening bid of $1299, you would probably have little to no bidding interest. For buyers, entering into a bidding situation at or near retail is a mental hurdle—they expect to get better than retail prices from an eBay auction. However, you can implement some pricing strategies to still uphold your manufacturer's contract and entice buyers to bid on your items.

Reserve Pricing   Start your auction low—say, $99, with a reserve of $1299 on the item. It is a well-known fact in the auction world that a buyer becomes emotionally vested upon placing a bid for an item—they feel that they now own that item. By creating emotional tension between buyers who are bidding at the lower pricing levels, you will eventually achieve an even higher price when you start out low than you would achieve in an auction that starts at a high price. In addition, the more people involved in the bidding of your item, the more attention your auction will receive due to the bidding activity, which will invite even more bidders to enter the sale.

This is a common phenomenon not only in the auction world, but in the brick-and-mortar world as well. If you walk into a department store during its half-yearly sale, which table are you drawn to first? Most shoppers head for the table with all of the customers flocking around it. While shoppers may not even know the contents of that table, the other customers provide a validation that it contains important or interesting merchandise, so others are more willing to spend time investigating. The same holds true for eBay. If many eBay bidders are participating in an auction, that can tell other buyers that it's worth their while to participate.

Promotions   You can also offer inducements for your customers that will not affect your contract. If you start your amplifier price at the $99 level with the $1299 reserve pricing, some customers may not see the benefit of buying it for the same price they can get it for at a brick-and-mortar store. However, you can show them the advantages in your description: the item is delivered to their door, with no wasted time finding a parking space at the busy mall, with a 100 percent money-back guarantee, an 800-number for customer service and installation help, and the ability to shop 24/7 with you on eBay. Also, you can offer advantages that don't break your stipulated contract with the manufacturer. These promotions could include free shipping of the amplifier, inclusion of a bonus wiring kit, or even a coupon for $50 off their next eBay purchase with you.

Stores   Having an eBay store (discussed in Part IV) is a phenomenal way of marketing not only your products, but a brand as well. With this strategy, you use eBay auctions to sell an item in high demand from your inventory. However, in the auction, you would also promote what you are selling in your eBay store. This could include the Chicago Silver amplifier priced for store inventory at a Buy It Now price of $1299, upholding your distributor contract. A person shopping for car audio equipment would see your auction for a highly desired product and then click over to your store to see the other items you are promoting. Prior to this, the customer may not have been aware of the Chicago Silver brand, and now you can educate them through your store's listings. If the customer is already aware of this brand, he or she may not have realized that you were the eBay authorized dealer of Chicago Silver products—now you have instant credibility that the manufacturer has given you its "stamp of approval" to sell its products. Finally, a potential buyer would now have the option of saving money on shipping, by combining purchase of two or more of your products.

Pass Along the Savings

Customers understand that when a company sells direct, the company saves money on the overhead of doing business: no distribution costs, no retail markup, less advertising, and so on. Therefore, buyers may expect to see a lower price on an item if it appears on eBay rather than in a typical retail channel. You can set your eBay price accordingly, declaring that you're passing the savings along to the customer, as shown in the sample auction page in Figure 4-2.

Description

Welcome! Here you will find ALL your writing needs AT FANTASTIC BELOW WHOLESALE PRICES. YOU SIMPLY CANNOT BUY PENS CHEAPER! On auction are 3 sealed packages of Zebra F 402 black ink refillable pens. Retail stores charge $6.49 each, or a total value of $19.50! DON'T PAY RETAIL BUY HERE FOR LESS

Buyer pays fixed shipping and handling of $2.95 with delivery conformation. Pay by PAYPAL Money Order or Checks. We ship via USPS with delivery conformation.

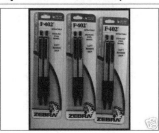

Thanks for
looking!
FREE Counters and Services from Andale

FIGURE 4-2   Declare the savings to the customer

> **NOTE** *We'll discuss some of the best ways to highlight the "extras" or "bonus savings" in your auction for your customers in Chapter 6.*

This strategy is most effective if your company plans to expand a direct-marketing effort and desires the one-on-one relationship with the customer. Plus, if you're a manufacturer, you would never receive the full retail value of your product anyway, as distributor and retail markups eat away at that juicy retail price. However, using eBay, you could find a happy medium and capture some of that value while passing along some savings to your customers.

Offer Free Shipping

If you're a retail outlet and you price your items the same on eBay as on your store shelves, the difference will be the shipping cost the customers have to pay if they use eBay. By offering free shipping, as shown in Figure 4-3, you essentially make it as easy (or easier) and cost-efficient for the customer to shop on eBay as it is to come into your store. You gain two key advantages by doing this:

■ Keep the customer shopping with you instead of someone else.

■ Reinforce the idea that the product still costs $X. When you lower the price to compensate for shipping, you devalue the price of the product, and later on, customers may expect that lower price to be in your retail outlet as well.

4

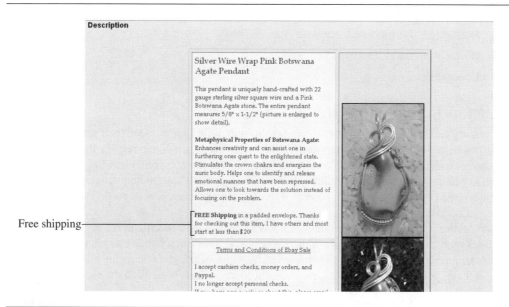

Free shipping

FIGURE 4-3   Offering free shipping on eBay

> NOTE   *Be aware that several parties will be a factor in what dual-channel strategies you can implement. Distributors, salespeople, and retail stores play a part based on their existing relationships with you. Your company may want to adapt your distribution channel contracts to include eBay as a territory.*

Decide Which Avenues Are Best Suited for eBay

Today's savvy companies know that the online auction marketplace at eBay provides a means for sellers to convert inventory into cash and for buyers to shop efficiently for a wide array of products. eBay has emerged as a solution to accelerate the sale of these assets while achieving higher returns over traditional liquidation methods. On the flip side, eBay has also proven to be a good place to showcase new products.

We've discussed different types of product to sell in Chapter 2. Here, we're going to revisit those categories briefly to see how they fit into a dual-channel strategy and how eBay can be the best fit:

- Refurbished, returned, recyclable items
- Inventory liquidated items
- New product lines

- Slow moving/off-season items
- Downsized, overproduced items
- Obsolete equipment/upgraded computers
- Unusual items

Returned/Refurbished Items

This category can be a great boon to companies who find it difficult to move their returned or refurbished items for a satisfactory amount. Most businesses are unable to restock these items on retail shelves with a low maintenance cost and achieve full retail prices for them. eBay listings can be used to generate more revenue per item. In many cases, your eBay strategy would allow you to move returned or refurbished items on the web site while keeping new items on shelves, creating an optimal dual-channel strategy.

Manufacturers have less complications with this strategy, unless specific terms in their contracts with distributors or retailers do not allow distributors to sell this merchandise or compete with the manufacturers. If the retailer or distributor returns these items, and you as the manufacturer refurbish them, your company should have the right to resell them directly to the consumer.

NOTE *You can check with your company's legal department to be sure that no contract restrictions prevent you from reselling these items.*

Inventory Liquidation

Typically, these types of items are supplies and not the main products of your company. Your company can achieve a much higher return on investment by using eBay than by using a typical wholesaler or liquidator. You can use that return to procure new supplies, as discussed in Chapter 5.

New Product Lines

Because the supply chain still relies on embedded relationships, some of your partners may stay in business or give you favorable discounts because of the implied understanding that you will provide new product lines to them first. Embedded relationships concern the linked relationships between vendors and their component suppliers.

Such businesses may suffer if you use eBay primarily for a new product line, and this should be taken into account before you make a decision to sell new product lines via eBay. One potential solution is to use eBay for product lines already rejected by your existing partners. If it takes off on eBay, your existing partners can't really object because you gave them that first opportunity and they passed. But don't sacrifice the power of the eBay channel for the sake of a previous business relationship. Your business solutions should take a look at the distribution of the 125 million eBay customers as well as the very low advertising expense for introducing a new product onto the site.

Slow-Moving/Seasonal Goods

Obviously, if the retail channels can't make a profit selling a particular item, they shouldn't mind you moving it via another channel. The only objection might be raised if the channel has an exclusive lock on a certain brand or type of product and would see eBay sales as "devaluing" the business because their status depends on exclusivity of your products. If, for example, potential buyers know that Department Store X is the *only* place to get Brand Y sweaters, and suddenly Brand Y is for sale on eBay, Department Store X loses that image and status that it hopefully paid for when agreeing to be the exclusive distributor. However, depending on your contract with that seller and via negotiations, you can often create an eBay avenue that works for everyone.

Obsolete Equipment/Computers

Unless your computer equipment supplier gives you a great discount if you trade in old equipment for new equipment, you should consider selling obsolete equipment on eBay. Typically, most Value Added Retailers or suppliers focus only on the company paying for the new equipment and don't want to bother reclaiming and reselling the older technology, so this "trade-in" option isn't offered.

eBay Success Story

Liquidation of Obsolete Equipment on eBay Isn't Just for Computers

Deep in America's heartland, the Douglas County, Kansas, government is using eBay to auction off old sheriff's cruisers. The idea is to dispose of old vehicles to make way for the purchase of new ones, while at the same time making money for the county. The outgoing fleet of automobiles features five 2001 Ford Crown Victorias and two 1997 Crown Vics.

"This is definitely a different approach for us," said Jackie Waggoner, the county's purchasing agent. "I think there are several entities and other Kansas City entities waiting on the sidelines to see how we do. Everybody's looking at it, but we're all kind of tiptoeing into it."

Normally the county sells its outdated vehicles and equipment at regional auctions, but a few months ago county officials decided to explore eBay as a way to cut costs and boost potential sales by broadening the market. The county's Buy It Now asking prices for the vehicles on eBay range from $5275 to $9950, well above the trade-in values, which range from $3900 to $7350, Waggoner said.

County officials set a reserve price for each vehicle, allowing the county to keep a car if the highest bid wouldn't pay off for the county. All those prices are above the trade-in values, Waggoner said, but won't be disclosed. "Now that we're getting to watch it, it's exciting. I look a couple times a day," Waggoner said. "Right now it looks pretty good…. We've got two dump trucks that will go to eBay if this is successful," she said.

County commissioners initially granted officials permission to sell vehicles at a site dedicated to selling surplus government equipment. But Waggoner and other officials discovered that the site's market was too small and its fees too high. They turned to eBay, the world's leader in online auctions. "Everybody knows eBay," Waggoner said. "They have the market."

This makes eBay a great avenue for reaching other businesses who can't afford that big upgrade. In fact, if you're leasing equipment, you may consider switching to an ownership situation since you can recoup some value at the end of life of the items. But that's a discussion for another time—let's focus on your current business operations and needs.

eBay helps you with selling your obsolete equipment and computers. Go to http://pcsellingcenter.ebay.com/ to find all the information you need to sell the computers as a company, or find another company who will sell them for you.

Unusual or Niche Items

Since unusual or niche items are not normally offered for sale, you're probably unaware of the inherent prices, cycles, or true values of the products. But this may actually give you an advantage—you probably won't require a profit margin that's similar to that for items in a more usual category, since the value of these types of items is totally dependent on idiosyncratic buyers. Because of this, you could get higher amounts for successfully listed items, which increases your revenue while filling some buyers' particular needs. Remember, do your research before your sale so you don't lose out on potential hidden value.

eBay Success Story

eBay as the New Bond Street—the Haute Couture Niche

Clothing and accessories are eBay's fastest growing niches, with *Vogue* magazine calling eBay "the new Bond Street." (The real Bond Street is in the heart of London's elegant shopping district.) But eBay is not new—it has been around since 1995, has over 125 million users worldwide, and has based its business on the never-ending drives of desire and consumption. However, today's eBay has a new fashion savvy, probably thanks to the early adopters who have made it the home of so many hot and hunted things. eBay now advertises front-of-book in American *Vogue* and has hired Constance White, formerly of US *Elle* magazine, as its style director and Hollywood stylist Philip Bloch as a columnist.

eBay has even held dedicated auctions of clothes by designers Narciso Rodriguez and Proenza Schouler, which has opened up possibilities for the future of fashion distribution and marketing.

It takes a lot of fashion sense and a good idea of what might constitute a good buy when all the usual shopping comforts are stripped away—particularly when you can't really see the clothes, let alone try them on. But eBay is no longer an obscure source of anything (although it is still the source of all things obscure), so the value of everything listed becomes self-determined, finding its own level.

The best attitude to bring to the site is a knowing sensibility and the foregone conclusion that you should be prepared to be surprised. After all, there is always someone, somewhere, who wants what you're selling.

The eBay Wholesale Category

eBay's wholesale categories, shown in Figure 4-4, also known as eBay Wholesale Lots, are specifically designed for manufacturers and distributors who are willing to offer excess merchandise or end-of-life products in bulk lots. Typically, these lots range from a couple items up to several thousand units, depending of course on the size and price of the goods being sold.

The Growing Wholesale Phenomenon

It may come as a surprise to you that, according to eBay's second quarter 2003 financial reports, wholesale lots have become a new force to be reckoned with when it comes to eBay. In fact, wholesale lots are among the fastest growing categories on eBay's site, with a jaw-dropping growth rate in annualized gross merchandise sales of 465 percent.

As of this writing, more than 200 wholesale lot categories exist on eBay, spanning a wide range of products. Since lot purchasers can find great savings on a wide range of goods from companies, it's natural to find buyers start-up companies here, seeking to set up a new company on the cheap.

The wholesale lot market has also attracted a host of small businesses who want to stock up on bulk inventory for the holiday season between Thanksgiving and New Year's Day. To cater to this demand, eBay will generally kick off a wholesale lots promotion on its site, usually starting around mid- to late September. Some categories of note include Office Products, Computers, Consumer Electronics, Building and Repair Materials, and Retail Equipment and Supplies.

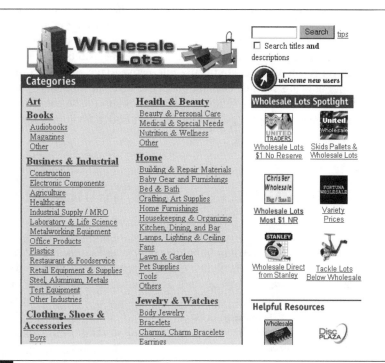

Karl Wiley, senior category manager of wholesale lots for eBay, notes that "Wholesale trading on eBay is a natural fit for our marketplace where we have a large audience of small businesses and individual sellers looking to find new sources of supply. Buyers of wholesale lots find eBay to be extremely flexible and convenient for finding great deals on inventory for their resale businesses, while sellers with large amounts of excess or closeout inventory are able to liquidate product easily."

More companies are starting to tap into the wholesale market opportunities on eBay's Wholesale Lots area. Some examples include Stanley Tools and chip-maker Newark Electronics. Perhaps the best known wholesale lot seller at present is the production house and movie distribution company Artisan Entertainment, which now sells DVD catalog titles on eBay's Wholesale Lots area, offering small business buyers a chance to stock up on Artisan's titles. The power of eBay here is that, previously, Artisan was unable to reach the small business buyer effectively through traditional channels. Using eBay makes Artisan products more accessible to everyone.

A Helping Hand for the Plunge into Wholesale

Suppose you're seriously looking into eBay Wholesale to increase your return on investment by quickly moving surplus or end-of-cycle products, but you want to outsource some of the setup tasks. You can get help in setting up your new sales channel from several firms.

For example, Marketworks (formerly Auctionworks.com, and discussed in detail in Chapter 17) launched a new division in 2003 that is dedicated to liquidating excess inventory for retailers, distributors, and manufacturers. Marketworks' stated goal is to enable retailers in efficiently listing or selling surplus product and product lines across online marketplaces such as eBay. (Incidentally, Marketworks started this division of the company because it bought the connection to eBay service from Accenture.) The Marketworks web page is shown in Figure 4-5.

Marketworks' services include inventory listing and management, sales strategy support, sales performance reports, integrated payment solutions, and fulfillment capabilities. By providing these services, Marketworks can offer a cost-effective alternative to typical forms of liquidation.

As a case in point for utilizing this dual-channel strategy to liquidate inventory, Artisan's Chief Operating Officer Bob Denton stated that "selling on eBay allows us to alleviate our inventory risks and at the same time realize a higher per-unit price than through traditional liquidators."

eBay Success Story

Lots of Success with Wholesale Lots

Wholesale lots on eBay can go beyond the selling of excess inventory and enable sellers to tap into a more global marketplace, simply by selling larger quantities of their goods.

The reseller United Traders retails apparel for a well-known department store chain. Recently, the company began selling wholesale lots of clothing on eBay. As reported by *Small Business Computing,* President Randy Hadeed noted, "In the past four months we've generated more in sales for our client than was achieved in all of 2002. By selling wholesale lots on eBay, we've revolutionized their business."

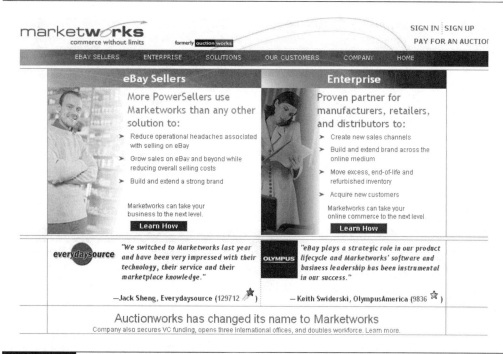

FIGURE 4-5   Marketworks' web site

Analyzing Wholesale versus Individual Price Points on eBay

If you're thinking about selling items under any of the wholesale categories, it's well worth your while to offer some analysis to see which is the most cost-effective way to do either of two things with your goods:

- Selling via a bulk listing
- Breaking out product and selling it piecemeal (via single or sub-unit sales)

Bulk Selling and Breakout Selling

Suppose you have numerous sets of 20 Italian charm tools, and your sales department has not been able to find a client in your existing customer base who is interested in purchasing them in bulk. Let's look at your eBay options.

You could sell all 20 products in a wholesale lot for one price of $99 each lot, as shown in Figure 4-6.

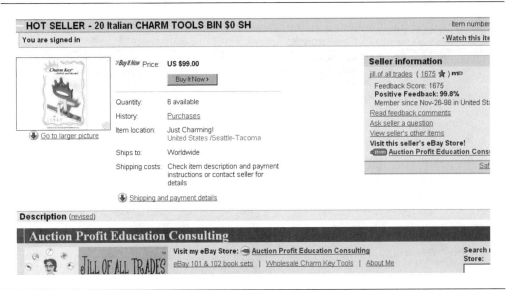

FIGURE 4-6   Selling by the whole lot

Conversely, you could sell each item individually, for a Buy It Now price of $7.95 each, as shown in Figure 4-7.

Before you post your items in an eBay auction, you need to do some research regarding which way will most likely result in the most income for your company. Of course, many of your decisions can be determined by common sense approaches; you could end up saving more just in storage costs by wholesaling bulky commodity items. But by researching before you list the auction, you can determine the best method to use.

Researching for Individual or Bulk Selling

Using the search skills you learned in Chapter 3, do some research on determining the price range for an individual item on eBay. Once you've properly reviewed how much your type of items on eBay are actually selling for, you can work out how high a price the market will bear if you sold these products individually.

There are two additional benefits of performing this review. First, you can roughly estimate the number of vendors on eBay who are selling in your market area. This can help you predict whether the market can sustain extra individual auctions or whether you'll have to wholesale this lot. Furthermore, you may be able to tell from their level of involvement on the site whether they are established firms, wholesalers, power users, or casual consumers who just want to offload their old models so they can buy new ones.

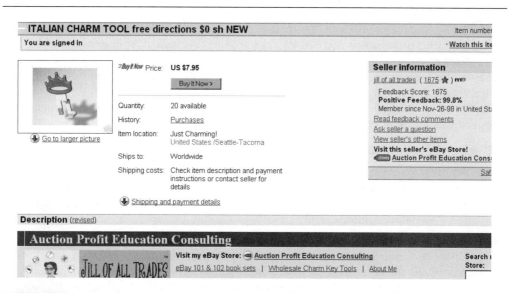

FIGURE 4-7   Selling the items individually

Second, you can judge the level of existing interest in your product area by looking at the bidding history on an item. Let's say that you notice that several items have gotten multiple bids— perhaps even a specific brand, model, or option that is attracting all the attention. If that's the case, you can pinpoint exactly what the customers want; you should probably ride that demand by selling your products slowly, through several individual auctions instead of the wholesale option.

By doing some research, you'll be able to tell what buyers are willing to pay for and just how much they are willing to pay for it. In that sense, eBay moves beyond a simple selling auction site to add to your dual-channel strategy—it also serves as a fine-tuned marketer's survey.

In the end, your research will help you determine which method is most effective for a better return. Let's look at an example to help demonstrate this. Suppose you have two sellers who both make $500,000 a month on eBay. One seller moves 700 individual computers per month, and the other moves 10 pallets, each full of computers, per month. The first seller is going to be spending time listing 700 auctions, taking 700 pictures, and shipping out up to 700 different packages per month. The other seller takes only a handful of pictures, lists a handful of auctions, and ships out a small quantity (of heavy items) each month. While the second seller has less work in the auction phase, that seller typically receives a lower price per computer.

So, the question becomes this: Does the extra work involved in breaking up a large lot and selling it piecemeal result in enough of a revenue increase to pay for this work? While the actual answer isn't revealed until your auctions are over, your research combined with some basic math should give you an excellent idea of which avenue to pursue. Take some time to figure this out, because the payout will be worth it.

Summary

Minimizing conflict between new and existing sales channels is essential for businesses seeking an eBay presence, because above all you want to avoid *cannibalization* of your existing sales. You'll avoid this by creating at the outset a *dual-channel* strategy. The three aspects of this are shipping, timing, and pricing.

Whether an item is ideally suited for sale on eBay depends on how it fits into a dual-channel strategy and whether eBay would be the best fit:

- ■ **Returned/refurbished items**   This avenue is best suited for companies that have trouble moving these items through traditional channels for a respectable return.

- ■ **Liquidated inventory**   You should achieve a much higher return on investment by selling through eBay than if you use a typical wholesaler or liquidator, and it should not affect your other channels.

- ■ **New product lines**   Because your supply chain probably still relies on embedded relationships, evaluate this area carefully. One potential solution is to use eBay for product lines already rejected by your existing partners. Your other option is to utilize the power of the eBay customer channel and inexpensive advertising solution to introduce a new product.

- ■ **Slow-moving/seasonal goods**   Obviously, if it's something the retail channels can't move and make a profit on, they shouldn't have a complaint with you moving it via another channel. The only objection could come if the channel has an exclusive lock on a certain brand or type of product.

- ■ **Obsolete equipment/liquidated computers**   Unless your computer equipment supplier gives you a great discount if you trade in old equipment for new equipment, eBay is a great avenue to reach other businesses who can't afford a big upgrade and are interested in buying your used items.

- ■ **Unusual items**   You could enjoy a high sell-through ratio and increase your revenue while filling your customer's needs. Do your research to achieve the highest amount of return as possible, and avoid losing out on potential hidden value.

Finally, the eBay Wholesale category is among fastest growing categories on eBay's site. Buyers of wholesale lots find eBay to be extremely flexible and convenient for discovering great deals on inventory for their resale businesses, while sellers with large amounts of excess or closeout inventory are able to liquidate product easily. Some firms, such as Marketworks, can help you set up your new sales channel.

Chapter 5

Cut Costs by Using eBay's B2B Channels

In this chapter...

- ■ Determine potential savings from using eBay
- ■ Change from a vendor to eBay
- ■ Consider more than cost when using eBay for procurement
- ■ Evaluate consistent needs versus "lumpy" needs
- ■ Save money on large equipment purchases with eBay
- ■ Find the right auctions, find the right sellers
- ■ Make business-to-business equipment sales

We've talked a lot about the benefits of posting company products for sale on eBay, so let's shift gears and discuss another huge benefit your company can reap from this trading marketplace—you can lower your company's procurement costs by buying on eBay. Millions of eBay sellers offer all kinds of products, and the range of products has moved beyond the "garage sale" inventory to include many everyday items such as consumer electronics, office supplies, business furniture, and high-tech equipment—items businesses need and use on a daily basis.

Determine Potential Savings from Using eBay

Because your company's eBay account allows your business not only to post items for sale, but to bid on products as well, you're already equipped and ready to start taking advantage of the deals eBay can offer your company. There's no extra fee to the buyer for placing bids or winning an item, and you can enjoy increased savings on purchases, with people and businesses around the world offering you discounts on commodity items, larger and one-time capital purchases that can help out in times of growth or development.

The eBay Business Marketplace

As mentioned in Chapter 1, eBay has created a portal site called eBay Business Marketplace (http://www.ebaybusiness.com), which presents a select subset of categories targeted to the business customer. The marketplace is a great starting point for researching areas to determine where you can lower your supply and equipment costs. Everything from computers to office supplies to industry-specific categories like Medical Equipment or Semiconductor Manufacturing can be found here, and based on the type of business your company operates, you can probably find at least one or more categories that fit your supply needs.

The easiest way to experiment with eBay purchasing power is to choose an item that your company has already planned and budgeted to buy and ask that it be purchased on eBay instead of from the normal supplier. Using your search skills, go to eBay Business Marketplace and search for that item. For example, the page shown in Figure 5-1 appears after you click the Networking & Telecom link on the Marketplace page. Continue searching for the particular item you want, and if multiple listings are found, compare their prices, the sellers' feedback, shipping costs, and other factors, and then bid on items that are acceptable.

FIGURE 5-1   Starting a search

NOTE   *As a rule, you should never pay more for an item on eBay than you would pay from another supplier, and the price you're considering should include any shipping and handling fees.*

After you've successfully purchased the item, go through the after-sales steps to procure it. Then, informally (or formally, as the case may be) poll the employees involved in the eBay purchase. You can also poll the people affected by the item you just acquired. After the goods are delivered, ask whether the supply is of the same and/or reasonable quality as supplies purchased from the normal supplier and if those involved in the purchasing process found that the eBay experience was reasonable or unreasonable. Using those results in conjunction with a simple price comparison will help you determine whether you should continue to purchase supplies from eBay.

NOTE   *In many cases, the equipment seller is a business, and this is another reason why you should always strive to maintain good relations with any sellers you encounter on eBay. One successful transaction could lead to a successful relationship of buying supplies directly from the other company at eBay prices.*

Changing from an Established Vendor to eBay

Suppose you're intrigued by the possibility of changing from a normal vendor to eBay as your primary procurement channel. Company management may also be in favor of the change but may want you to conduct a "test case" and then write up a report outlining why this new venture makes sense for your company. In the following example, we walk through the analysis of switching from an exclusive supplier for cellular phones to outsourcing your needs using eBay.

Let's say you're currently purchasing 200 cellular phones per year for your employees. Your supplier has recently established a per phone cost of $82, due to supply issues and other market demands. This amount does not include a shipping and handling surcharge of $3 per phone, making your total $85 per cell phone.

You log onto eBay Business and go to the Consumer Electronics area; then you click the Cell Phones link, and then click Wholesale & Large Lots. You search for *Motorola v60** and 33 items are found. In going through these listings, you notice that several listings look exactly the same. This could mean that one seller is offering a number of the same items for sale. This seller may post several auctions a week, so that the item is always available for sale, even if the seller's other auctions for the same item end.

You discover that this seller has the same brand of cell phone that your company uses— a Motorola v60t phone, as shown in Figure 5-2. You need to determine whether this seller can help fill your sourcing needs.

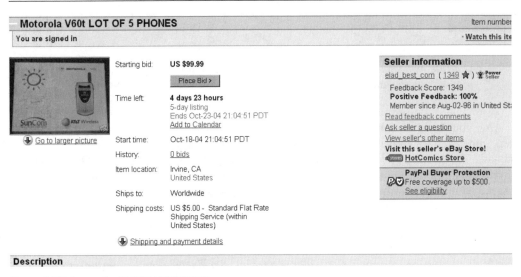

FIGURE 5-2 The seller's listing with the merchandise you need

First, you click View Seller's Other Items to see how many phones the seller has listed. You can also see what other lots he or she has been selling, giving you options if, for example, this person specializes in lots of different phones. Then you click Search Completed Items and discover that the same lot has been sold five times in the last two weeks and never sold for more than $301 for a lot of seven phones—or $43 each.

This tells you two important factors: the availability of the phones and the average price. If you're going to depend on eBay to supply you with an important item, you want to be sure that you'll always be able to find it when you need it. Looking at the prices realized for these lots gives you an idea of how much you'll need to spend over the long run to keep the phones in the hands of your company's employees.

You learn that the shipping cost averaged to $20 per lot of seven phones. Therefore, you would be able to get seven cell phones for $321, which works out to about $46 per phone. Of course, you have to see whether this seller could offer you a bigger lot, or you could shop around for more lots to reach the 200 phones you need, but if you can swing the deal and average $46 per phone as your acquisition cost, you could save your company quite a bit of money. In this example, your annual savings would work out to $7800 (200 × [$85 − $46]). Therefore, you could save your company $7800 just by outsourcing one product purchase from your list of regular equipment from your current supplier to eBay suppliers.

When you submit your report to management, you can make the case in the best way possible—by using concrete examples, objectively chosen amounts for your calculations, and an easy demonstration as to how eBay positively affects the bottom line.

Other Considerations

Of course, you must consider factors other than gross savings when purchasing an item. While you may save money buying items from a seller on eBay, headaches and problems of an inferior purchase (such as a defective cell phone) could cost your company twice or three times the savings to fix the problem. As you test out and shift over to eBay for procuring supplies, consider the following factors:

Timeliness

How quickly are your items arriving through your new eBay suppliers? Are they shipped right away or does the seller make you wait for a while? While most auctions come with shipping policy explanations, the reality is that small sellers may not have enough time or manpower to send their products every day, so they may ship only once or twice a week.

TIP *Keep in mind that occasionally a small business seller's shipments might be affected by an unforeseen event that occurs in the seller's life. While this is not common on eBay or for its sellers, you need to factor this possibility into your risk analysis when changing to eBay vendors. If you start a business relationship by purchasing supplies from a specific vendor, you may consider querying that seller about his or her business operations to make sure the seller can continue delivering orders in case unusual circumstances occur.*

Dependability

Since businesses of any size can set up an eBay identity, you need more information than just a listing to gauge the dependability of this seller's ability to deliver consistent service to you. In this case, the place to go is the Feedback Forum, where you can track the history of the seller's interactions.

NOTE *Remember that the feedback rating consists of a numerical tally of comments, as well as the actual comments from each person who dealt with this seller. This feedback rating is shown on the right side of the listing by the seller's name.*

It's important that you read the comments to determine whether the seller has been prompt, courteous, and communicative with their buyers, and whether the products are of good quality.

Consistent Needs versus "Lumpy" Needs

The term *lumpy* refers to your need of a lump sum of a given good only once in a while, as opposed to a consistent need for *X* amount of supplies per week or month. For example, a lumpy need may require that you purchase a new network server to handle increases in network traffic as your company continues to expand. On the other hand, a consistent need for a similar company might be a supply of high-quality, glossy paper for the graphics department's laser printer.

If you're buying from eBay suppliers and you base your purchases only on lowest price, the strategy of using eBay for procurement may work best if your company's supply need is lumpy. Once you see a great price posted on one of eBay's auctions, you can bid on it and stock up on the items you need. Then you can sit back and wait until the next great deal appears.

eBay
Success Story

Procuring for a Small Aerospace Company

Robert Maple, owner of Owen Aerospace, a $1 million-a-year company that builds parts for big aircraft manufacturers, purchases everything he needs for his business, even heavy equipment, on eBay.

"eBay has saved me so much money it's pathetic," he says. The numbers are startling: In the course of slightly more than 300 transactions, he has spent about $300,000 on goods. Had he purchased the same goods used, the cost would have been $3 million. And purchasing them new would have cost an astronomical $9 million.

The savings are evident in each transaction. For example, Maple recently used eBay to purchase a used computer numerical control device for $500. Retail price? $250,000.

Being able to keep costs down by buying equipment at bargain-basement prices on eBay makes the difference in being able to buy the equipment he needs to keep ahead of his competition. It keeps Owen Aerospace from having to take out a loan or simply making do without the needed goods.

"I don't have to go all over the place to find what I need," says Maple. "I just go to eBay."

Of course, if your supply need is more consistent, look to see how many auctions for the item appear per week. Search under Completed Items to see whether the same sellers list these items week after week and whether they list multiple lots per week. If you see this behavior, it should increase the likelihood of using lowest-price eBay suppliers for a consistently needed supply, since you can be fairly sure of getting the same great deal, week after week.

Add everything up, and the cost savings can be small, medium, or large. The more time and effort you put into your eBay searches and purchases, the more you can save.

Save Money on Large Equipment Purchases

In the past, businesses shopped from a limited number of equipment resellers, because only a few resellers could afford to keep specific high-dollar equipment in stock for when a new or growing business would need it. Nowadays, due to eBay's large audience, chances are that at least one eBay seller will have the item you need for sale when you need it.

After all, eBay's loyal and growing user base ensures that a broad variety of items are listed every day. As more and more businesses are discovering the value of making large purchases from eBay and saving huge amounts of money, this encourages more sellers to turn to eBay first and increase the supply available. eBay's supply and demand atmosphere works to solidify eBay's position in this newer market.

The savings a business enjoys by using eBay are critical, especially for small businesses just starting out or businesses about to grow to the next level. As Jordan Glazier, general manager of eBay's business unit, said to *Fortune Small Business* magazine, "You see companies in the early stages and they can't afford to buy an original set of capital equipment. They are more often price sensitive and capital constrained and more concerned with making their nest eggs go as far as they can go."

Identifying the Best Avenues

Given your timetable and budget for an acquisition, eBay can assist you in locating the equipment you need quickly and at considerable savings. In some cases, the actual items will be on sale in a particular category for you to bid on. In other cases, eBay can help put you in touch with the busy sellers who spend their time buying and reselling equipment, as perhaps these sellers have the equipment you need or can locate it for you. Lastly, you could use eBay's community forum features to connect to other business owners who can help you put together the right purchase.

Finding the Right Auctions

The eBay Business Marketplace is an excellent place to start finding business equipment, but while the Office Technology subcategory contains many leads for commodity items such as office supplies, the Industry Marketplaces are excellent sources for heavier, more expensive capital equipment. This section organizes the products sold by their intended use, such as Medical Equipment, Metalworking, and Semiconductor Manufacturing. Subcategories are broken down by the properties of their specific marketplace, whether it's by machine capacity, OEM brand name, or where the equipment will operate—from the kitchen to the front office.

For example, suppose your company decides to open an in-house print shop to do all its printing internally, instead of relying on an outside supplier. You want to minimize your outlay on capital equipment to get this division off the ground, but you still need to equip it properly to handle all the output the shop needs to deliver. By going to the Printing & Graphic Arts Industry Marketplace, as shown in Figure 5-3, you can see the specific categories—bindery equipment, commercial printing presses, high volume copiers, or other items.

Notice the links and graphics on the right side of the page. eBay will create images and offer links to its most popular subcategories. In this case, items such as finishing equipment, copy machines, and ink and toner are featured, as well as specific eBay stores in areas such as sign cutters and laser engravers.

If you scroll down the page, you'll see three items that will be particularly useful to you, which are shown in Figure 5-4:

- **Related Categories**   Provides other ideas about where to look for your specific equipment needs

- **Popular Searches**   Gives you an idea of what people are always looking for with defined searches

- **Featured Items**   Shows items listed by people who invested money to get out those listings for buyers like you

FIGURE 5-3   An example of specific category listings

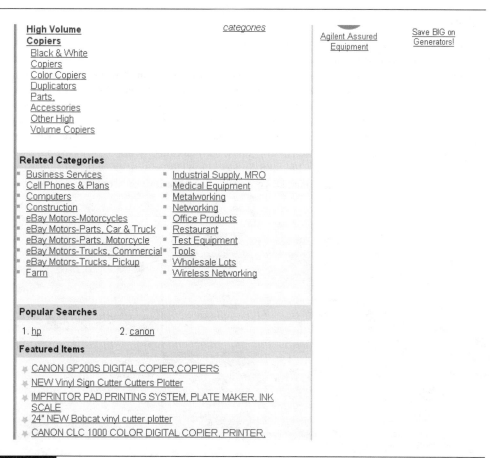

FIGURE 5-4   Related Categories, Popular Searches, and Featured Items

Of course, the best way to sift through these endless pages of products is by using the Search box at the top of the Printing & Graphic Arts Marketplace page. Make sure the Search Within Printing & Graphic Arts checkbox is checked so that your search is refined and returns quality leads for you.

If you think that sellers of your searched items may have used different terms than your search queries use to describe their items, you can check the Search In Titles & Descriptions box to get more listings, and you might see items you wouldn't have found just by searching the titles. In addition, you could find equipment that is equivalent to the model number you're searching for—something that can do the job but that is perhaps selling for less money. Keeping your options open and being flexible is a key to saving money using eBay for procurement.

Finding the Right Sellers

While the right product may not be offered on eBay at the exact moment you're looking, chances are that at least one seller is using eBay to sell products that are similar or related to the one that you want. Finding this seller can be just as helpful as finding the right product in the long run, since many sellers carry multiple models of equipment. For example, if you're looking for a specific brand of copy machine and you find a seller that has dealt in all kinds of copiers over the last year, it's worth inquiring with that seller as to when he or she might come across the one you want.

In this way, finding the right source can lead to a healthy sourcing agreement for both parties. To help foster these types of connections, eBay has a feature called Seller Showcase on the eBay Business Marketplace home page (see Figure 5-5). Here, you can browse the various categories and find the sellers who deal in the merchandise you want to acquire for your company.

FIGURE 5-5   The Seller Showcase feature on the Business Marketplace home page

These sellers could help you find the equipment you want, or they can use their network to find that item and sell it to you. Even if you can't find the specific model or models you're looking for, continue to search for similar items, even if you have to look at another manufacturer's goods. From that list of items, notice similarities in either the titles of the auctions or the style of the descriptions, and notice that some of the seller names show up again and again.

> **TIP** *We've mentioned doing searches for Completed Item auctions, and you'll see us recommending this again before the end of the book. This is because such searches are useful for analyzing prior bidding activity and looking for common patterns. Always consider using a search under Completed Items when you're interested in uncovering a repeating sale pattern, determining how prior items have fared, or defining limits on price or timing for products.*

After you've identified sellers who offer items similar to those you're looking for, search on that seller and all their Completed Items over the past 30 days. Ask yourself (and your company colleagues) if the items the seller offers are suitable alternatives for what you're looking to purchase. You can click the Ask Seller A Question link to ask the seller questions that would test whether their product will serve the same goal as the equipment you wish to purchase. This link, shown in Figure 5-6, is located on an individual auction page as part of the seller's information box. This may help you find merchandise that will save you money and suit your needs.

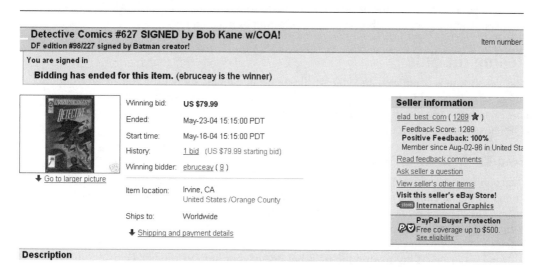

FIGURE 5-6   eBay's Ask Seller A Question link

eBay Success Story

Procurement via eBay Helps a Small Business Start up and Thrive

PyX Technologies, which builds and maintains data storage solutions, was started by Andre M. Hedrick and three co-founders in 2001. The company's successful startup was greatly assisted via procurement purchases made through eBay.

According to Hedrick, PyX Technologies saved at least $60,000 by purchasing necessary gear and equipment on eBay. The founders used the savings that buying through eBay provided to grow the business, and the eBay gear is still being used to demonstrate PyX technologies at tradeshows.

"We decided to do our own startup from scratch and turned to eBay to buy gigabit cards and switches for our research and development lab," Hedrick said. "The cost savings were tremendous—we bought world-class equipment for a couple of hundred dollars. These things were selling for $1000-plus new. If eBay wasn't available, I don't think we could have pulled it off."

As you use eBay to replace a normal procurement processes, ask yourself this: Is the cost savings I could enjoy worth the effort? If you could save thousands, or even tens of thousands, of dollars by hunting around a bit, your answer should be a definite *yes*.

Closing the Sale

After the auction is completed and you are the final and winning bidder (or you've agreed to a seller's fixed price or Buy It Now price), it's time to settle up and close the deal. However, unlike most eBay listings, a big-item sale probably won't be settled with a quick PayPal payment and a UPS box showing up on your doorstep the next week.

From Their Door to Yours

When purchasing equipment, especially the heavy, toxic, or fragile kind, you need to keep shipping in mind. Is the purchase something that has to be carefully shipped or should it be picked up in person? The choice here depends on what the seller is offering, the distance between you and the seller, and the relative costs of using a shipping service versus the cost of you bringing the appropriate vehicles and labor to arrange shipment yourself.

If the seller is willing to ship the item but needs your help to choose a carrier and pay for shipping, eBay provides some tools to help you find a shipping quote. Working with freightquote.com, shown in Figure 5-7, eBay has created a special portal to help eBay buyers and sellers obtain shipping quotes for items. However, when you use this feature, you'll need to know the exact dimensions of the item, the item's weight, the seller's zip code, the contents of the package, how securely the items will be packed, and the dollar value amount of this purchase.

FIGURE 5-7   The freightquote.com page

If you must pick up the item or you have to arrange the shipping details, consider the following:

■ *Does our company fleet have a truck and personnel that can pick up this item?* If so, contact the appropriate person, find out how to reserve the person's time, and then contact the seller to work out a time for the pickup to happen and notify your people of the time.

■ *Does the seller know of a shipper he or she can recommend?* If you can't arrange shipment, don't waste time jumping into searches to find a moving service or contractor to handle this. The seller may have sold similar equipment in the past and may know which companies can handle the specifics of shipping your newly purchased equipment.

■ *Does my company have a preferred shipper or moving company?* Ask your corporate HR or facilities department who handles company moves. If you outsource some of your equipment, such as industrial copiers, to another company, ask someone from that company who they use to haul equipment.

■ *Can I handle this shipment within my own department?* Usually this is the last-resort method, but sometimes you've grabbed such a good deal that you'll have to figure out a solution by yourself. Get an idea of who owns a pickup truck or a van, or rent a truck from a rental company. Gather some of your stronger coworkers, buy them lunch, and ask for their help in moving the equipment.

Paying for the Item

Typically, businesses are accustomed to dealing with purchase orders, invoices, and payment deals where they can pay for the item after it's been delivered. In eBay, you often get a good deal because you pay up front before you take possession of the equipment. Chances are the seller won't be eager to whip up an invoice and grant a complete stranger credit terms for a quick sale. Therefore, if you're looking for serious bargains on serious equipment, you need some serious cash that's readily available.

Our first piece of advice is simple but often overlooked by inexperienced bidders: Know the terms of the auction before you bid. Find out what payment options the seller accepts. Don't be afraid to send the seller a question via e-mail and offer alternatives. Naturally, questions should be sent before the auction ends, if possible, so that you know before you bid whether you can honor the terms of the sale.

If you present your case clearly and openly to the seller, and you're flexible to different options, you can probably negotiate a payment plan, which you'd use if you become the high bidder. Based on those discussions, go back to your company execs, especially the finance department, to see whether your company can accommodate the seller's needs before placing a bid.

Our second big piece of advice is common sense: Set up a PayPal (http://www.paypal.com) account and be ready to roll. PayPal (see Figure 5-8) enables buyers to store, receive, and spend

FIGURE 5-8   PayPal's home page

"electronic money" from a bank or credit card account. Many sellers accept PayPal, even for bigger purchases. Because the PayPal setup process can take a few days, it's better to set up the account early and have it ready before you bid on something.

NOTE   *The process for setting up a PayPal account is discussed in detail in Chapter 6.*

PayPal is typically used for small purchases, especially for commodity items. Normally, if you buy something that's more than just a typical supply purchase, your company's financial officers arrange for the bank to do some sort of wire transfer or electronic payment based on an invoice. The problem is that you're usually at the mercy of the banks and their slow timetable to close the deal.

Your PayPal account will be able to link up immediately with the company bank account—and best of all, the seller is notified immediately when you start the process, and PayPal notifies the seller immediately when the cash is cleared. If PayPal pays a seller directly from the buyer's bank account, an Echeck (Figure 5-9) can be used, which also takes a few days to clear. The seller is always informed, which puts the burden of responsibility on PayPal, not your company.

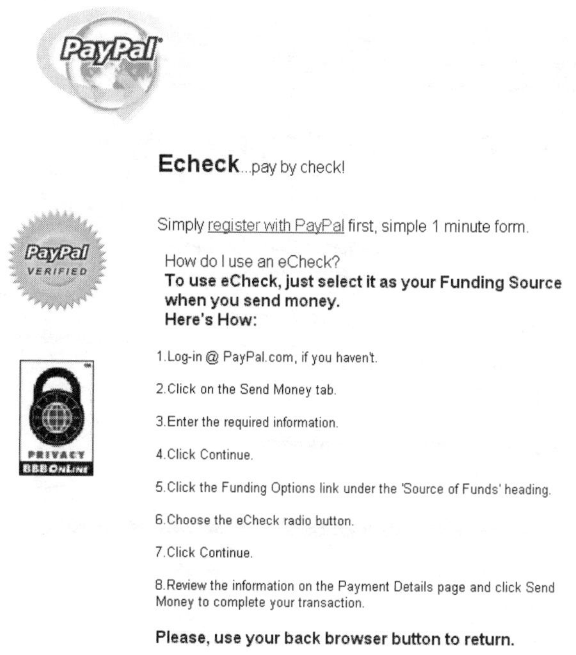

5

Echeck...pay by check!

Simply register with PayPal first, simple 1 minute form.

How do I use an eCheck?
**To use eCheck, just select it as your Funding Source
when you send money.
Here's How:**

1.Log-in @ PayPal.com, if you haven't.

2.Click on the Send Money tab.

3.Enter the required information.

4.Click Continue.

5.Click the Funding Options link under the 'Source of Funds' heading.

6.Choose the eCheck radio button.

7.Click Continue.

8.Review the information on the Payment Details page and click Send Money to complete your transaction.

Please, use your back browser button to return.

FIGURE 5-9   About Echecks from PayPal

Next, look into a feature called Equipment Financing for eBay, as shown in Figure 5-10. This feature is powered by a financial company called Direct Capital, which offers eBay buyers and sellers the chance to use its services to finance the purchase of expensive equipment on eBay. Several features are offered to the seller, including the reimbursement of the seller's Final Value Fees and PayPal fees if the buyer finances through Direct Capital, to encourage sellers to include this option within their eBay listing.

As an eBay buyer in this case, Direct Capital can offer 100 percent financing, an option for no down payments, startup finance options, and flexible payment terms such as deferred, seasonal, and skip payments. The company can accommodate a full range of credit types and equipment costs, based on the setup of your business. Plus, since Direct Capital is handling the financing, you can structure your payment terms with them regardless of the seller's requirements, since they will arrange immediate payment to the seller.

NOTE   *Direct Capital can cover financing anywhere in the United States except Puerto Rico, but it requires a $2000 minimum level of financing.*

FIGURE 5-10   The Equipment Financing page

If you think you'll need financing for a purchase, you can prequalify with Direct Capital before the auction is closed. Then, once you place a bid on a listing and are hopeful of winning the auction, you would notify Direct Capital to start the final approving process. The Prequalification application review takes approximately 30 minutes, while the final approval process depends on how quickly Direct Capital gets the item number and seller information—this typically can be accomplished within the same business day. If you're curious as to what kinds of equipment you can finance, check out the listings in Figure 5-11.

In the end, consult with your company's finance department or whoever holds the company purse strings. If you're looking for expensive equipment, you've probably already asked for formal approval to spend that kind of corporate cash, so you can consult with them as to how to resolve this purchase. Whether it's a meeting with your company's assigned banker or your CFO making a few phone calls, there's usually a way to make the payment process happen. The best news is that once you've done the first transaction, you'll know how to handle future transactions, and that's when the real savings can come into play.

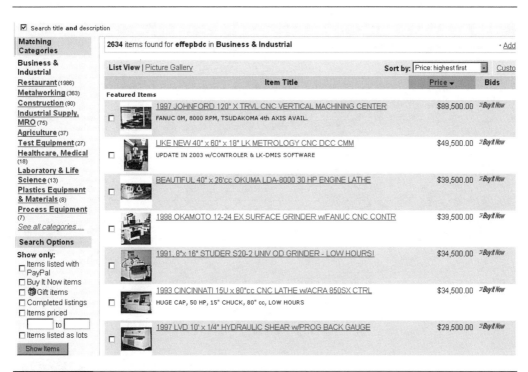

FIGURE 5-11 Types of equipment that can be financed

Summary

The Industry Marketplaces section of eBay is incredibly useful for finding both commodity items and large-scale equipment for your company needs.

Identify the appropriate areas of eBay to find the business supplies you need. Look for both auctions and sellers when it comes to researching purchases, and ask lots of questions. Be flexible in your search for cheaper suppliers. Consider items that do the same job or function similarly to the original item with about the same or better quality.

Take the time to compute costs of eBay purchases versus your current costs with existing suppliers. Make sure the cost saving justifies the time and effort put in to procure these items. Consider the other costs, such as dependability, reliability, and internal demand of the supply you're procuring.

Be ready to consider multiple shipping and payment options when it comes to larger equipment purchases. Know the seller's terms before you buy, and know the methods you plan to use to satisfy the after-sales process. Research your company's abilities when it comes to shipping and freight, as well as payment options.

Part II

Bring Your Business to eBay

Chapter 6

Lay the Groundwork for Your eBay Identity

In this chapter…

- ■ Choose your eBay coordinator
- ■ Take the first steps toward becoming an eBay seller
- ■ Register an account with eBay
- ■ Build up feedback by buying items on eBay
- ■ Highlight your company using About Me

You've taken a good look at your company's products and have a good idea of the amount and range of goods you can offer for sale on eBay. You've checked out the eBay web site and familiarized yourself with how an eBay auction looks and operates, and you've seen how to search through the millions of listings to find a set of items. You've also learned how to buy goods on eBay. Now it's time to look at the other side of that transaction: the seller's side.

In this chapter, you walk through the basic steps you'll need to take to establish your corporate eBay identity to sell selected goods.

Choose Your eBay Coordinator

Before you go through the eBay registration process, it's critical that someone in your company be designated as the official eBay coordinator. Perhaps it's you, or maybe the title should belong to someone else. Often, an edict is issued that the company should hop on eBay and someone, somewhere, should start listing items. Before you know it, a host of items has been offered and sold, but the initial lister has problems accessing the inventory, doesn't know how to ship the products, doesn't have the support of the shipping department, and can't handle the flood of e-mails that arrive!

That's why we recommend selecting an eBay coordinator *before* you continue any further with the process—don't just choose someone who's handy once the fires start burning. After the coordinator has been chosen, he or she should follow the steps presented in this chapter. That way, you're not duplicating efforts or causing confusion with multiple accounts and user IDs. And always remember that a successful eBay strategy depends on a strong team supporting the eBay coordinator.

Why the Coordinator Matters

You may be asking "Why do we need a specific eBay coordinator? Can't a group of people contribute equal time to get the job done? It's all on the computer, right?" That's a simplified way of looking at the situation, but it's not a realistic one.

First off, an eBay account can have only *one* e-mail address attached to it. That means that any e-mails from the eBay staff; any e-mails from customers asking about an item for sale; any e-mails showing the listing, closing price, and after-sale information for an item posted on eBay;

and any billing or payment e-mails tied to eBay will be sent to this account. Even if a new e-mail account is set up to handle eBay issues, if multiple people are responsible for dealing with the account, it can be difficult to coordinate who has read a particular e-mail and whether a question has been answered. What if no one checks the account for a couple of days? What if someone checks the account and accidentally deletes a message someone else needed to file away? Having one person receive, redirect, and file this information can save your company a lot of frustration and troubles.

> **TIP** *The eBay coordinator should ask IT to create a new e-mail account specifically for eBay usage, so the coordinator's e-mail regarding other work and personal matters doesn't get mixed up with e-mail regarding eBay matters. And although you and/or your coordinator may want to create your own personal accounts on eBay, remember that if you use a personal e-mail address for the eBay corporate account, you can't reuse it for a personal eBay account.*

6

Secondly, the e-mail information flow needs to be coordinated by someone who sees everything that's coming up and knows either how it was handled or to whom the matter was redirected to be resolved. Although the eBay coordinator should not be expected to answer every single e-mail that comes into the eBay account's inbox, if one person does all the redirecting, filing, and occasional answering, that person will know the status of every issue that occurs via e-mail.

It's very common, for example, for some buyers to send repeated e-mails asking about the status of a listing. Today, with eBay's expansive communication system, almost all e-mails are forwarded with precise listing information. Without a specified coordinator, whoever receives such e-mail might have to spend an inordinate amount of time figuring out the status of a particular transaction. Or, for example, if management wants to know how many listings were put up this month, the eBay coordinator can simply log onto eBay, access the My eBay section, and click the Seller tab to provide a quick and precise answer.

The coordinator can monitor high bid prices as they come in, react quickly if an auction ends early due to a certain preset price being realized (which is discussed in Chapter 8), and get a feel for which auctions are outperforming others based on bid activity and the number of customer questions regarding the listing.

Identify Ideal Coordinator Candidates

If the company has already decided that you are the best candidate, choose teammates from different departments to work with as you coordinate your eBay strategy. However, if you're searching for a coordinator, look for a person who is eager to accept new projects and who understands how eBay can help the company. The coordinator should understand the importance of management buy-in and support and should be a trustworthy person who can handle a new project. The coordinator should be flexible enough to handle change and keep track, via documentation, of aspects of new processes so others will be able to track what has been done if necessary.

Getting Outside Help

One popular option for many aspiring eBay sellers is to have an experienced eBay user sell *for* them. This service is provided by two types of sellers on eBay: the trading assistant and the trading post.

The *trading assistant* is an individual who is registered with eBay to sell merchandise for others on eBay. You can choose a trading assistant for your specific situation by visiting http://www.ebay.com/tradingassistants and selecting a person according to his or her area code, zip code, or selling specialty. A trading assistant can benefit your company in a variety of ways, from helping get you started setting up your listings all the way up to running your eBay business from top to bottom.

A *trading post* is an actual brick-and-mortar location where either you bring in the items you want to sell or someone picks up your merchandise. Registered trading posts in your area that meet eBay's strict selling standards can be found by using the Trading Assistants Directory and selecting the checkbox that says Show Only Trading Assistants Who Have Drop-Off Locations.

Become an eBay Seller

At this point, you're ready to get in front of a computer and create an eBay seller's account. Let's walk through the steps you need to follow. We'll discuss how to create the user ID for the new account and consider the setup information you may need in association with your new eBay account.

Choose an eBay User ID

Your user ID is the name every buyer is going to see in each of your auction listings. In essence, it's your eBay "brand name" as you build a reputation.

Today, with over 125 million registered eBay users, a lot of user ID combinations exist, and it's getting difficult to find a unique ID when you register. Many people use either parts of their name, their favorite science fiction or television character, their favorite hobby, or the name of a collectible they sell to help build a user ID. However, you, as a company account, bring an advantage to the table that very few eBay sellers have—an existing business name. Part of the value of using eBay is that your company brings its reputation and brand name with the account, and it's perfectly legal (and encouraged) to use that name in your eBay dealings. For example, IBM's user ID is very simple—*ibm*.

Some companies like to add in words, such as *auctions, sales,* or so on, to keep separate IDs for separate types of sales. Or words are added to business names to prevent confusion with other businesses that use the same or a similar name. For example, several Atomic Comics comic book stores exist across the country. Since the physical shop locations serve primarily a local or regional audience, comic book shoppers who visit the actual store know exactly from where they're buying. But on eBay, owners of stores with similar names may find it necessary to create individual IDs to separate their businesses from others with the same name, so they may use IDs such as atomiccomics, atomic-comics, atomiccomicauctions, and atomic-comic-auctions.

NOTE *When it comes time to enter a user ID, think of something simple that conveys your company name or brand and that's easy for people to remember. Be prepared to try different combinations if your first choice is unavailable.*

Did you know?

eBay User ID History

In the beginning, eBay users simply used their e-mail addresses as their user IDs, so sellers wouldn't have to remember yet another user ID and buyers and other users could freely contact one another with questions or concerns. However, as eBay grew in participant size and number of listings, spammers started collecting these publicly displayed e-mail addresses and flooding them with tons of unsolicited junk e-mail.

More dangerous, however, were the group of malicious spammers who contacted eBay users posing as eBay staff. These spammers' e-mails would con unsuspecting users into giving up personal information such as passwords and credit card account numbers, which resulted in cases of identity theft, siphoned financial accounts, and more. Eventually, eBay began requiring all buyers and sellers to create a user ID that was not an e-mail address. Today, all eBay buyers and sellers have their own registered user IDs and passwords.

Register on eBay

One of eBay's principles is that everyone is an equal seller on an equal platform. Therefore, everyone from the beginning user to the biggest corporation goes through the same steps to register as an eBay seller. For your company, registration is handled by the eBay coordinator.

The Registration Process

Let's get started with the step-by-step creation of a new account:

1. Use an Internet web browser to go to eBay's home page at http://www.ebay.com.

2. In the upper text navigation area, click Register.

3. In the Registration screen shown in Figure 6-1, fill in the information requested:

    ■ eBay coordinator's first and last name

    ■ Company street address

    ■ City, state, and zip code

    ■ Primary and secondary telephone numbers for your eBay coordinator

    ■ E-mail address for your eBay account (you'll enter this twice)

    ■ Date of birth

TIP

For the Date Of Birth field, consider using a more generic date, such as the company founding date or the CEO's birth date. Remember that this date must be such that it shows you are at least 18 years old in order to register.

Register: Enter Information | Help
1 **Enter Information**   2. Choose User ID & Password   3. Check Your Email

If you want to bid or buy on eBay, you'll need to register first. It's easy and **free**.

First name

Last name

Street address

City

State
Select State

Zip code

Country
United States

Primary telephone
( ) - ext.:

Secondary telephone (Optional)
( ) - ext.:

Date of Birth
–Month– –Day– Year

Important: A valid email address is required to complete registration.

Email address

Examples: myname@yahoo.com, myname@example.com, etc.

Re-enter email address

FIGURE 6-1   Enter information into the Registration screen

4. You will also be asked to review and agree to eBay's User Agreement and Privacy Policy. Once you have read through the policy, click the checkbox next to the words "I agree to the following." Then, click Continue, and you'll be asked to enter a user ID and password. eBay gives you some options for passwords as well.

NOTE   *Depending on the size of your company, you may want your legal department to go through eBay's policies to make sure they do not conflict with company rules and regulations. You'll note hypertext links for Printer-Friendly Version. Click that link and print out the resulting pages, and show them to your legal department. We recommend that you go ahead and complete the registration, and if Legal tells you there's a problem, you can cancel the account later.*

5. You'll also be asked to select from a list of secret questions and provide an answer. This is a mechanism that eBay created to help a user who forgets his or her password (a common occurrence, which will probably happen as coordinators change and more people become involved). If you forget your password when you log on, you'll simply click the appropriate button and eBay will send you an e-mail with the secret question and ask you for the answer. If you provide the correct answer, eBay will send you an e-mail containing your eBay password.

<table>
<tr><td>TIP</td><td>Choose a question with an answer related to the company rather than to your personal life. That way, if other authorized people need access to the account, you're not revealing personal data that you may have used to set up personal accounts and passwords. For example, for the question "What street did you grow up on?" you might type in the street of your corporate headquarters. For questions like "What is your pet's name?" or "What is your school mascot?" think of an animal that is associated with your company or division—maybe an actual mascot or the name of the boss's dog.</td></tr>
</table>

6. After you've entered information into all the fields on this page, click the Continue button. If the user ID you typed in is already in use by someone else, you will be prompted in a new screen to build a unique eBay user ID. It will ask you for three words associated with your business and offer a few combinations of letters and numbers from which you can choose as your unique eBay user ID. You may also be required to type in a new password if the one you typed in doesn't meet eBay's criteria.

7. If the user ID you selected has not been used, you will be taken to the third and final step of the Registration process, involving your e-mail account. Because eBay needs to know that the e-mail address you provided is a valid e-mail address, eBay will send you an e-mail asking you to click a special link that's sent back to eBay. Follow the instructions provided in that e-mail to confirm your account and complete this process. After you do this, your e-mail account and other registration information will be entered into eBay's database as a valid user.

<table>
<tr><td>CAUTION</td><td>The confirmation e-mail may not show up immediately after you register. In some cases, it may take hours or even a day for this e-mail to arrive in your inbox, depending on the efficiency of your corporate e-mail system and eBay's level of activity. If you don't receive this e-mail within 24 hours, go to this web address: http://pages.ebay.com/services/ registration/reqtemppass.html. You'll be asked to type in your e-mail information again so that eBay can send you confirmation.</td></tr>
</table>

Add Financial Information

At this point, you will have a functioning eBay account, so you can go online and bid on any item listed. However, before you can sell an item, you'll need to take a few more steps to establish an automatic method for eBay to collect its auction fees, as well as verify your identity.

1. Once you have confirmed your account, click the link to set up your Seller's account. The Registration will appear in a new window. From the Registration confirmation screen, click the link to Set Up Your Sellers Account.

2. You will be taken to a three-part process called Seller Account: Verify Information. In part 1 of this process, you verify the address, telephone, and birth date information you provided in the registration process. Once you are done, click the Continue button.

3. In part 2 of this process, you are asked to Provide Credit Card Verification. In this step, you need to input a credit or debit card number, the card identification number, expiration date, and card holder name. In addition, the billing address for this credit card must match the address on file with eBay. If necessary, you can change your address during this step to match the credit card number you use. Once you have completed all this information, click the Continue button.

> **NOTE**   *Because free e-mail accounts from services such as Yahoo! or Hotmail do not verify your identity, if you supplied an e-mail address from one of these services, you are required to type in a credit card number before you finish the buyer's registration. That credit card number is the default used for the seller registration process, though you can change it during this step.*

4. You will be asked to add checking account information. You need to input your bank name, routing number, and checking account number in this step. Once that is all entered, click the Continue button.

5. In the third and final step of this process, select which financial method will be used to pay for any eventual charges using eBay, such as the fee for listing an auction or the final fee for selling an item. You can choose between your checking account or your credit card account. Once you've chosen your automatic payment method, click the Continue button.

You have now completed the Seller Registration process and are able to start selling items on eBay. These steps help to ensure the security of the buying community. Here is what eBay posted when it changed its policy a few years ago:

Why does eBay have additional requirements in order to sell?
As of June 11, 2001, the requirements to sell at eBay have changed to ensure that we provide a safe environment for the eBay community. eBay now requires a credit/debit card and bank account information to help ensure that:
   Sellers are of a legal age.
   Sellers are serious about listing an item on eBay.
   You are further protected from fraudulent sellers.

eBay has really good reasons for asking for credit card information from sellers. A single fraudulent seller can ruin the eBay experience of a potential buyer (meaning the buyer may not use the eBay service again) and taint the reputations of honest sellers. eBay needs to protect its users and sellers to stay in business. Additionally, hoax listings, such as the sale of a human kidney that was posted a few years back, only serve to clutter the listings for serious buyers and sellers like you.

If the eBay coordinator has a corporate credit card, he or she can use that card and get reimbursed for any eBay fees. However, if you're part of a smaller organization that doesn't use corporate credit cards, you will need to work with your comptroller or accountant to establish a subaccount to be used primarily for eBay revenue and expenses or have your company bank account tied directly to your eBay account.

Set Up Financial Accounts

Depending on the level of financial accounts your organization has established, you may want to consider a couple of extra options to help your company while it conducts business on eBay. The "currency" used on eBay is the electronic kind: paperless, fast, and easy to access.

Although other payment forms used to be accepted, as eBay became a more efficient marketplace and people began to rely on it for more than just collectibles, the need for efficient payment methods grew. The standard method of payment has therefore become the credit card. Sellers not interested in waiting for a check to clear or a money order to get sent through the mail—and/or those looking to be as flexible as possible in terms of payment options—quickly adopted and promoted online payment options and found ways to accept credit cards. Consumers, accustomed to using credit cards in daily shopping, increased their online usage of credit cards after card issuers like MasterCard and Visa sharply increased their fraud protection efforts and eBay augmented its insurance programs, all to encourage online credit card usage. (As it turns out, payment by credit card is a good thing for eBay sellers, because survey results have indicated that eBay shoppers tend to spend more money when they're given the option of paying by credit card.)

PayPal

With over 56 million users, PayPal has been widely adopted as the online method for credit card support for the eBay Marketplace. An online payment service that started six years ago, PayPal enables people to store "electronic money" in their accounts. Payment is gathered from their bank or credit card and sent via e-mail to other PayPal members to pay for merchandise. If merchandise is returned, money goes back into the buyer's PayPal account.

NOTE *PayPal now offers an ATM/debit card that draws against the PayPal account. This debit card also has a MasterCard number and can act as a small company's corporate credit card. A 1.5% user incentive award is a great benefit of this card.*

Today, eBay owns PayPal and has fully integrated its capabilities into auction listings. PayPal and eBay offer promotions and incentives for sellers to accept only PayPal as a payment option. It's the preferred standard, and loyal eBay buyers have said in surveys that they tend to shop more with auction sellers that offer PayPal as a payment method. In fact over 75% of the listings on eBay end with PayPal as the form of payment.

Using an Existing Merchant Account   Taking credit card payments online is vital to your success in an e-commerce business. Your customers expect this level of ease and security. Also, studies have shown that by being able to use credit cards as a form of payment, customers spend more money than with other forms of payment.

If your company currently has a merchant account for accepting credit cards—whether it's for e-commerce operations from the company web site or for dealing with small vendors—you should be able with that account to accept online payments using a secure web page and/or take a credit card payment over the phone at your company's toll-free number. Even if you already

How to ... Enroll in PayPal

If your company currently does not have a merchant account or the ability to accept credit cards, we strongly urge you to consider getting a PayPal account for your eBay business. Even if your company *does* have a merchant account, using PayPal can help to generate confidence among potential buyers because of the protections it offers.

PayPal offers various kinds of accounts, depending on how much revenue you generate during the course of your online buying and selling. Typically, you need to get a PayPal business/merchant account. With this account, you'll be able to receive credit card payments and send payments to anyone with an e-mail address under the name of your business. Signing up is very simple:

1. Go to http://www.paypal.com.

2. Click the Sign Up button under New User.

3. The Sign Up screen will appear, as shown next, allowing you to select a personal or business account and your country of origin. Choose Business Account In and select your country of origin. Then click Continue.

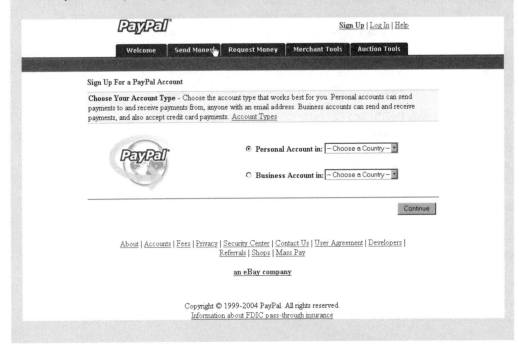

4. Enter your business information on the following screen in the fields provided, and then click Continue.

5. You'll be asked to provide some personal information on the next screen, where among other things you'll want to list a specific e-mail address for your business (this can be the same e-mail address you used for eBay registration). Click Continue to finish up.

6. Finally, PayPal will process the information and send you a confirmation e-mail. After you receive this e-mail, open it and click the link to confirm your e-mail and activate your PayPal account.

have an eBay merchant account, you'll want to offer your customers the opportunity to pay through PayPal. The eBay community has grown to trust the ease and security of using PayPal with credit cards as well as e-checks. Signing up for an account is easy, as we've explained. By offering PayPal as an additional form of payment, you are giving your customers flexibility in their payment methods.

eBay Success Story

PayPal Pays

Janelle Elms, co-author of this book, conducted a little test with one of her clients to see how much eBay buyers respond to the option of using PayPal as a means of payment. Her client, a well-known and successful businesswoman in the antiques business, had a merchant account that allowed her to take credit card payments in her physical store location. Janelle recommended that she open a PayPal account, but the client could not see the benefit of having two companies through which she could accept credit cards.

The two then decided to conduct a test: The first week, they ran professional-looking listings, complete with beautiful pictures, creative and telling descriptions, competitive terms of service, and the option for bidders to call her toll-free number with any questions about the items for sale, as well as the option to pay by credit card through her merchant account. Nothing sold that week. The second week, they ran the exact same listings but added that the seller would also accept PayPal as an additional form of payment. Not only did everything sell, but most items sold for a higher price than the seller was expecting. Clearly, PayPal is a recognized and trusted form of payment for many eBay buyers.

Build Feedback Ratings by Buying on eBay

One of the best protections eBay members enjoy is the feedback rating system, which allows people to leave positive and negative comments based on their transactions with other buyers and sellers. Sellers and buyers gain reputations based on their interactions, and on eBay, these reputations count for everything: future sales can be influenced by a good record as well as a poor one.

While your existing business brings with it an established reputation, some people still want to see how your eBay behavior will affect an interaction. After all, it usually takes only one bad incident to make a consumer cautious, and while most consumers may know how to handle problems with companies that have a brick-and-mortar physical presence, they might be less than familiar with how an online transaction might be handled.

To avoid some of this buyer hesitancy, you can establish a feedback record even before you make your first big push as a seller. The easiest way to do this is to buy items on eBay. Purchase items that either you or your company can use and make sure you can pay the seller quickly. Some sellers even state in their auction listing that "fast payers get instant positive feedback." Those are traits to look for when choosing goods to purchase. Buy office supplies for your company, start holiday shopping early, or buy office birthday gifts. Best of all, this interaction will help you get familiar with how eBay operates, which will make for a wiser interaction once your company is an eBay seller. This will also allow you to see, from a buyer's standpoint, what you like and don't like about sellers in the eBay community. Getting used to the feedback system, and earning a good reputation, will make you a stronger seller.

Highlight Your Company Using About Me

One of the founding aspects of eBay is the sense of community that it helps generate, the chance for users not only to buy and sell goods, but to meet people with similar interests, hobbies, and goals. eBay lets users establish a "home page" of sorts as a way to express themselves and provide a central focus for users, highlighting their feedback records and current auctions available. This page is visible to the world and has a fixed web address, so you can advertise yourself to others and they can find out more about you. It's called About Me, and it's a free function for any eBay registered user.

More important, for businesses, your About Me page is one of the few places you're allowed to provide web links back to your existing company's web site and other contact information. Your About Me page allows you to establish your credibility on the site. You may have owned a hobby store for 25 years in the real world, but you are a newbie on eBay and to its community. This page offers you a chance to talk about your quarter of a century experience, discuss your expertise of radio-controlled planes, and display a picture of your brick and mortar. Also, because of the fixed nature of the web page address, it's a great starting point for customers you want to introduce to your eBay auctions and goods. While some of the items on this page are provided by eBay, such as a list of the most recent feedback comments and current auctions, the rest is designed by you.

You can stick to eBay's template designs, or you can create your own:

■ From the eBay home page, click Services in the upper text navigation bar. Then scroll down the page and look in the left column, under Member Reputation, for a link to the About Me page. Log into your My eBay page, click the Preferences tab, and under the About Me page heading, click Create A Personal 'About Me' Page. From here, you can use the template to create a page.

■ If you want to create your own page design, go straight to this web page URL: http://members.ebay.com/ws2/eBayISAPI.dll?AboutMeLogin. You'll see the About Me screen shown in Figure 6-2. Click the Create Or Edit Your Page button.

Create the About Me Page

If you decide to create an About Me page, eBay has organized the process into three steps in which you choose the layout of the page, create the content for your page, and then review and submit your page. eBay assists you by offering several layouts so you don't have to know much about HTML. (But you can use all sorts of programming tricks to make your About Me page as complex or as simple as you'd like.)

Choose a Layout

Your first decision is what kind of layout you'd like to use for your About Me page. eBay presents you with three options, as shown in Figure 6-3:

■ Centered layout

■ Two-column layout

■ Multi-column layout

About Me starting screen

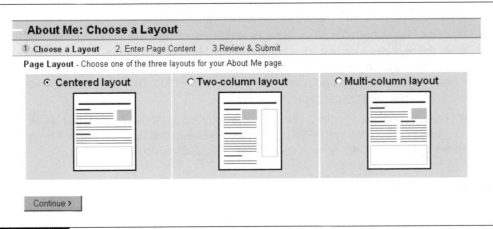

FIGURE 6-3   Choose a layout

There is no right or wrong choice in this case. If you're going to keep the page simple, a centered layout is probably your best bet. If you think you might want to offer special deals on your About Me page to new visitors, a two-column layout could provide a handy sidebar for changing deals, while the main column stays the same. Of course, if your account is going to encompass multiple categories of items, a multi-column layout would allow to summarize each section on one unifying page.

Enter Page Content

Here's where you get to fill in the information about your company and the products that you sell—both your eBay and non-eBay sales. You'll see fields such as the following:

Page Title   Use the name of your company and indicate whether you're focusing on auctions, fixed pricing, or maintaining an eBay store (more on the eBay store in Chapter 13). If you look at other companies' About Me pages, you'll see page titles such as "IBM Authorized Auctions" or "Sun Microsystems eBay Store." You can name your site something similar if you want.

Subtitle   Each paragraph in your layout will start with a subtitle. Appropriate subtitle choices are things like "About my company," "History," or "Company Facts." Give your titles and subtitles a bit of thought—you'll use these to grab the buyer's attention and draw them in.

Paragraph   Enter anything from a paragraph or two of text to a complex table filled with pictures, links, and information. Be warned, however, that while fast Internet access via methods like cable modem or DSL are being adopted in the United States, most people (50 percent as of this writing) still use dial-up Internet access. If you make an About Me page that's too loaded with large graphics, and it takes too long to load onto a viewer's screen, a potential customer may get tired of waiting and go elsewhere.

The key is to present information that's going to matter to your consumers. What should people know about you? Can you show how reliable, inexpensive, innovative, exciting, or necessary your products are? Use the fact that your business is established and go through some company history to prove you're not just some fly-by-night operation that may disappear with a buyer's money. Finally, if you want to make your page more fancy, consult with your IT or creative services department to have them help you use HTML (Hypertext Markup Language, the language of the World Wide Web) to make this About Me page stand out from the rest.

TIP *A great source of material for your About Me page may already exist if your company has a web site. You can copy information about your company from your company's site onto your About Me page.*

Label of Picture   eBay's default settings allow you to display an image on the About Me page. Of course, you can add more pictures by referencing them in the Paragraph section, but especially for the beginning user, a picture is a handy way to display the company logo if you have no HTML knowledge. Simply type in the label you'd like to appear with the image.

Link to Your Picture   Fill in the URL that points to your company logo. Typically, this logo will be found on the home page of your company web site. If your company is still building a web site, or the current site is being designed, you can store your logo (or another picture) and provide the URL address here.

TIP *If you want to use a logo or picture from your company web site, the easiest way to find the URL address of that logo is to bring up your company home page, right-click the logo, and choose Properties. The URL address will be under Address in the window that opens.*

Show Your eBay Activity   Your last few choices customize what options are automatically presented on your About Me page, as you can see in Figure 6-4. eBay allows you to decide how much feedback and how many current listings appear on your page. While anybody could discover this information about your account by clicking around the eBay listings, including the information here makes it easy for buyers to evaluate your eBay presence.

Show Feedback You've Received   You can either show 0, 10, 25, 50, or 100 feedback comments on your About Me page. We recommend selecting between 10 and 25 comments. These "personal recommendations" to potential buyers will provide credibility to your online selling presence. The feedback rating is plainly available and people can click it to investigate further; however, having 10 or more positive feedback comments appear on your page can instantly prove your credibility as a seller.

TIP *If you use one of the standard templates, you should always use the 10 feedback comments per page setting. Showing credibility with other customers gives you instant credibility with the buyer reading your About Me page. Studies have shown that including feedback information in your listing can increase your final auction price.*

6

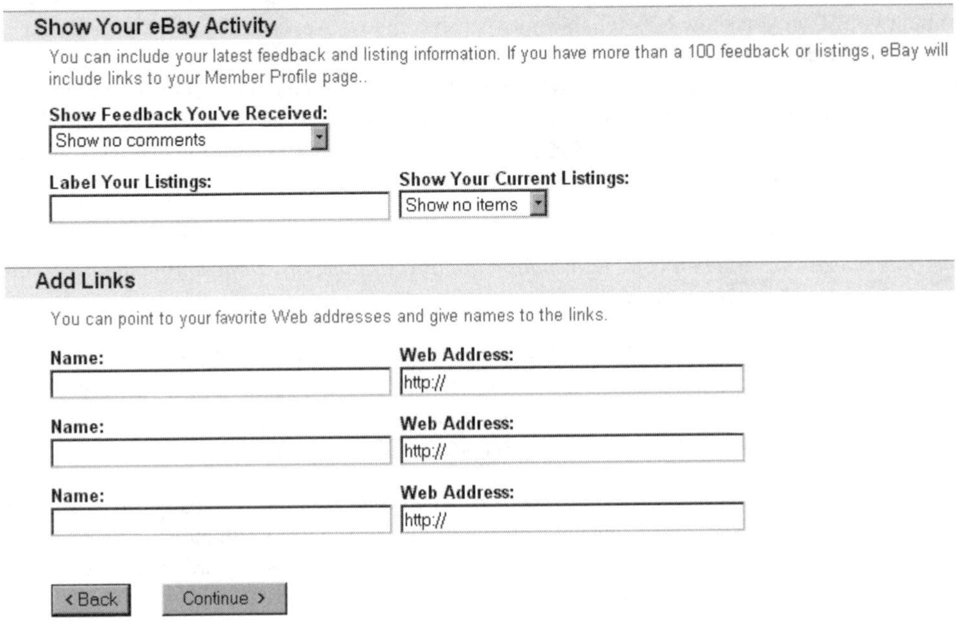

Show Your eBay Activity

You can include your latest feedback and listing information. If you have more than a 100 feedback or listings, eBay will include links to your Member Profile page..

Show Feedback You've Received:

[Show no comments ▾]

Label Your Listings:

[   ]

Show Your Current Listings:

[Show no items ▾]

Add Links

You can point to your favorite Web addresses and give names to the links.

Name: **Web Address:**

[   ]   [http://   ]

Name: **Web Address:**

[   ]   [http://   ]

Name: **Web Address:**

[   ]   [http://   ]

[< Back]   [Continue >]

FIGURE 6-4   Show your eBay activity

Label Your Listings   Labels can be as simple as "Items for Sale" or "Current Items for Sale," or as creative as anything you can imagine: "Fabulous Deals," "Once in A Lifetime Purchasing Opportunities," "What Fell Off the Back of the Truck." Your About Me page is a *huge* part of your eBay persona.

> **TIP**   *In developing a marketing plan for your online business, it is essential that you carry through with that plan in everything that you put out there about your company.*

Show Your Current Listings   Like feedback, you can show 0, 10, 25, 50, or 100 of your listings. We strongly recommend that you show at least 10 listings, if not more. You're hoping at this point—especially if you use your About Me page as a portal for new customers—that people have read through your company's description and are interested in buying products from you. You want them to be able to act on that interest, and if they see a list of items for sale, they can click through directly to an item and place a bid. As far as how many listings to include, either 10 or 25 is a safe number to start off with. (You can always come back and change it later.)

Add Links   This section allows you to add web links to your About Me page. It's not used very often, since many sellers create their own links within the paragraphs of the page. But it's a great place to reference any partners in your strategy or perhaps direct viewers to a section of your company's web site. The Name field contains the text a person will see and click, and the Web Address field is the actual web address that takes viewers to a specific page.

Once you're done, click the Continue button and review your work. If you like what you see, click the Submit button to activate your page. Once your About Me page is active, a little Me icon will appear next to your eBay user ID every time you list an auction, which viewers can click to see your About Me page.

Summary

It's critical that someone in your company serve as the official eBay coordinator. Selecting an eBay coordinator before you continue with the listing process is wiser than just choosing someone who's handy once the auction fires start burning. Once the coordinator has been chosen, that person should create a plan that avoids duplicating effort or causing confusion with multiple accounts and user IDs. Although one coordinator oversees the eBay program, this is still a team effort, and the coordinator will need all the help he or she can get.

One of the foundations for healthy eBay sales lies in the feedback rating system, which allows people to leave positive and negative comments based on transactions with other parties. Since future sales can be influenced by either a positive or a negative record, you should establish a feedback record before you make your big push as a seller. The easiest way to do that is to purchase items on eBay that you or your company can use, and make sure you pay the seller quickly.

If your company currently accepts credit cards online, whether for e-commerce operations from the company web site or for dealing with small vendors, you should have the ability to accept online payments using a secure web page. Consider PayPal as an additional option, since PayPal has a lot of credibility among buyers because of its reputation and the buyer protections it offers.

After you set up your account, eBay helps build your credibility on the site by making the process of creating an About Me page easy. It's organized it into a three-step process in which you choose the layout of the page, create the content for your page, and then review and submit your page. eBay assists you by offering several preprogrammed layouts so you don't have to know anything about HTML. But you can also add HTML to the page if you want.

6

Chapter 7

Define How Your Business Will Work

In this chapter...

- Decide policies for auctions
- Determine shipping strategy
- Use in-house or outsourced shipping
- Offer international shipping

By this point, your business is already a couple steps ahead of the competition in that you've taken the time to lay the groundwork for your eBay online presence. After your eBay coordinator is selected, the next move is to determine how to perform the necessary steps to make your entry into this new sales channel a self-sustaining one. In this chapter, we cover what you should keep in mind when planning your first set of auctions, some suggestions on how to attract more sales on the eBay site, and how to fulfill those sales once the customer enters the portals of your e-commerce shop.

Decide Auction Policies

As you've probably noticed by this point in the book, we're extremely big on carefully planning out your moves before executing them. We certainly don't mean to temper your enthusiasm—in fact, we're sure that now that you've reached this chapter, you're itching to get truckloads of items up for auction on eBay. However, there's a great deal of difference between the eBay dilettante who dreams of riches by selling items from the attic and watching reruns of *Antiques Roadshow* on PBS, and a disciplined, prepared, and bottom-line conscious company like yours.

Therefore, let's take awhile to think about the auction policies you'll implement when you enter the eBay pool of buyers and sellers. The policy you set will affect many aspects of your eBay venture: the attention your listings get, fulfillment of customers, and timeliness of payments received from buyers. Therefore, it's more than worth your time now to decide how your eBay strategy is going to handle typical seller situations.

TIP   *Depending on the size and the corporate style of your firm, you may not have all of the answers or authority you need to make final decisions on company policy. Treat eBay as you would any other new sales channel, and make sure that you—or your eBay coordinator—are able to talk with people in your shipping, sales, accounts payable, and invoicing departments to get the job done effectively.*

Shipping Policies—Multiple Options, Combining Items

Shipping policies are extremely important, and single-item or single-lot sales should move through your company's shipping department in exactly the same way, whether the sale came from your account manager or direct from the eBay web site. However, to encourage your company's eBay sales, it's common practice to combine freight costs when shipping items purchased in multiple listings.

Often, a prospective customer may want to purchase more than the single item or lot that you have available, placing bids on both. Or, if you have a suite of products available on eBay, a customer will choose to buy complementary goods from you. For example, you may sell a set of office desks to a client, and to complete the outfitting of his department in the same style, he will successfully bid for matching computer tables, file cabinets, and cubicle partitions.

Stating Your Policy Up Front

It's a good idea to state up front that winning multiple auctions will result in a bonus savings on shipping costs. This will encourage greater sales and customer loyalty. Make sure that something similar to the following appears on the page under each item you post on eBay:

We are more than happy to save you money on shipping by combining your orders. Please assist us in keeping these shipping prices low by:

1) Making sure that all of your combinable auctions have closed within a three-day period.

2) Sending one payment for the entire shipment. This is easier on your bookkeeping as well as ours.

You might also consider basing your policy on what you see in the verbiage of successful auction sellers. Some examples of shipping policies are shown in Figures 7-1, 7-2, and 7-3.

Shipping information

THIS IS A VERY NICE LOT OF MISCELLANEOUS CRAFT BOOKS, CROCHET, KNIT, PLASTIC CANVAS, AND OTHER CRAFTS....ALL ARE BRAND NEW...FROM ANNIE'S ATTIC, HOUSE OF WHITE BIRCHES, NEEDLECRAFT SHOP ETC..... SHIPPING IS MEDIA RATE (8.00 PLUS INSURANCE)....WILL GLADY ANSWER YOUR EMAILS...

CHECK OUT MY FREE SHIPPING WITH PURCHASES OF 5 OR MORE CRAFT BOOKS.... will accept Money orders and PayPal for same day shipping, personal checks must be cleared, takes about 7 - l0 days.....DEFINITE PAYMENT ARRANGEMENTS MUST BE MADE WITHIN 10 DAYS and if my terms of communication or payment are not met, I will relist , I try to present my merchandise as fairly as possible..... Mailing costs are for U.S.A. only, international rates will be figured at the request of a bidder or when auction is over..... ... Insurance is optional but my responsibility ends at the post office. AUCTIONS CAN BE COMBINED TO SAVE ON POSTAGE....IT IS A GREAT WAY TO BUY EXTRAS....PLEASE NOTIFY ME IF YOU ARE BUYING SEVERAL ITEMS OR EMAIL ME FOR POSTAGE. PLEASE DO NOT PAY FOR ITEMS WITHOUT ADDING SHIPPING, I REFUND THE PAYMENT. IF YOU DO NOT KNOW WHAT THE SHIPPING IS, PLEASE EMAIL ME. I WILL SEND AN INVOICE. PLEASE CHECK MY OTHER CRAFT AUCTIONS, THANKS!!!! .

FIGURE 7-1   Shipping policy example

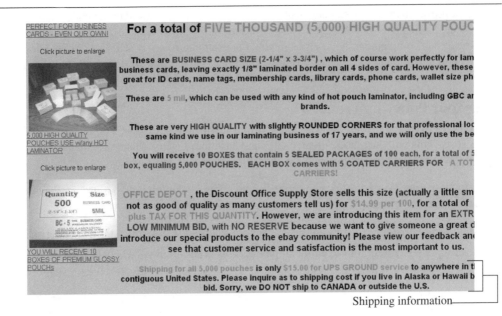

PERFECT FOR BUSINESS CARDS - EVEN OUR OWN!

Click picture to enlarge

5,000 HIGH QUALITY POUCHES USE w/any HOT LAMINATOR

Click picture to enlarge

YOU WILL RECEIVE 10 BOXES OF PREMIUM GLOSSY POUCHs

For a total of FIVE THOUSAND (5,000) HIGH QUALITY POUC

These are **BUSINESS CARD SIZE (2-1/4" x 3-3/4")**, which of course work perfectly for lam business card, leaving exactly 1/8" laminated border on all 4 sides of card. However, these great for ID cards, name tags, membership cards, library cards, phone cards, wallet size ph

These are 5 mil, which can be used with any kind of hot pouch laminator, including GBC a brands.

These are very **HIGH QUALITY** with slightly **ROUNDED CORNERS** for that professional loc same kind we use in our laminating business of 17 years, and we will only use the be

You will receive **10 BOXES** that contain **5 SEALED PACKAGES of 100** each, for a total of 5 box, equaling **5,000 POUCHES**. **EACH BOX comes with 5 COATED CARRIERS FOR** A TOT CARRIERS!

OFFICE DEPOT , the Discount Office Supply Store sells this size (actually a little sm not as good of quality as many customers tell us) for $14.99 per 100, for a total of 5 plus TAX FOR THIS QUANTITY. However, we are introducing this item for an EXTR LOW MINIMUM BID, with **NO RESERVE** because we want to give someone a great d introduce our special products to the ebay community! Please view our feedback an see that customer service and satisfaction is the most important to us.

Shipping for all 5,000 pouches **is only** $15.00 for UPS GROUND service **to anywhere in t contiguous United States. Please inquire as to shipping cost if you live in Alaska or Hawaii b bid. Sorry, we DO NOT ship to CANADA or outside the U.S.**

Shipping information

Shipping policy example

* Shipping Discounts are offered directly from the seller.

Shipping and payment details

Shipping and handling: Standard shipping service: US $40.00
(within United States)

   📦 **Pay only $2.00 shipping** **for each additional item!***
   (Shipping Discounts are offered directly from the seller.)

Shipping insurance: US $10.00 (Optional)

Sales tax: 0.600% (only in KY)

Will ship worldwide.

Shipping information

Shipping policy example

Consider Listing Other Items to Encourage Sales

Work with your shipping department to determine the costs involved when combining shipments. You should make these costs available to potential buyers by placing this information on the item's auction listing. The goal in providing this level of transparency is to make it more appealing for a buyer to purchase multiple products from you.

Following is an example of how you might list your formula:

XYZ Company combines freight charged under the following formula:
– For one item, you pay 100% of the fixed freight amount for that item.
– If you buy two to five items, you pay 100% of the first freight amount, plus 50% of the fixed freight amount for the additional items.
– If you buy more than five items, you pay only 25% of the fixed freight amount for each item.

Did you know?

7

The eBay Shipping Calculator

Built into the Sell Your Item form is a shipping calculator. This allows you to simply enter the weight of your item, your zip code, and which shipping carrier's service you would like to use; it then figures the shipping costs for your potential buyers.

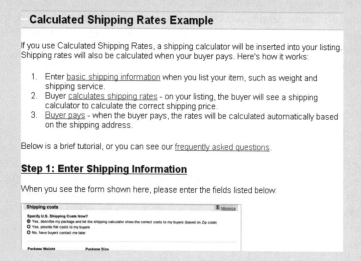

Calculated Shipping Rates Example

If you use Calculated Shipping Rates, a shipping calculator will be inserted into your listing. Shipping rates will also be calculated when your buyer pays. Here's how it works:

1. Enter <u>basic shipping information</u> when you list your item, such as weight and shipping service.
2. Buyer <u>calculates shipping rates</u> - on your listing, the buyer will see a shipping calculator to calculate the correct shipping price.
3. <u>Buyer pays</u> - when the buyer pays, the rates will be calculated automatically based on the shipping address.

Below is a brief tutorial, or you can see our <u>frequently asked questions</u>.

Step 1: Enter Shipping Information

When you see the form shown here, please enter the fields listed below:

Shipping costs   ✕ Minimize

Specify U.S. Shipping Costs Now?
◉ Yes, describe my package and let the shipping calculator show the correct costs to my buyers (based on Zip code)
○ Yes, provide flat costs to my buyers
○ No, have buyers contact me later

Package Weight   Package Size

If your shipping formula is based on weight versus the number of items purchased, you may be better off developing an interactive freight calculator and placing it as a hyperlink on the listing, like so:

If you're bidding on multiple auctions, try our <u>online shipping calculator</u>. Note that the shipping calculator can be used for computing postage for both domestic and international packages.

Payment Policies

Consult your company's finance or accounting department to set up policies for payment of eBay auction items. At first, your goal should be to ensure that you're following acceptable company procedures when offering certain methods of payment from clients, installment payments, and the like. You should also consider the following services when developing the payment policies for your eBay channel.

PayPal

PayPal had 56.7 million total accounts at the end of the Third Quarter of 2004, a 61 percent increase from the 35.2 million reported in the same quarter of 2003. PayPal has competitive merchant fees when compared to those of banks, with no setup fees, no monthly fees, and a very low per-transaction fee. In addition, since PayPal accepts currency from more than 45 countries, you can easily conduct numerous types of foreign money exchanges on eBay. PayPal provides a service that is as valuable to a Fortune 500 company as it is to a garage-based startup: it makes it easier for buyers to purchase items and it makes it easier for you to collect funds from eBay buyers.

PayPal provides the Winning Buyer Notification, which automatically sends an e-mail invoice to a buyer, including all listing details. Not only does this remove some of the work from your hands, but since the transaction is done electronically, it's much faster, which means that you'll receive payment more quickly.

Finally, PayPal offers several reporting tools that work with different accounting programs. We discuss this further in Chapter 11.

Escrow Services

One service eBay offers that may be slightly lesser known is its connection with Escrow.com, whose web site is shown in Figure 7-4. As a result of eBay's stepped-up efforts to protect consumers and sellers so that they can confidently deal with high-end items, eBay recommends that you use its escrow services with any transaction that involves goods costing more than $500.

eBay's partnership with Escrow.com allows that agency to protect both buyer and seller by acting as a trusted third-party during the transaction. As with any normal escrow agency, it manages the client's payment process (for a fee) from the beginning of the transaction until its completion. For more information on Escrow.com, see Chapter 10.

CAUTION   *Be aware that many fraudulent escrow agencies purport to be legitimate. To be safe, we recommend that if you require escrow, consider using the services of Escrow.com only.*

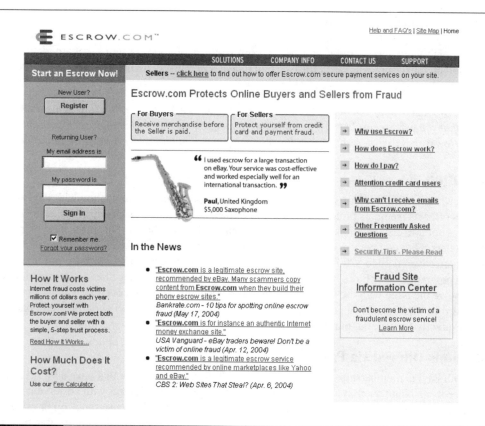

7

FIGURE 7-4   Escrow.com

Equipment Financing for eBay

One of the recurring requests of eBay customers has been to make purchasing large-ticket items easier. eBay has responded by offering financing via a seller's listings through the Equipment Financing for eBay program. Using this program, you will be able to close transactions more quickly and reduce the costs of transactions.

Return/Refund Policies

If your business is already established, you probably have set up return policies. You should determine acceptable return or refund policies for your eBay sales as well. Policies such as these are extremely product dependent, for obvious reasons—they'll vary tremendously depending on whether you ship metal back braces or live-culture French cheese, for example.

The key to applying an effective return or refund policy with eBay is to ensure that you conspicuously state your policy in each auction, no matter whether you're selling a lot of 1000 items or a single high-value piece. And if you deal in high volumes of goods or items that are identical to one another, make sure you've set up a system that can effectively identify or track all of the goods shipped.

If you list in your auction a 100 percent money-back guarantee, eBay research shows that you will receive bids 6 percent higher than auctions that do not offer such guarantees. However, only 1 percent of the eBay community will actually take you up on that offer.

Insurance

As of this writing, eBay does not offer a shipping insurance program. In conjunction with PayPal, eBay does offer its members protection against loss from non-delivery or misrepresentation. The coverage is not universal, but it is sufficient for the majority of purchases. This protection plan is free for sellers; your company does not have to provide insurance at this level.

Items are covered up to $200 (minus a $25 processing fee) under eBay's standard purchase-protection program. Since eBay's business relies on keeping its community together, eBay encourages you to resolve the issue with the seller rather than filing a claim. And, of course, if PayPal or a credit card was used during a purchase, you're encouraged to contact PayPal or the credit card company directly to work out purchase details.

Protections Offered via PayPal

Sellers with PayPal memberships with a minimum of 50 items of feedback that have a 98 percent positive feedback rating on eBay will be able to offer buyers $500 in coverage, with no service fee. PayPal also offers a money-back guarantee program. Buyers can purchase insurance on physical goods for transactions of less than $1000 from qualified sellers. Since PayPal is the insurance holder, sellers are not held liable for buyer claims made under the plan.

> **CAUTION**   *This service is available only for purchasers in the United States. Be careful that you don't include any verbiage in your offers that implies that international buyers will be covered under this program.*

The SquareTrade Seal of Approval

One final service you can offer a potential client is the SquareTrade seal. More than half a million items on eBay feature this seal, and knowledgeable buyers recognize this as an additional indication that they can feel safe purchasing items, particularly high-cost items, from a seller.

Full details of qualifying for the SquareTrade seal are available at http://www.squaretrade.com (see Figure 7-5), but they include research into your company's identity verification, your selling standards, and customer dispute resolution history. As an added benefit, SquareTrade offers a Fraud Protection guarantee where seal members can be covered up to $250.

FIGURE 7-5   The SquareTrade web site

Determine Shipping Strategy

Though often an afterthought, shipping operations are crucial to the success of e-commerce companies. As businesses both big and small have become more sophisticated through the course of experience in serving the online ordering public, the need to improve fulfillment methods has become a major challenge—or opportunity, depending on how you look at it.

Fulfillment problems have been an ongoing nightmare for many e-tailers. A study by Accenture released after the 2001 holiday season found that during the crucial Halloween-to-Christmas holiday period, as many as 67 percent of online deliveries were not received as ordered, and more than 10 percent were not received in time for the Christmas holiday. That same year, e-tailers faced an estimated loss of some $11 billion in sales due to fulfillment problems.

Those figures may sound off-putting, but consider this: in the time since those reports were issued, more and more options have been opening up for firms, no matter what their size, to help them ship their product on time. And if other companies (your competition) are still having problems promptly fulfilling orders, thanks to eBay's customer feedback system, you've got an opportunity to steal those customers away from your competition for good.

That said, you're way ahead of the game if you've figured out your shipping strategy for your products in advance of the wave of orders you're going to develop from the eBay site. Let's take a look at a couple of the options available.

Use In-house or Outsourced Shipping

You need to decide whether to keep your shipping in-house or to outsource it to another company. Of course, in theory you'll have more control over product release if you keep shipping in-house, and it may appear less expensive at first glance. However, if you're an up-and-coming company with limited staff, you should realize that energy spent on shipping product in-house may be diverting time and overhead away from production or other areas.

This is particularly noticeable in startup companies without a formalized structure, where everyone does a little bit of everything. At some point, especially if you begin to generate mass sales on eBay, it makes less and less sense to have your $50/hour contracts manager or $75/hour code designer spend a couple hours a day packing boxes for shipment.

In addition, what often makes the crucial difference is simply the nature of the product. For example, if you ship a product that needs little or no packaging and comes in one standard size, keeping things in-house may be ideal. However, if you run a company that produces goods that are fragile, perishable, and come in all sorts of bizarre shapes and sizes, you may be better off handing over the operation to a specialist firm.

TIP   *If your business ships extremely heavy items that shippers such as UPS and FedEx won't touch, consider checking out eBay's Freight Resource Center, at http:// ebay.freightquote.com. You'll be able to find multiple shipping options and rate calculators depending on your specific needs at your location.*

United Parcel Service

One of the ways that eBay has shifted the playing field to favor your use of outside shippers has been its standing deals with firms such as UPS. As far back as 2000, eBay began to give its users direct access to UPS shipping options through the eBay web site.

The partnership is designed to make it easier for eBay users to ship packages by providing services to encourage the use of UPS. For example, the UPS section of the eBay site enables users to calculate shipping costs, arrange for package pick-up and drop-off, print labels, and track packages. The link to the UPS Shipping Zone, shown in Figure 7-6, is at http://pages.ebay.com/ ups/home.html.

Of course, eBay still removes itself from the post-sale negotiations. Buyers and sellers must determine which shipping arrangements will best suit them, so be sure to mention in all of your posted auctions what shipping times or options are available to your buyers to manage your customer's expectations.

UPS has several advantages over regular US Postal Service mail, which makes it an attractive option. Detailed tracking information is available on every package, and up to $100 of package insurance is automatically included in the price of each shipment. Perhaps most important in managing customer expectations, UPS can guarantee a specific day of delivery, which is especially helpful when shipping perishable or time-critical goods.

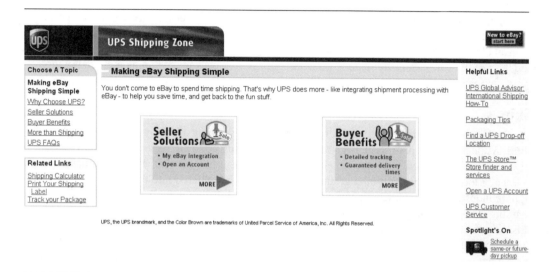

FIGURE 7-6   The UPS Shipping Zone

TIP   *UPS was one of the first shippers to be integrated with eBay, since it also allows you to print labels directly from PayPal. Today, the USPS is also highly integrated with eBay.*

US Postal Service

The USPS also has its links in the eBay site to encourage shipping where speed may not be of the essence but coverage is. eBay provides its users direct access to USPS shipping options through the eBay site.

TIP   *If the majority of your customers' shipping addresses are residential or they use post office boxes, the USPS may be your best choice for two reasons: First, the USPS will deliver to PO boxes when FedEx won't. Second, only the USPS does not add a surcharge for Saturday delivery or a delivery to a residence. Also, if you are shipping items that are under 4 lbs, the USPS becomes a more cost-effective shipping method for your buyer.*

Federal Express

Like UPS, FedEx offers package services with global capabilities, tracking numbers, insurance, and guaranteed ship times (services that are not offered by the USPS). Perhaps the biggest advantage to using FedEx is that the shipper has the strongest brand recognition and client integration in the United States. Many companies already use FedEx, are familiar with the company's shipping process, and have integrated their systems to create labels online, print the shipping labels, and get their product to one of innumerable drop boxes across the United States.

A special advantage for business eBay users is their newer home delivery service. Both FedEx ground and home delivery allow you to ship items at a quick, but not blazingly fast, four- to five-day ground shipment speed at a much lower cost than the speedier air-delivery rate. In addition, like UPS, FedEx carries an automatic $100 insurance on each package, which is included in the cost of shipping.

uShip

uShip has become the largest peer-to-peer marketplace for shipping and moving goods purchased online. While traditional package delivery companies like FedEx and UPS specialize in efficiently delivering small packages, their shipping costs rise as much as 500 percent when a shipment is too large or too heavy for traditional ground service. uShip has entered into this segment of the shipping industry by providing an alternative to extremely high commercial freight prices.

uShip uses professional movers or independent drivers who have space available in their cargo holds, shipment trucks, or the back of their personal vehicles and who are traveling along the route of the shipment. By utilizing these available spaces, a shipper can save as much as 80 percent over regular shipping charges. uShip members list their shipment details on the uShip web site at http://www.uship.com, along with an offer price, and they are notified when their delivery is selected by a driver. After reviewing each driver's feedback and trip details, members have the option to accept or decline the offer.

International Shipping

If you'll be selling products to be shipped overseas, keep in mind that while the United States has efficient and established shipping companies, service and reliability can vary from country to country when dealing with overseas companies and foreign governments. Today, about 46 percent of the business conducted on eBay is international—and it's growing annually.

 You'll encounter a great variance of service and reliability when sending goods outside the United States, even to our friendly neighbors in Canada or Mexico.

The best way to prepare for international sales is to understand the customs, duties, and paperwork that can slow down your competition but gain you access to a tremendous and eager buyer pool. Because you are shipping goods as a corporation, as opposed to an individual seller, more information is required for the various shipping and customs forms. Thankfully, the larger, established shipping companies can help you sort it out and prepare accordingly. Whether you plan to sell millions of dollars' worth of product to an international distributor in a one-time sale or make lots of smaller sales directly to international consumers, encourage your shipping department to work with companies that handle these types of transactions and that can help you with the paperwork.

Customs Forms   Dealing with customs forms requires a dash of common sense and a fair amount of persistence. Depending on the shipping company requirements, you'll have to be precise in the quantity and description of goods and the value for customs purposes. Also, be sure that the nature of the item (gift, merchandise, samples, and so on) has been explicitly stated. If you do plan on shipping internationally, be sure to ask your shipping company for a copy of the paperwork before you send items out the door.

CAUTION *Make sure your shipping information is accurate. If the destination country inspects the package and finds the custom form to be fraudulent, the buyer can face unexpected fees and penalties that in turn can affect your feedback and customer relationship. You can also be convicted in the US (or other countries) for mail fraud.*

Be sure that you know which countries are handled by the shipping service you choose—not every overseas shipping company goes to every country overseas. Even more common, your services will vary by country, or even by the particular region of the country. Keep in mind that where you can track, register, certify, and insure your package will also vary depending on where your packages are shipped.

CAUTION *Beware of buyers who ask you to lie on customs forms so they can avoid duty taxes. The last thing you need is to have your shipment seized by customs, your business barred from selling, or being reported to the authorities.*

Payment   Sometimes collecting payment for an item shipped overseas can be difficult. To remedy this, PayPal is expanding its foreign money exchange services. Currently, PayPal offers such currencies as Euros, Pounds Sterling, Yen, and Canadian dollars. Some of your customers may want to send cash, as getting a money order isn't as handy in some countries as it is in North America.

Create a Plan for a Series of Listings

Before you start a series of listings, decide on a product "test group." Using a search of completed auctions, as detailed in Chapter 3, do some research to gather a range of prices based on past selling behavior. This should give you a rough idea of the following statistics:

- Revenues
- Margin
- Number of units sold

Select a product group that matches or is similar to the one in your study for the initial auctions. Set objectives for 30, 60, and 90 days based on your target price range, the expected versus actual margin attained, and the number of units sold via your eBay sales channel.

Choose the Best Products to Auction

As a new entrant into the eBay marketplace, your primary goal is to create excitement around your item, which you hope will develop into a bidding frenzy among buyers. Generating this excitement is what will turn a loss leader into a profit leader.

Many new sellers prefer to set an opening bid below what the item is actually worth. This can jump-start bidding activity and ultimately produce a higher selling price. Human psychology being what it is, other buyers are generally more likely to jump in to an auction if they see that bids on an item have already been made.

As we discussed earlier, start by searching completed listings for similar items to gauge what similar items have sold for before setting your opening bid. Look for two types of criteria:

- Items that are listed many times but have an acceptable range of closing prices where a healthy margin is enjoyed.
- Items you can sell that are not commonly listed on the eBay site.

In the first case, even though you are competing against many sellers, see whether the closing bid range is still an acceptable number for you. If so, eBay has enough demand to handle the additional supply you would be bringing to the marketplace. In the second case, you can sell products without much competition and hopefully the buyers who see it will fight to grab it. This causes the closing bid to go up, and you'll enjoy a healthier return on your investment.

In either case, try to choose some of your company's most popular items to list on eBay in your initial offerings. Your goal should not necessarily be limited to making money, but you should strive to introduce your company to the millions of eBay users. Once you have their attention on one of your auction pages, you can easily redirect them to your other listings, which may be as valuable but less "buzz-worthy."

Summary

State your shipping policy up front in your eBay listings. Work with your shipping department to determine the formula that will be used when combining shipments. If your shipping formula is necessarily based on weight versus number of items, you may be wise to utilize eBay's shipping calculator.

Consider PayPal and eBay Escrow services when developing your payment policies on your eBay channel. PayPal allows consumers to draw funds from their checking or credit card accounts to purchase items. eBay's partnership with Escrow.com allows that agency to act as a trusted third party during the transaction.

To encourage your company's eBay sales, it's common practice to combine freight with multiple auctions. This may result in customers who choose to buy complementary goods from you to save on shipping.

Determine whether you want to keep your shipping in-house or outsource it. If you're an up-and-coming company with limited staff, pay attention to the fact that energy spent on shipping product in-house may divert time and overhead away from production or other areas.

If you're considering doing a substantial portion of your business overseas, you'll have to be precise in the quantity and description of goods and the value for customs purposes. If you do plan on shipping internationally, be sure to ask your shipping company for a copy of the paperwork before you ship. Also be sure that you know which countries are handled by the service you choose.

Create a plan for a series of initial auctions by first using a search of completed auctions to come up with a range of prices based on past selling behavior. Select a product group that matches or is similar to the one in your study for the initial auctions. Set objectives for 30, 60, and 90 days based on your target price range, the expected versus actual margin attained, and the number of units sold via your eBay sales channel.

Chapter 8

Prepare an Excellent Auction Listing

In this chapter...

- ■ Set listing start and end times
- ■ Use the Sell Your Item form
- ■ Relist your item

In Chapter 3, we showed you how to research your products utilizing eBay's extensive product pricing and marketing information. In addition to creating compelling listing descriptions and marketing your products well, you can use certain listing strategies to increase the number of visitors to your listings, convert those visitors into buyers, and position your products to attain maximum final sales prices.

Set Listing Start and End Times

One of the most important strategies for driving traffic to your listings and creating sales is setting the timing of your listings. When you begin and end your listing is one of the most important factors in drawing the highest number of buyers and attaining the best final sales price. The same product listed on different days with different ending times can produce dramatically different final sales results. The parameters to consider while setting beginning and endings times for your listing include both the day of the week and the time of day that your listing is scheduled to begin and end.

> **NOTE** *While "popular" eBay advice says to end your eBay listings on a Sunday evening at 7 PM, the truth is that you cannot select one universal time to start and end all listings.*

The *most important factors* to consider when determining when to start and end your listing are

- ■ The kind of item you are selling
- ■ Who your target market is

For example, if you end your listing for a Canon Professional Office Copier on a Sunday evening or Friday afternoon, you most likely will not produce the optimal sales results that you could achieve by ending your listing on a Wednesday afternoon, as shown in Figure 8-1.

Why is this? Because your product is a professional copier that will most likely be purchased by a business during business hours. Your target market is the office professional who is more likely to be shopping for office products during the business week rather than during the weekend or evening.

So how do you determine what the best time to start and end a listing for your particular product is? First, your original research for the product will give you a good indication of when the highest priced winning listings are ending. But you should never rely solely on previous marketing data from the site. You should always follow up with your own testing of the product. Testing the starting and ending times for each product that you sell is a critical step in preparing your

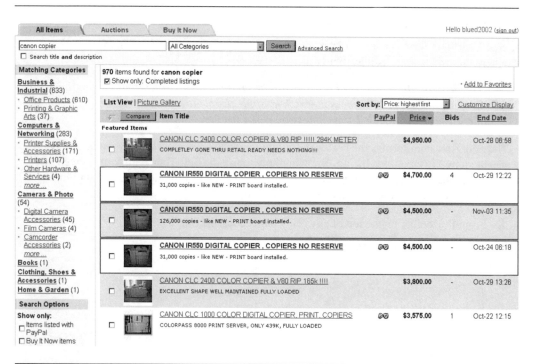

FIGURE 8-1 Sales results from different days of the week

products for online sales success. To do this, you must run the same listings scheduled to end on different days of the week and different times of the day. With the end of each listing, track the results of its performance—analyze how many visitors your listing received, how many bids were placed on the item, and what the final sales price was.

After testing several listings with different ending days and times, you will see the buying patterns of your target market. Once you have tested and tracked this valuable information, you can build a listing timing strategy based on testing, metrics, and fulfilling the needs of your target market.

> **TIP** *eBay always displays its time in Pacific time. So if you're not located in this time zone, make your time calculations accordingly. Try to choose a window of time that accommodates buyers from as many locations as possible.*

Now that you have done your research, you have all of the crucial details you need to list your first item. You know the keywords you want to use in your title, how you are going to present your product and business personality in your description, and what pricing strategy you will use to maximize your profit for the item. You also have the images you are going to display for this listing saved on your computer.

Use the eBay Sell Your Item Form

The Sell Your Item form is the most basic of eBay's listing tools. Easy to use and free of charge, it can help you create your listings in no time.

NOTE *The Sell Your Item form is best if you will be creating your listing from start to finish all in one session. For a business in which multiple people are creating different parts of the listing, using the Sell Your Item form is not the best option.*

The Sell Your Item form is the best way for you to educate yourself quickly and easily on the steps required in creating a listing. Knowing how to use the Sell Your Item form as well as understanding the selling psychology and strategies behind the information that you will input into the form are important in creating a successful listing.

1. From the toolbar on the top of any eBay page, click the Sell tab.

2. Choose the type of listing you want, as shown next:

Sell

How would you like to sell your item?
- Online Auction - Allow bidding or offer a Buy it Now price.
- Fixed Price - Let buyers purchase your item at a set price.
- Store Inventory - Lower fees & longer duration but appears only in your Store.
- Real Estate - Advertise property to generate multiple leads.

Sell Your Item >

3. Select the appropriate category for your item. Based on your research, you should already know which of the 50,000 categories on eBay is going to maximize your profits for this particular listing. You are offered four options to help you locate the appropriate category:

   - Browse the categories in the hierarchical browsing section on the Sell Your Item form.
   - Search for a category by keywords.
   - Enter a category number (you would need to know the category number).
   - Select a previously used category.

4. Complete the prefilled information page (if applicable). This page will not be displayed for all categories of merchandise. However, for certain categories, eBay provides drop-down menus to assist you in selecting product-specific features.

TIP *Use as many of the drop-down menu items as you can. If your buyers use Item Specifics to search for their items and you haven't completed this part of the form, your item won't show up in the search results, even if the type of item matches their search.*

5. Create your listing title (see the section "Crafting a Winning Title"). Look at the titles used for closed listings that garnered the highest final sales prices. This can be a good starting point for you to craft a winning listing title.

6. Enter your item description (see "Crafting Your Description").

7. Enter a price (see "Setting a Starting Price"). Enter your item's starting price as well as a Buy It Now price (see "Using Buy It Now") if you choose to use one, as shown in Figure 8-2. You can also set a reserve price (see "Using Reserve Listings").

NOTE *As discussed in Chapter 3, test your starting prices to see at which price point you generate the most attention for your listing as well as which brings you the highest final sales value.*

8. Schedule your listing (see "Scheduling Your Listing") by setting a duration and start time.

9. Enter a Quantity, the number of individual items you are selling. This can be a bit confusing for new sellers. If, for example, you are selling a box filled with 20 business card scanners, your quantity is 1—you will have one winning bidder for the lot. However, if you have 20 of the exact same item—same condition, size, color, and so on—you could expect to have up to 20 winners. Your quantity number would be 20.

8

Sell Your Item: Enter Pictures & Item Details   ⊙ Live help
1. Category 2. Title & Description 3. **Pictures & Details** 4. Payment & Shipping 5. Review & Submit

Title
Collectible

Store Category *Required
[Other ⌄]
Edit Store Categories in the Store Builder

Pricing and duration
Price your item competitively to increase your chance of a successful sale.
NEW! Get ideas about pricing by searching completed items...

Starting price *   **Reserve price** (fee varies)
$ [   ]   No reserve price. Add
A lower starting price can encourage more bids.

Buy It Now price ($0.05)
$ [   ]
Sell to the first buyer who meets your Buy It Now price

Duration *   **Private auction**
[7 days ⌄]   No private auction. Add
When to use a 1-day duration.

Start time
⊙ Start listing when submitted
○ Schedule start time ($0.10) [Select a date... ⌄] [Select a time... ⌄] PST
   Learn more about scheduled listings

FIGURE 8-2   Setting a starting price and Buy It Now price

10. Add pictures. eBay gives you the option of adding one or more images to your listing. The first picture is free, and each additional picture costs 15 cents. Always use the free picture option. The item's image should be clear, close up, and have a clean background. Your company's marketing or sales department may also have professional pictures ready for you to use.

11. You have the option to utilize Listing Designer. For an additional 10 cents, Listing Designer will allow you to add a special theme and a layout to your listing. Listing Designer is optional.

12. Add special features (see "Adding Special Features").

13. The next step is to add a counter. This option is free. The counter will track the number of visitors to your listing.

14. Choose a payment method. The Payment Methods screen, shown next, gives you the option to choose what kind of payments you will accept.

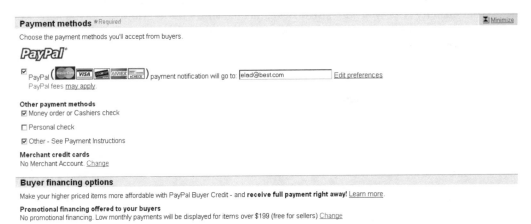

Your preferred method of payment for your eBay sales should be PayPal. Accepting PayPal not only enhances customer trust of your business, but studies show that sellers who accept PayPal, and specifically credit cards payments via PayPal, will have more sales and high final sales prices. You can also choose to accept personal checks, money orders, and payments using your existing merchant account.

15. Specify domestic and international shipping costs. You can provide flat shipping costs or use eBay's powerful shipping calculators. If you choose to provide a flat shipping cost to your buyers, you will be able to enter the exact cost. However, using the shipping calculators eBay provides free, by inputting your package's weight, shipping zip code, top three shipping preferences, and a reasonable handling cost, the shipping calculator will figure your potential winner's shipping cost for you. This will allow your domestic and international bidders the opportunity to realize the shipping/handling cost up front before the bid. This will also help to alleviate additional, "how much is shipping" e-mails.

NOTE *The Shipping Cost screen also provides a valuable Shipping Resource section that lets you research various shipping options.*

16. Add any payment instructions or detail your return policy. Use this section as a good marketing and retention tool. Your instructions will be sent to your winning bidder. Here's an example:

> *Thank you so much for your purchase! We know that you have many online shopping options and appreciate that you chose our quality and customer service. Now, let us save you some money! Check out our other listings at www.stores.ebay.com/ AuctionProfitEducationConsulting. If you purchase additional items, we would be happy not only to combine shipping for you, but we will also take 10% off your total order! Questions? We are only an e-mail away!*

This is one of the last things that your buyer will see before he or she completes a purchase with you, and it is your opportunity to extend special discounts and thank the buyer for the purchase.

17. Select Ship to locations. Specify your shipping parameters. Unless your merchandise is too large to ship worldwide, we recommend that you make your eBay business a global one.

8

NOTE *International sales are one of eBay's fastest growing markets. And if you are not doing business internationally, you are missing out on at least 25 percent or more potential sales.*

18. Review your listing and submit.

Crafting a Winning Title

The title contains the 55 most valuable characters of "real estate" in your entire eBay listing. Use all 55 characters and fill those 55 characters with searchable words that your buyers will use. For example, buyers will search for words like *camping stove, Coleman, gas burner, REI,* or *gas stove.* They will *not* search for words like *wow, l@@k, must see,* or *it's a beauty.* Fill your listing title with searchable keywords and you will draw more visitors and buyers to your listings.

NOTE *eBay gives you the option of adding a subtitle to your listings. For an additional 50 cents per listing, you can now expand your title by another 55 characters. This can be a valuable tool for you if you need to add critical information to your titles that won't fit in the first 55 characters. However, keep in mind that subtitles are not searchable as title keywords at this time, so you will want to put your primary search terms in the title.*

Though it might be easy to think that the listing title is an "automatic" thing, based on model numbers, brand names, serial numbers, and other specific bits of information, realize that with a 55-character limit on the listing title, you can't go on forever about the product. You do have a lot of flexibility in what and how you choose to present your product, though.

NOTE *While users can choose to search items based on title and description, many users choose to stick to titles-only searches first so they're not overwhelmed with choices.*

Your listing title must contain the keywords, spelled correctly, that users are most likely to search for. If common variations, or common misspellings, such as *Wedgwood* and *Wedgewood*, occur for a word's spelling, offer those variations as space allows. For example, someone selling an older printer might include both *HP* and *Hewlett Packard* in the listing title, to be sure that both keyword searches point to their listing.

NOTE *Do not use an ALL CAPITAL LETTERS in your listing title because your title will be hard to read—plus, on the computer, capital letters imply that you are shouting at your customer.*

Crafting Your Description

When buyers look at your listing description, you have about 3 seconds in which to catch their attention and make them want to keep reading. Therefore, the format and content of your description is important in hooking the interest of your buyers and enticing them to learn more about your product. A well-written listing will provide enough features and benefits about the product you are selling in a format that is easy to read and scan. Bullet points, white space, and no more than two font styles or colors are key components of a visually pleasing listing.

When entering your item description, you can either use the WYSIWYG (What You See is What You Get) editor (same as typing in a word processor such as Word) in the Sell Your Item form, as shown in Figure 8-3, or you can click the HTML tab and paste in a template. If your company has already created a standard template for your listing, you will want to use the HTML option. In WYSIWYG, type in your text, and then you are free to make creative changes such as changing the font color, bolding, or highlighting the text and changing the font style and size.

When writing your listing description, be clear and concise and provide your potential buyers with all the information that they need to select your item as their product of choice. Listing the benefits of the item as well as the features will help buyers understand why they need your item. For example, instead of saying "This crock pot has a self-timer" and leaving it at that, you could say, "This crock pot has a self-timer that will save you time and effort when preparing your meals. All you need to do is set it and forget it and dinner will be cooked for just the right amount of time and ready to eat when you get home."

You also want to pay close attention to the formatting of your listing. Typing all your text in one paragraph with the same font size makes it difficult to read. Using enough white space to break up the text and draw your bidders' eyes into the key points will help them quickly make the decision to buy your product.

In addition to describing your item, include your customer service policies in your listing description. Your terms of service are an important part of persuading your buyers to purchase from you rather than your competitors.

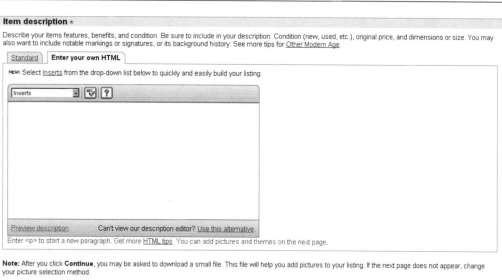

FIGURE 8-3   The WYSIWYG editor for the eBay Item Description box

Some key points to include in your customer service policies are as follows:

- **Terms of Service—100% Money Back Guarantee**   Studies show that listings with the words *100% Money Back Guarantee* produce 6 percent higher bids. Yet only 1 percent of buyers actually use the money-back guarantee.

- **Feedback will be left for every transaction**   eBay studies show that posting these words in your listings effectively attract more buyers. Additionally, the honest buyer will look forward to receiving positive feedback and those buyers who have a penchant for bidding and not paying for products will be more inclined to stay away.

- **Gold Customer Service**   Let your buyers know up front that you provide the best customer service on eBay. All additional value-added services that you provide should be included so that your buyers know exactly who they are dealing with and what customer service practices to expect. These could include a 1-800 customer service phone number, shipping to additional store locations for your buyer, and warranty information.

Your description is your online salesperson—how your description is presented is how your customer will judge your company and its products.

Using a Standard Template

Designing a standard template for all your eBay listings—one that provides the same look and feel for all your listings—is very effective in building brand name presence for your products and company. A listing template can be created in standard HTML and used with the Sell Your Item form as well as other automated listing tools. Once you've designed the template, you'll need to change only a few paragraphs describing each item. Everything else—such as your policies for the listing, payment information, and other information that's consistent from sale to sale—is the same for every listing.

You may have noticed that retail chain stores always set up each store in the same way, rather than leaving it up to a store manager's discretion. You can do the same thing on your auction site via an listing template. By having a template, your customers always know where to find what they're looking for—quantity, description, condition, sizes, and other information. This lets them shop faster (thus spending more money) because they are already familiar with where you place such details.

Setting a Starting Price

The following pricing strategies are the rules of buyer's bidding psychology, not the exceptions. By understanding your buyer's bidding thought process and adjusting your pricing strategies accordingly, you will become a more effective and successful seller.

One of the most effective pricing strategies is using a low opening bid. With a low opening bid, you are required to sell your item at this price (should the item not get bid higher); however, a low opening bid will generally attract the most buyers and generate greater excitement for your listing. Numerous tests show that a low opening bid will create emotional tension among buyers and will drive up the bids on your item.

Most importantly, once a buyer has bid on a listing, he or she becomes what marketers and psychologists call *vested* in that listing and will follow it through its duration and try to win the item, sometimes spending more by small incremental bidding than he or she would have spent if the starting price was too high.

Conversely a high opening bid can often create a "mental hurdle" in which your buyer is intimidated by the high opening bid. For example, in the case of the same item, exact same listing, but with an opening bid of $9.99 versus $100.00, the $9.99 seller will create excitement, drive up the bids on the listing, and generate additional interest, while the seller who opened the item at $100.00 may not even get a bid.

Using Buy It Now

eBay offers the option for sellers to list their items using Buy It Now pricing rather than auction-style pricing. Buy It Now means that you set the price you want for your item and your customer can purchase the item at that price, with no bidding involved. Additionally, with a Buy It Now listing, the purchase can be made immediately—there is no waiting time for the listing to end.

You can use Buy It Now in two ways:

- As a stand-alone price; your item lists only the Buy It Now price
- As a Buy It Now price in conjunction with a starting bid price

In the first scenario, for example, you list your blender for $54.99 and your buyers have a chance to buy the item immediately at that price. In the second scenario, a bidder has an option to place a starting bid on the item or purchase it using Buy It Now. Once a bid is placed on the item, the Buy It Now option is removed.

When using Buy It Now, you must use your eBay market research to determine the appropriate Buy It Now price. Depending on your merchandise and the time of the year, you can also increase your Buy It Now price to reflect growing market demand of a product.

The Buy It Now feature is an excellent option if you want to turn merchandise over faster, offer purchasing opportunities to buyers who do not want to participate in the bidding process, or set a consistent selling price for your item.

Using Reserve Listings

In a reserve listing, you set the minimum sales price for an item, and you are not required to sell the item below that price. The purpose of a reserve listing is to protect your investment on a product that you are not sure has sufficient market demand to command your desired price.

While at first glance a reserve listing sounds like a good option, the reality of it is quite different. As a general rule, eBay buyers do not like reserve listings. In fact, the mere use of a reserve listing can sometimes drive away buyers, who may have otherwise had an interest in your item. This is buyer psychology at work.

Nevertheless, there is an appropriate time and strategy for using a reserve listing. If you need to protect your investment while testing marketing strategies for your product, a reserve used with "information" is the approach to take. Making your reserve price as transparent as possible allows potential buyers to bid on your listing with the knowledge that they have a chance of at least being in the ballpark with their bid. Buyers don't want to waste their time bidding on items that they have no chance of winning.

Add comments in the description area of your listing page for each reserve item; this gives your buyers the information they need to know while allowing you to protect your selling price. Here are some examples:

- My reserve is one-half of retail.
- Our reserve price is less than $500.
- The reserve on this item is $749.

NOTE   *Reserve price auction fees can be fully refundable. At the end of the listing, if a buyer reaches or exceeds the reserve price in bidding for your product, the reserve price auction fee is refunded to your account.*

Scheduling Your Listing

Enter the duration of your listing (1, 3, 5, 7, or 10 days), as shown in Figure 8-4, and the start time (immediately or in the future). As discussed earlier in the chapter, when you schedule your listing has a definite impact on your final sales price.

In many cases, you will be creating a listing prior to the time you are ready to schedule it. You will want to schedule your listing to start at a future date and time. The Sell Your Item form (and other automated auction-management systems) will allow you to choose a date and time in the future to start your listings, and for a small fee (10 cents) will start your listings for you later.

Adding Special Features

When you are almost through creating your listing, you can add the "bells and whistles" to make your listing even more special.

 eBay offers many unique promotional features that you can add to your listing. The drawback is that they all cost an additional fee and can quickly deduct from your profit margin. Use Special Features sparingly and use only those that increase your sales or your final sales price.

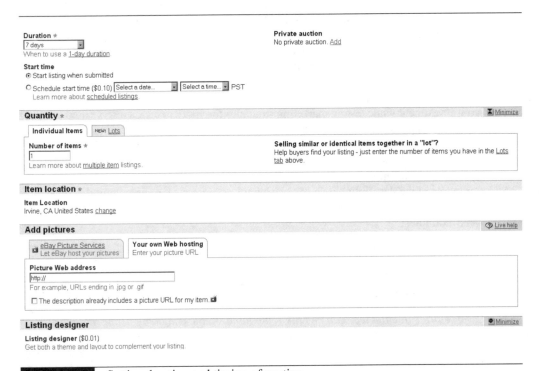

FIGURE 8-4   Setting duration and timing of auction

Did you know?

Take a Loss and Win Big

Some eBay sellers successfully use many features and actually take a loss on a particular auction. They are accounting for the fees spent (such as a $39.95 feature) as an *advertising cost*. A company can put out a loss-leading item (or a really popular or hot item) and use that featured auction to promote other listings and make more sales in their store.

One add-on that you *do* want to use every time is the Gallery feature, shown in Figure 8-5. The Gallery feature is like an inviting storefront window display. For 25 cents, eBay will add a small thumbnail of your item picture next to your listing. *This add-on is a must.* A gallery photo can increase your final price by as much as 19 percent.

8

Gallery Examples

Gallery items let buyers see what's being offered without another click. When buyers search for an item using keywords, or browse through our categories, Gallery photos appear directly in the result lists. When buyers click the Gallery Items Only tab, they see a catalog-like page showing photos of Gallery items.

Gallery costs only **25 cents per listing**.

Note: Gallery photos must be JPEG (.jpg) files.

Example 1 - Gallery Photo in result list.

| FIGURE 8-5 | eBay listing Gallery option |

The Gallery option also doubles the height of your listing in the search results. Your item having more space than your competitors' items helps to set it apart and adds a visual enticement for your buyers. We recommend that you budget this as part of your costs on eBay.

Review and Submit Your Listing

Congratulations, you have created an eBay listing. You can now review your listing, make any needed changes, and submit your listings. Once you have reviewed your listing and are satisfied with it, click the Submit button and your listing will be up and running on eBay.

Creating the best listing for your merchandise is a combination of strategies, using buyer psychology, testing and tracking. As you create more listings and evaluate your sales results, you will be able to adjust your listings to maximize sales.

Selling Similar Items

After you've listed your first auction, you'll see a button on the confirmation screen called Sell A Similar Item. By clicking this button, everything you added into your first auction is automatically copied into a new listing. This feature is extremely helpful if you're selling similar items with only one or two small differences, such as different colors, model numbers, or sizes. Just change any of the following information as needed:

- Title
- Description
- Price
- Photo Listing
- Category (unlikely to change if you're selling a similar item)

Complete this, and your second item will be ready to sell in a fraction of the time it took to create the first. The Sell A Similar Item function is a great way to save time while posting auctions using the Sell Your Item form.

Summary

The timing of your listing can mean the difference between an optimal final sales price and a marginal one. Researching, testing, and tracking the results of ending listings on different days and times will provide you with the information you need to schedule your listing on the best day for long-term success.

The eBay Sell Your Item form is the most basic of the eBay listing creation tools. Free of charge and easy to use, you can create a complete listing quickly and efficiently. However, this tool should only be a starting point for listing creation strategies. Automated tools such as Turbo Lister or one of the many other auction-management services (which we will discuss in the next chapter) will be necessary to automate your business for the long term.

Writing a searchable listing title is the most important success factor in designing an order pulling listing. Before people can buy your products, they must be able to find your listing. Creating a listing title that is filled with a variety of searchable keywords will allow the maximum amount of future buyers to find your listing.

You have approximately 3 seconds when a buyer first looks at your listing to capture their attention and entice them to read more about your product. Easily scannable listings that include plenty of white space as well as bullet points will draw your bidder in and invite them to stay. Always provide enough information in your listings to describe the key features and benefits of the item.

Your listing description should provide a "one-stop shopping" experience for your buyer. Adding your customer service information into your listing means that your customer is not left guessing about your policies and who you are as a business. Including the words *100% Money Back Guarantee* will offer buyers the confidence they need to bid on your products as well as increase the number of bids and final sales price.

A lower starting price for your products will excite buyers and generate enthusiasm for your merchandise. Once a buyer places a bid, they are now vested emotionally in winning that listing. Additionally, studies show that listings that have at least one bid will garner more bids—rather than listings that sit there for the duration of the listing time with no bids. Before determining your starting bid price, you must always do your research for price point and market demand on eBay.

Reserve listings should be used only when it is necessary to protect your investment in a product. Making the reserve price known in your item description will instantly make your product more accessible and appealing in the minds of your buyers.

Special features added to your listing can add excess cost to your bottom line and should be used only when your tests show that they are increasing your sales or your final sales price. The one exception to that is the Gallery picture, which has been shown to increase the number of bids and a final selling price by 19 percent.

By using specific listing strategies, buyer psychology, and testing and tracking your results, you will be able to maximize your number of bids per product as well as your final sales price.

You can easily relist items for which you have depth of inventory. This can be done using the Sell A Similar Item function.

8

Chapter 9

Automate Your Business with Auction-Management Tools

In this chapter...

- ■ Use eBay auction-management tools
- ■ Track listings with My eBay
- ■ Upload listings with Turbo Lister
- ■ Get help from Selling Manager
- ■ Use Selling Manager Pro
- ■ Partner with ChannelAdvisor
- ■ Take advantage of Marketworks
- ■ Access eBay Developers Program

You have listed your first auction and congratulations are in order! Now let's take a look at some of the management tools that will help you keep track of your listings as well as automate your business for future items. The auction-management solution you use will depend on the type and volume of items that you will be listing. Also, keep in mind that the tools that best suit your business will change over time as your eBay business grows and evolves.

Use eBay Software Tools

eBay software designers have come up with several solutions you can use to manage your listings. Most of the tools that eBay provides are free or cost only a small fee. They include My eBay, Turbo Lister, Selling Manager, Selling Manager Pro, and more.

Table 9-1 offers a full comparison of the features included with each of these services.

Track Listings with My eBay

You have just finished listing your first item; now let's keep track of your listing's progress. As soon as you register on eBay, you are given a free, personal, password-protected landing page called My eBay. This page is automatically set up for you and is currently keeping track of your selling transactions, purchases, feedback, and all of your other eBay activities. As shown next, My eBay is available from the toolbar at the top of any page on the site.

home | pay | register | sign out | services | site map | help

| Browse | Search | Sell | My eBay | Community | Powered By IBM |

My eBay makes managing your buying, selling, and account activities a quick and easy process. Your My eBay page is also customizable, allowing you to select which information you want to view and in what format you want to view it.

Feature	My eBay 2.0	Turbo Lister/ Selling Manager	Selling Manager Pro	Seller's Assistant Basic	Seller's Assistant Pro
Offline access		TL only		X	X
Online access via eBay.com	X	SM only	X		
Create bulk item listings		TL only	X	X	X
Create fixed-price listings for stores		TL only	X	X	X
eBay Picture Services		TL only	X	X	X
Templates for listing creation		TL only	X	X	X
Schedule listing submission		TL only	X	X	X
Organize saved items in folders		TL only	X	X	X
Preview listings before submission		TL only	X	X	X
Create listings for multiple sites		TL only	X	X	X
Multiple user profiles		TL only			X
Automatic inventory increment/decrement			X		X
Alert when restock needed			X		X
Create listings linked to product			X		X
Track unsold items	X	SM only	X	X	X
Edit, reschedule, cancel scheduled items	X	SM only	X	X	X
Store sales and customer information		SM only	X	X	X
Track buyer communication and payment		SM only	X		
Track active listings in real time	X	SM only	X	X	X
Customize views	X	SM only	X		
Print shipping label/invoice		SM only	X		X
Monthly view of archived sales		SM only	X		X

TABLE 9-1 Comparison of eBay Auction Management Tool Systems

9

Feature	My eBay 2.0	Turbo Lister/ Selling Manager	Selling Manager Pro	Seller's Assistant Basic	Seller's Assistant Pro
Notification sent on receipt of auto-payment or item shipment			X		
How long data is available	62 days	120 days	120 days	Unlimited	Unlimited
Download size*	No download required	TL: 2.5–14MB SM: No download required	No download required	15.3MB	18.1MB
Price per month	Free	TL: Free SM: $4.99	$15.99 Free with Featured & Anchor stores	$9.99	$24.99

* The time spent downloading will vary depending on your connection speed.

TABLE 9-1   Comparison of eBay Auction Management Tool Systems (Continued)

My eBay 2.0's easy-to-use features are organized into the following sections:

- **My Summary**   This is the main section of your My eBay page. It includes information about all of your buying and selling activity. This is where you will receive all eBay announcements.

- **Managing Buying with My eBay 2.0**   Your All Buying section will allow you to keep track of your bids, purchases, and items that you are "watching" on the site. This is a great portal page for your purchasing division to have access for all your additional eBay acquisitions.

- **Managing Selling with My eBay 2.0**   All Selling will track your listings, bidder activity, unsold items, and sales. Other sections of My eBay include:

  - **Tracking Favorites with My eBay 2.0**   Choose and view your favorite categories, searches, and eBay sellers.

  - **Managing Your Account with My eBay 2.0**   See and update your personal information, eBay preferences, feedback, seller account information, and PayPal account information.

  - **eBay Preferences**   Your unique settings for using and viewing My eBay and eBay as a whole.

  - **Viewing and Leaving Feedback with My eBay 2.0**   Find all the transactions for which you need to leave feedback from this section. Or view the feedback you've recently received.

NOTE *My eBay is discussed in detail in Chapter 10.*

Turbo Lister

One of the most powerful tools from eBay is Turbo Lister, shown in Figure 9-1. Turbo Lister is a free, easy-to-use software program that helps you create collections of listings on your computer and upload them to sell on eBay.

With Turbo Lister, you can work with the program offline to create, manage, and fine-tune your listings before uploading them directly to the eBay site. You can start work on creating a listing and then stop midway, save the information, and come back to complete it at a later date. If you're working with a group to put together your eBay listings, using Turbo Lister and working offline also allows several people to access the program and work with the listings before they're posted.

Turbo Lister isn't limited to working with HTML, which many nontechnical users may find difficult and cumbersome to implement. Instead you can create your listing in Turbo Lister using the WYSIWYG (What You See Is What You Get) editor.

A WYSIWYG editor is the same as a word processor editor. You type in your text and then use the options on the toolbar to format your listing and add special effects such as bold, highlight, or font colors.

9

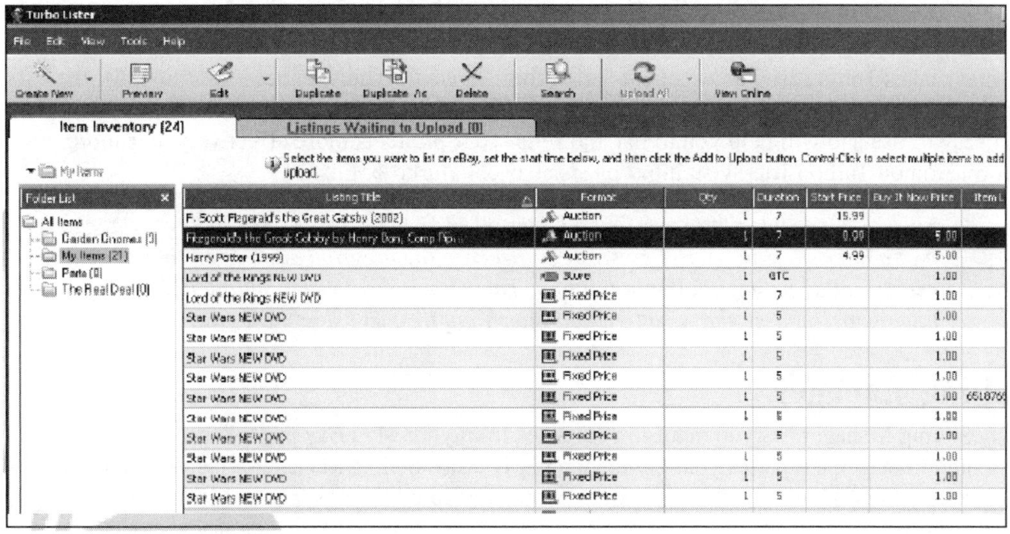

FIGURE 9-1   eBay's Turbo Lister tool

Additionally, Turbo Lister can work with files constructed in what is called CSV (comma-separated values) format. The vast majority of self-constructed or commercially available database programs use this format or can save to it. Therefore, you can open, save, import, and export the data you'll use to create listings between your database program and Turbo Lister with little or no difficulty or technical knowledge.

Turbo Lister has several automated features including the following, which let you

- Duplicate listings into the same or a different format
- Easily fill in item specifics
- Automatically back up your listings
- Define the order in which you would like your items to be uploaded
- Use default settings for every listing
- Sort your listings into separately named folders
- Create multiple users to manage your listings
- Use the activity log to keep records of what you have updated and when
- Preview your eBay fees before your listings go live
- Schedule your listings in advance
- Include hyperlinks in your description without having to know HTML
- Insert images into your descriptions without using HTML or templates

The ability to automate much of the listing process as well as have multiple users create listings makes Turbo Lister an excellent listing tool choice for your business. Additionally, the use of Turbo Lister is free and therefore very cost effective. Turbo Lister is reliable, quick, and easy to use and will help you to list and relist your products more effectively. For more information on Turbo Lister, visit http://pages.ebay.com/turbo%5Flister/.

NOTE   *Even if you decide not to use Turbo Lister when you start your eBay listings, you can try it at a later stage in your eBay strategy, because the program allows you to import your existing eBay listing information into it. This allows you to keep selling items without having to "reinvent the wheel" if you later want to start using the software.*

Selling Manager

eBay Selling Manager lets you manage your sales from your My eBay page. When you subscribe to Selling Manager, it replaces your Selling tab in My eBay. Selling Manager separates all of your eBay listings into views to help you manage your scheduled listings, active listings, and post-sales activities.

Selling Manager comes in two forms: Basic ($4.95 per month) and the higher-end Selling Manager Pro ($15.99 per month). Selling Manager separates your eBay listings according to their status. These separations are called *views*. You can move among the six Selling Manager views by using the corresponding links in the Manage Listings box. The view that you are currently using is highlighted in bold.

Selling Manager maintains the following information in your listings:

- **Summary View**   Your Selling Manager home page. The Summary View gives you a quick overview of your selling activities as well as reminders of what sales activities you need to do that day.

- **Pending Listings View**   Displays all listings that you have created but have set to start at a later date and time—they are not yet active on eBay.

- **Active Listings View**   Shows all of your listings that are active on eBay, including your store inventory.

- **Sold Listings View**   Shows all of the listings that have successfully sold. At a glance, the listing icons will show whether the buyer has used checkout, paid you, if you have shipped the item, and if feedback has been left by either party.

- **Unsold Listings View**   Shows all of the listings that did not have a successful bidder.

- **Archived Listings View**   Shows all listings that you have chosen to archive. Selling Manager will also automatically archive listings after 60 days from the Sold Listings View.

In addition to a snapshot of your current listing activities on eBay, this program also automates many of your daily selling tasks, saving you time. This includes automated e-mail templates to make your "after-sale" communication with your buyers a snap. You can also bulk-relist your listings as well as leave bulk feedback for your winning buyers. From Selling Manager, you can print out labels and invoices for your customers. Selling Manager also allows your accounting department to download your sales into a CSV file. You can find out more about Selling Manager at http://pages.ebay.com/selling%5Fmanager/.

> TIP   *The combination of Selling Manager and Turbo Lister provides an inexpensive, easy to use, reliable method for creating and managing your listings.*

Selling Manager Pro

Selling Manger Pro is a more robust and feature-rich version of Selling Manager. As with Selling Manager, when you subscribe to Selling Manager Pro, it replaces the Selling tab in My eBay. Selling Manager Pro separates your products and all of your eBay listings and reports into views to help you manage products, schedule listings, monitor active listings, and perform post-sales activities. Selling Manager Pro also allows you to customize your e-mail templates for more efficient communications.

In addition to the Summary, Pending Listings, Active Listings, Sold Listings, Unsold Listings and Archived Listings views, Selling Manager Pro offers two additional views.

Product Inventory View   This is your first stop in the listing process on eBay, where you will log in the entire eBay inventory that you will be selling. This page also tracks the success ratio of your listings as well as their average selling price. Product Inventory can be used as a valuable marketing tool. By analyzing when your items were submitted, how many were available versus how many sold, and the average selling price, you will be able to more effectively price and list your item in the future.

Reporting View   This view allows you to see a monthly summary of profit and loss for all of your listings. You can also view the previous three months in separate reports. This simplified profit and loss statement based on your eBay listings takes into account your eBay fees, cost per item, actual shipping costs, and total revenue generated by the completed listing.

This version allows you access to easy, automated e-mail and feedback communications with your buyers. However, with the Pro version, you do not have to send one type of communication out to a single buyer. You can click the 28 winning customer records who purchased your product that day and send them all, with a click of one button, a personalized "We have shipped your item" e-mail. You can also leave those same 28 winning buyers feedback with just one click. You can find out more about Selling Manager Pro at http://pages.ebay.com/selling%5Fmanager%5Fpro/.

Additional Sites to Help You Manage Your Listings

Given the growing number of businesses using eBay as their online sales site, the related field of software-based seller assistance has also increased in size. While many different services are available—and more are being developed all the time—we profile a couple of them here: ChannelAdvisor and Marketworks.

ChannelAdvisor

One of the growing leaders in the auction-management service industry is ChannelAdvisor (http://www.channeladvisor.com/), a company that offers software services and components that can be tailored to specific businesses seeking to manage mass numbers of eBay listings. Their customers make up more than 90 percent of the large enterprises selling on eBay, such as Sears, Best Buy, Sharper Image, and Ritz Camera. An especially exciting development from the business perspective is the ChannelAdvisor Enterprise Solution, which comes in three editions: a Public Marketplace edition that helps enterprises reach customers on marketplaces such as eBay or Amazon, a Private Marketplace edition that allows companies to host their own transactions with their suppliers, and a Catalog Syndication edition that helps coordinate product and pricing data among numerous online shopping sites and search engines. In addition, ChannelAdvisor offers a Merchant edition for mid-sized businesses and ChannelAdvisor Pro for PowerSellers and smaller companies. The ChannelAdvisor home page is shown in Figure 9-2.

ChannelAdvisor tailors its services to fit clients' needs while the Enterprise Solution combines powerful software with an active account team that works directly with the client, and Merchant Pro allows a company to customize the software to fit its listing needs. Clients of ChannelAdvisor can then focus on gaining new customers, extending the power of their brand, and creating healthier streams of revenue for excess, refurbished, returned, or unusual inventory.

Marketworks

Marketworks, "Commerce without Limits," has been successful in working with businesses on the larger end of the scale by allowing them to integrate eBay with the rest of their sales channels. The company's best-known clients include Home Depot, Genco, Disney Auctions, and Olympus

FIGURE 9-2 ChannelAdvisor's home page demonstrates enterprise solutions and case studies of companies that use its tools.

Camera. Marketworks also claims to have more than 2000 small and medium-sized business customers.

Marketworks made its name in 1999 by being the first to develop fixed-price storefronts with integrated eBay item checkout and combined shipping for multiple purchases. As of today, it has added automated non-paying bidder reporting, customer communications, one-payment integration, and other valuable services to its suite of offerings.

TIP

While we've profiled only two of the most visible listing service sites here, you should be aware that many more services are available. Your choice should depend on what services the company offers and whether it caters to your company's product or market segment. When you're making your final decision, be sure that the company has a strong record of success—not just in general, but when working with companies that are similar to yours in regard to development and market area.

Marketworks and MJR Sales Apparel

Using Marketworks software, apparel seller MJR Sales doubled its eBay business in less than six months. In 2003, MJR Sales was awarded eBay's "Entrepreneur of the Year" award by eBay CEO Meg Whitman in San Francisco during the eBay Seller Summit.

MJR Sales first registered on eBay in March 2001 but didn't start thinking of it as a serious business opportunity until late in 2002. "We were just getting started and really didn't know much about selling on eBay," said Mark Mendelson, MJR Sales director of operations and the man charged with working with eBay. "We worked with another eBay Preferred Solution Provider before settling on Marketworks in December of 2002."

He added, "Marketworks has been instrumental in helping us become the leading apparel seller on eBay. The Marketworks team helped improve our eBay operations, their software has enabled us to increase listings by over 500 percent and process over 20,000 transactions each month, and their account management team has been outstanding in providing leadership for our business."

eBay Developers Program

Just as pre-packaged accounting solutions may not work for your particular method of doing business, the same may hold true for auction-automation software. Many third-party service providers have created tools and solutions for your eBay business. You can find these at http://www.solutions.ebay.com. Even these solutions may not be specific or detailed enough for your business needs. If your company is interested in developing a custom application that will interface with eBay, the application programming interface can provide a custom interface, functionality, and specialized operations not otherwise accessible by the standard eBay online interface.

The eBay API is the heart of the eBay Developers Program. Normally, users buy and sell items using eBay's online interface. But with the eBay API you can communicate directly with the eBay database in XML format. To access the eBay API, you must first join the eBay Developers Program. For more information about the eBay API go to http://developer.ebay.com/DevProgram/developer/api.asp.

Summary

The auction-management solution you use will depend on the type and volume of items that you will be listing. Also, keep in mind that the tools that best suit your business will change over time as your eBay business grows and evolves.

My eBay is a personal, password-protected page that is automatically set up for you and keeps track of your selling transactions, purchases, feedback, and all your other eBay activities.

eBay Turbo Lister is a powerful, free, easy-to-use software program that helps you create and automate multiple eBay listings.

Selling Manager software separates your eBay listings according to their status and lists them in views. When you subscribe to Selling Manager, it replaces the information in your My eBay tab.

Selling Manager Pro is a more robust and feature-rich version of Selling Manager. In addition to all the standard features of Selling Manager, Selling Manager Pro offers a Product Inventory view and a Reporting view.

Channel Advisor and Marketworks are two of the more sophisticated and effective auction-management tools available. Both products are scalable for the mid- to large-size business.

The eBay API allows your company to create custom applications that interact directly with eBay's database. To access the eBay API, you must first join the eBay Developers Program.

9

Chapter 10

Refine Your eBay Presence

In this chapter...

- ■ Manage existing listings
- ■ Use the My eBay function
- ■ Refine auction listings
- ■ Prepare after-sales processes
- ■ Use escrow services
- ■ Communicate with your buyer
- ■ Relist existing listings and Second Chance offers

You've figured out what you're going to sell, created auction listings, and thrown open the bidding. The most difficult part of taking that first step is over, and now you can move on to the next phase—improving on that success.

In this chapter, we cover various tools that eBay offers to help you keep track of your listings and monitor your early activity; by using that experience, you'll integrate the lessons learned into your next set of listings. We also talk about the after-sale process—when the listing finishes, the highest bidder has emerged, and it's time for you to finish the deal, arrange payment and shipping, and keep that customer for future transactions. Now that the pipeline of items has been created, it's time for you to manage it.

Manage Your Existing Listings

It can be very satisfying to create a host of listings, knowing that you're about to convert surplus equipment into a healthy cash reserve, clear out warehouse space, and expand your sales potential without hiring more sales personnel. After you've created and listed these listings, however, your job is not done. You must manage these sales throughout the bidding process and wrap up the details after the sale.

While a retail customer can simply show up at the checkout stand, pay for the item, and leave the store, an eBay customer must communicate with you from another location, pay through certain mechanisms, and ask you to ship the purchase and typically offer them a way to monitor that shipment process. By learning and using a few tricks, you can significantly reduce the time it takes to monitor all these open listings and increase the amount of listings you can list each week.

The My eBay Function

In Chapter 6, you learned about the About Me page, which is a home base for the world to monitor your eBay presence. eBay has also created a home base for *you* to monitor your eBay activity, My eBay. My eBay allows you to coordinate all your buying and selling activity from one location.

You can also set a range of preferences, manage your feedback activity, update your account specifics, and create favorites regarding categories, search terms, and sellers that are important for your company to monitor on eBay.

On the My eBay My Summary page, shown in Figure 10-1, a precise summary of your buying and selling activity is presented first, reminding you of how many items you need to pay for (as a buyer) and leave feedback for, as well as a list of what shipments you need to send out (as a seller) and which of your buyers need a precise total. Below that you will find important eBay announcements that could affect your listing activity.

The rest of the page contains subsections showing your bidding activity, items you've won, items you haven't won, items you're currently selling, and items that have sold. If you look at the left column on this web page, you'll see that My eBay is organized under five different page views: My Summary, All Buying, All Selling, All Favorites, and My Account. Let's take a look at some of these subsections.

All Buying

This page, shown in Figure 10-2, coordinates all the information related to your bidding and buying activity on eBay. After a handy reminder summary, similar to the one on the My Summary page, you're presented with four groupings of eBay listings: Items I'm Watching, Items I'm Bidding On,

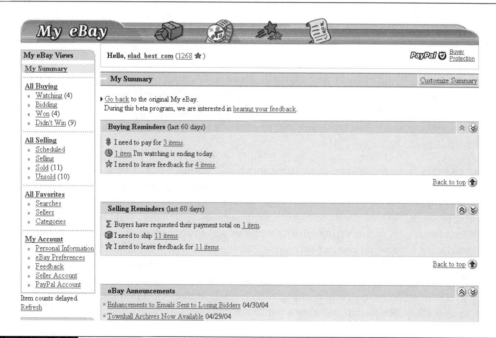

FIGURE 10-1   My eBay My Summary page

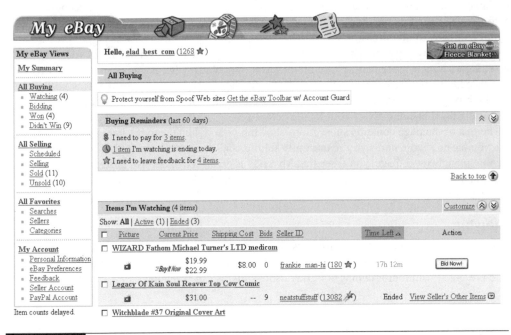

FIGURE 10-2 My eBay All Buying page

Items I've Won, and Items I Didn't Win. If, for example, you've bid on an item and the listing is still open, you'd see that listing under the Items I'm Bidding On list. Once that listing closes, the listing gets moved either to the Items I've Won list or the Items I Didn't Win list. Finally, for listings you're not actively pursuing but for which you're interested in the outcome, you can use the eBay Watch List feature.

Watching a Listing   As mentioned throughout this book, research is a critical component to a successful eBay strategy. As you study listings related to your products, you gain insight into pricing, supply and demand, and sometimes find sources for information you can reuse in your listing. You may want to monitor these listings without bidding on them. Watching a listing is a tremendous boost to your marketing efforts: it allows you to keep track of your competitors' listings, marketing mixes, and product inventories. In the brick-and-mortar business world, it can take days or sometimes weeks to know what your competition is doing in the marketplace. By watching listings on eBay, you can know instantly whether your competitor is offering free shipping as a holiday promotion or has changed its pricing strategy on a particular product. You can also keep track of new sellers entering a particular category.

While you can use your Internet browser to bookmark competitors' pages so you can return to them, eBay's Watch This Auction feature lets you click the Add To Watch List link near the top right corner of any eBay page, and eBay will store that item in your watch list for future reference and return you to the listing you were studying:

After you click the link, the reference near the top right corner changes to This Item Is Being Tracked In My eBay and shows you the new total of how many items are being watched:

NOTE   *eBay allows you to watch up to 100 items simultaneously. When the listing end date is 30 days past, that item drops off your Watch List.*

You can access your Watch List by opening the My eBay All Buying Summary page and perusing the list. While you can now customize your Items I'm Watching section to show any combination of nine elements regarding the product listing, your page will probably look something like Figure 10-3. You'll see the title of the listing, the current price of that item, the shipping cost, the number of bids that listing item has received, and the seller's eBay user ID. You can also see the time remaining in the listing and choose to view the seller's other items.

TIP   *You can look at three versions of your Watch List: all items, items that are still active, and items for which the bidding has ended. If you want to study realized prices for similar items, click the Show Ended link. You can also click the Customize link to see other critical information.*

10

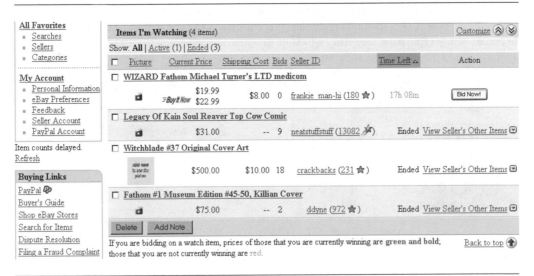

FIGURE 10-3   My eBay Items I'm Watching

Monitoring Your Buying Activity   After bidding ends, you need to close the deal, make sure to pay the seller, and make sure you get the product. eBay has added more features to record these steps electronically, and the Items I've Won list now shows a series of icons representing the after-sales process and gives you a visual checklist of sorts so you can see in one row where you are in the after-sale process for each item you purchase using eBay. These icons are shown on the right side of the screen in Figure 10-4.

If a particular after-sales step has been completed, the icon appears in color. If the particular step has not been completed, meaning eBay doesn't have the information to know that it's been completed, the icon appears gray and in shadow. The three icons are shown in the following table.

Icon	Meaning	How eBay Tracks It
	Paid	Buyer used PayPal or marked item as paid if money order or check was sent
	Feedback left	Buyer entered feedback for seller
	Feedback received	Seller entered feedback for buyer

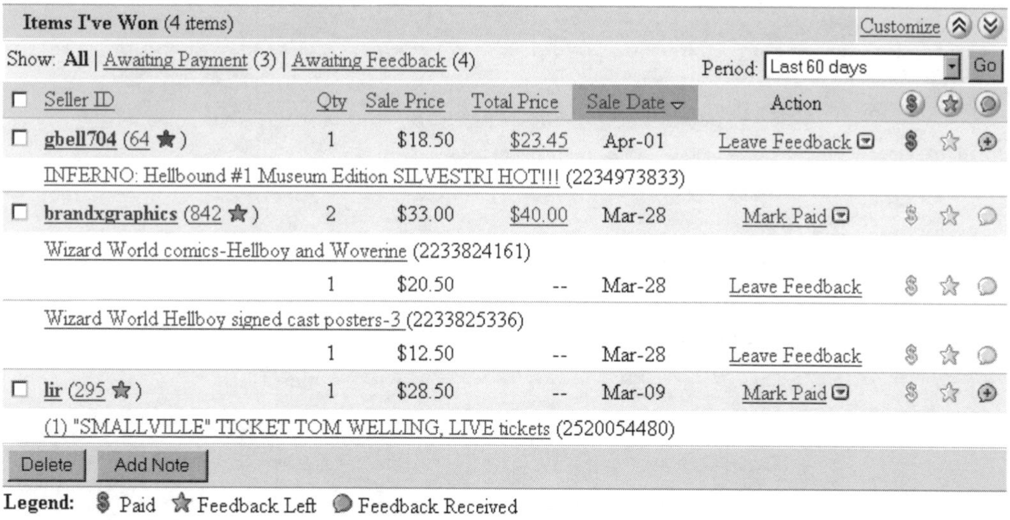

Items I've Won (4 items)						Customize ⊗ ⊗		
Show: **All** | Awaiting Payment (3) | Awaiting Feedback (4)					Period: Last 60 days ▾	Go		
☐ Seller ID	Qty	Sale Price	Total Price	Sale Date ▽	Action	⑧	☆	◯
☐ **gbell704** (64 ★)	1	$18.50	$23.45	Apr-01	Leave Feedback ▾	$	☆	⊕
INFERNO: Hellbound #1 Museum Edition SILVESTRI HOT!!! (2234973833)								
☐ **brandxgraphics** (842 ★)	2	$33.00	$40.00	Mar-28	Mark Paid ▾	$	☆	◯
Wizard World comics-Hellboy and Woverine (2233824161)								
	1	$20.50	--	Mar-28	Leave Feedback	$	☆	◯
Wizard World Hellboy signed cast posters-3 (2233825336)								
	1	$12.50	--	Mar-28	Leave Feedback	$	☆	◯
☐ **lir** (295 ★)	1	$28.50	--	Mar-09	Mark Paid ▾	$	☆	⊕
(1) "SMALLVILLE" TICKET TOM WELLING, LIVE tickets (2520054480)								
Delete Add Note								

Legend: $ Paid ★ Feedback Left ◯ Feedback Received

FIGURE 10-4   The Items I've Won list shows the action and after-sale process icons.

For each item, the appropriate action is also offered. If you've already paid for the item, the Action column may say Leave Feedback. If no payment information has been received, you may see a Mark Paid link. Finally, you can see subsets of Items I've Won, based on whether the seller is awaiting payment or awaiting your feedback.

All Selling

Let's shift gears and talk about selling. If you click the All Selling link from the My Summary page, you'll see a screen that looks similar to Figure 10-5. You should see a handy list of Selling Reminders, followed by four groupings of items that you as a seller have created: Scheduled Items, Items I'm Selling, Items I've Sold, and Unsold Items.

When you create an auction listing and you start the listing immediately, that listing appears under Items I'm Selling. If you create a listing but schedule a later date or time, perhaps due to delayed listing timing, this listing appears under Scheduled Items. When your listing has closed, the item appears under Items I've Sold, unless the reserve was not met or no one placed a bid—in which case you would see it under Unsold Items.

Monitoring Your Selling Activity   Just as the Items I've Won list under the All Buying page offers you a visual guide to the after-sales steps as a buyer, the Items I've Sold list on the All Selling page offers you a checklist to the important after-sales seller processes. A seller should now consider five processes to complete each listing successfully, as you can see in Figure 10-6. The icons representing these processes are shown in Table 10-1.

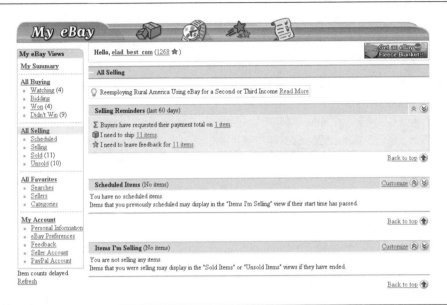

FIGURE 10-5   My eBay All Selling page

FIGURE 10-6   The Items I've Sold list—note the Action and five after-sales processes

Icon	Meaning	How eBay Tracks It
	Checkout	Buyer and seller followed checkout instructions to give precise total to buyer
	Paid	Buyer used PayPal to pay seller
	Shipped	Seller entered tracking number into buyer's PayPal record
	Feedback Left	Seller entered feedback for buyer
	Feedback Received	Buyer entered feedback for seller

TABLE 10-1   Icons for Seller Processes

For each item, the appropriate Action is also offered up next to the icons. If the buyer has already checked out and paid for the item, the Action may be Print Shipping Label. If you've already shipped out the item and the buyer has left feedback, you may see a Leave Feedback link. Finally, you can see subsets of Items I've Sold, based on whether you as the seller are awaiting payment, the buyer is awaiting shipment of the item, or the buyer is awaiting your feedback.

TIP *One excellent form of marketing feedback in the selling section indicates how many people are watching your listing. This is a new option with My eBay 2.0 and is a good indication of the great last-minute "snipers" that drive up the price of your listing.*

10

Did you know?   eBay World Tops Real World

In the real world, it is difficult to amass information quickly about your competitors and their products. However, on eBay, at a moment's notice you can access all of that information. In addition, eBay will even e-mail you marketing information on your competitors on a daily basis.

All Favorites

When you click the All Favorites link, you'll see a page similar to Figure 10-7. You'll also see three main groupings: My Favorite Searches, My Favorite Sellers, and My Favorite Categories.

Based on all the research you've already started, you should execute certain searches regularly on eBay to keep track of relevant and competing products, categories, and sellers. Rather than having to keep notes and type in those searches every time, you can set up all the criteria for your search, save it under a specific name, and simply click a link under My Favorite Searches to run that search any time you want. It's a definite time-saver and a way to share these searches with others who help you set up your company's eBay strategy and can log into the company eBay account.

After a few listings have ended, you should begin to see patterns in the selling behavior for your products. You may also find other eBay sellers who specialize or focus on products in your product areas. Using My Favorite Sellers, you can store a list of sellers' user IDs and easily peruse their items for sale on eBay at any given time. Using this function allows you to study multiple sellers without having to flip through different screens or start a search all over again with a different seller.

Finally, based on the products you've decided to sell for your company on eBay, you can create a "short list" of categories for which you conduct your searches—specific categories that hold the listings you're interested in studying. You can use the My Favorite Categories function to store a list of those categories and go back to them from one handy nexus.

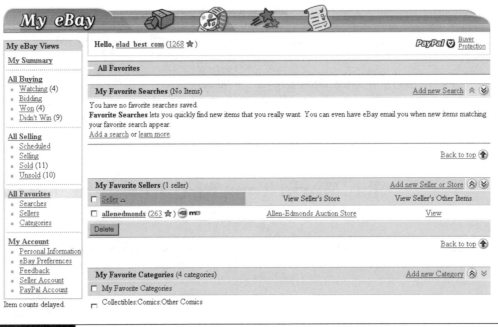

FIGURE 10-7   All Favorites page

How to ... Have eBay E-mail You Product and Company Searches

You can have eBay e-mail these valuable marketing searches to you.

1. Click the Advanced Search link at the upper-right of any eBay page.

2. Using the Search options, set up search parameters (such as seller ID, keywords, categories, or pricing).

3. Submit that search, and you'll receive the current eBay results. At the upper-right of the search page, click Add To Favorites.

4. eBay will ask whether you want the search not only saved in your My eBay, but e-mailed to you as well. Choose a timeline between seven days and 12 months for which you want e-mail sent.

My Account

The My Account page, shown in Figure 10-8, organizes a lot of functions used for doing administrative maintenance on your eBay account. Click the My Account link to access the page. You'll see links that let you check the PayPal account you've tied to your eBay account. You'll also see an account summary, showing your last invoice amount for eBay fees, payments, or credits in the last month, and any new charges and fees added to your account since the last invoice.

Next are links offering you a chance to set up automatic payments for your eBay fees with your checking account or credit card. You are also prompted to make a one-time payment to pay off your current eBay fee balance. Finally, the page shows some recent feedback that your eBay account has received from other eBay users.

Auction Listing Refinements

While you invested a lot of thought, effort, and time into building the perfect listing, there's always room for improvement. The good news is that you can get lots of free help in this area from your eBay bidders. After you post your items for sale, you may receive questions from potential bidders asking for more details or about something you've stated in the listing. The most popular questions have to do with such things as overseas shipping costs, condition of the item (if it's not stated in the listing or not stated clearly), and sometimes how quickly an item can be shipped once the payment has been received.

NOTE *Some eBay buyers ask questions regardless of whether they need to ask them, simply to test a seller's responsiveness.*

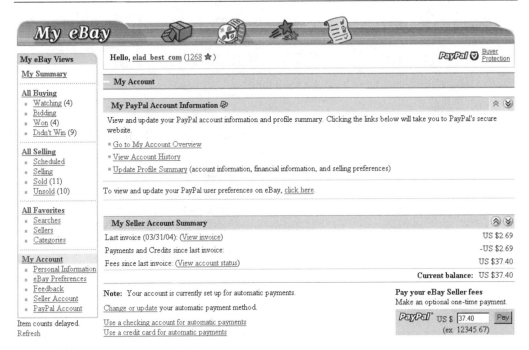

FIGURE 10-8 Use the My Account page to coordinate all administrative aspects of your eBay account from one spot.

In most cases, potential buyers' questions are legitimate and are intended to help the buyers determine whether they want to buy an item. Questions are a good sign, because it means that the buyer has read your description and has invested the time to write you an e-mail about it, which means he or she may be considering buying your item, depending on your answer to the question.

NOTE *Remember, an e-mail in the e-commerce world is like a phone call in the brick-and-mortar world. It's important to answer customer e-mails in a timely manner.*

When it comes to responding to listing questions, keep two important rules in mind:

- Answer as quickly as possible.
- Keep track of those questions.

The first rule is obvious: you want to hook the buyer quickly, before the listing ends and before he or she finds another item similar to yours and buys that one. The second rule is more important in the long term, especially if you're going to be listing a lot of similar items. Your main goal with a great listing is to provide all the information a buyer needs to make an informed bid on your product. You want to capture and retain the buyer's interest, and capture that bid before the buyer moves on and either forgets, finds another item, or goes to a store and buys it there. By keeping track of these questions, you may begin to notice patterns of the same or similar questions. You can use this information to improve your listings and your sales.

TIP   *Sometimes the item number or name of the listing will not appear in an e-mail message that a bidder sends to you, and the buyer's question may be too generic for you to answer appropriately. In such a case, politely reply to the e-mail and ask for more information about what listing he or she is interested in, so that you can help accordingly. (It's likely eBay will update this feature in the future so that listing info is automatically included in e-mails, but until that happens it's best to ask the customer for this information.)*

eBay Success Story

Jillian Distributors and the Process of Refining What You Do on eBay

When Brent and Priscilla Crouch of Greenbrier, Tennessee, heard about a neighbor's teenaged son earning $15 to $20 a week reselling products on eBay, it made them think. Could they do the same thing on a slightly larger scale and turn it into a viable small business for Priscilla to run from their home? Three years later, with their company, Jillian Distributors, on track to hit $200,000 in annual revenues, the answer is a resounding yes. Nevertheless, despite the remarkable success of startups like Jillian Distributors, eBay remains an often-overlooked resource for small and medium-sized businesses.

The e-commerce services provider has more to offer than just a forum for auctioning unwanted personal items. After the Crouches' eBay awakening three years ago, they experimented with auctioning unwanted household items. But they quickly progressed to buying products from wholesalers—end-of-line and off-brand watches, leather goods, dollar store items, anything they could find—and auctioning them on eBay. Eventually, they formed Jillian Distributors. Today the company also sells wholesale to other eBay and flea market vendors from its own web site—and it maintains an eBay store.

Jillian had sales of $25,000 a couple years ago. The next year it jumped to $97,000. Currently, with 70 percent of sales coming from eBay and 30 percent from the web site it launched last year, the company is on target to bring in close to $200,000 in revenues.

"For us, it's a trial-and-error process," says Brett Crouch. "When we find a new [supplier], we look for items of interest. Of every ten items we try [on eBay] maybe only two end up being winners. So then we try another fifteen items. In the end, we're just left with what sells." Jillian pays a flat monthly fee of only $10 for a basic eBay store. It costs 5 cents to list each item—as opposed to more than $3 to list an item in a regular eBay auction. At those prices, the Crouches can afford to let the store run on its own, which for the most part it does, while still accounting for about 10 percent of total sales.

Not only are costs lower, but the Crouches discovered they could set prices slightly higher than what they expect buyers to pay in listings, and the store also attracts customers interested in buying more than one item at a time. "It's a lot more profitable," Brett Crouch says.

10

When it's time to relist a listing or sell a similar item, take the time to edit the listing description by adding details relating to the queries you received. Remember to make appropriate changes to similar listing items—but keep in mind that the answer to one listing bidder's question may be different for other items, especially if the question involves weight, dimensions, or value of the item.

> **TIP** *If you plan to offer overseas shipping, either utilize eBay's international shipping calculator or describe the shipping costs to various countries. Listing revisions help here, too, because you should add information for users from countries for which you reveive the most questions. For example, if you're constantly being asked "How much is shipping to the UK?," be sure to provide that information in all your listings, not just the listing from which the question originated.*

Of course, the ultimate test to determine whether this strategy is working is to monitor the stream of questions from newer listings. If the questions have stopped or you are receiving unrelated questions, that means you've clearly updated your listing to convey the questioned information. If the questions keep coming, you may want to look at how you updated your listing description and see about adding those changes with more emphasis.

In the end, you won't get rid of 100 percent of the questions. But the more automated you can make this process, the more time you can spend on other aspects of your eBay strategy and the more profit this strategy can provide. Answering fewer questions means decreasing customer service time.

> **TIP** *Always include a link back to the listing item—as well as to your eBay store—in your reply e-mail.*

Prepare After-Sales Processes

When it comes to retail sales, most of the seller's work happens before the actual sales transaction occurs—the retailer orders, receives, and displays the goods for sale. After an item is sold, the retailer hands over a receipt and some change, and moves on to the next sale. In an eBay transaction, when the listing ends, that point-of-sale moment is followed up by several processes that ensure a smooth operation and repeat business.

After the high bidder has been identified, the buyer and seller work out the details of the sale, making sure that payment has been made and the product gets delivered. In addition, other events occur, such as submitting feedback for both parties on eBay's Feedback Forum, and the seller gets a chance to capture additional sales through mechanisms such as Second Chance offers (discussed later in this chapter).

Escrow Services

Anyone who's bought a home can remember what the word *escrow* means to them. Whether it's the contracts, negotiations, fees, wait times, or the annoyance of a difficult party, everyone usually puts up with the escrow because, essentially, it is meant to protect the buyer while the negotiations are in place and the sale of the house goes through. For expensive items on eBay, escrow is an option as well. Escrow provides a safety net to buyers purchasing large items—the escrow service provides them with confidence in their purchase.

Given that many transactions occur between buyers and sellers who "meet" online for the first time, a level of trust isn't always present, regardless of the feedback ratings of the seller and buyer. If your business plans to sell high-priced items on eBay, you should expect that some buyers will ask whether you will accept an escrow process to handle the ensuing sale. Before you're asked that question, though, let's walk through how the online escrow process works on eBay so you can consider all the facts.

Escrow Overview

Escrow.com acts as a secure mediator, monitoring the progress of each deal by communicating with both the buyer and seller along the way and protecting each party with a series of checks and balances. The escrow process, at http://www.escrow.com, involves five steps:

1. The buyer and seller register at http://www.escrow.com and agree to the terms of the deal, so there is no doubt as to who will pay the fee, what is the condition of the item, and other considerations.

2. The buyer sends the money to Escrow.com via a check, money order, wire transfer, or online credit card. Escrow.com then verifies the payment.

3. After the payment is verified, Escrow.com notifies the seller to ship the merchandise, which the seller should do immediately after receiving that notice. (The seller should *always* use a shipping service with a tracking number and signature confirmation of some sort.)

4. The buyer receives the merchandise, inspects it to make sure it fits the terms of the deal as stated in step 1, and notifies eBay that the merchandise will be accepted or rejected. The buyer has a limited number of days to do this, and if no objection is received by Escrow.com, it is assumed that the merchandise is sound.

5. Escrow.com sends the seller the money once the buyer has approved the merchandise.

10

TIP
Consult eBay's help page for more information on approved escrow services for both domestic and international transactions at http://pages.ebay.com/help/confidence/payment-escrow.html.

Communicating with Your Buyer

eBay gives you several opportunities to correspond with your buyer. With some preparation and experience, you can use these interactions to build relationships with your customers, and not just over particular purchases that buyers have made.

E-mail is the standard form of communication among eBay buyers and sellers. It's the quickest form of correspondence, and it can help close a sale and provide the buyer with a sense of immediate satisfaction following a purchase. The benefits of this to a business are that e-mail does not incur a higher operational cost like phone calls or standard mail can, and e-mail correspondence offers a clear electronic record of the transaction in case of problems; plus, just about everybody has access to e-mail nowadays.

At least two or three types of e-mails should always be sent when an item is sold on eBay: an e-mail informing the buyer that he or she won the item, with a total cost included; a payment reminder e-mail if the buyer doesn't respond quickly; and an e-mail stating that the payment has been received and the item has been shipped successfully, sometimes with tracking information from the shipper.

You can automate these steps with little customization. Chances are, your shipping policies are relatively the same no matter what item you've sold. Your payment address and information should be consistent for most of these listings, and the only differences are the types of items sold, the actual closing prices (which depend on the bidding), and the shipping costs (which depend on where the item is shipped).

> TIP
>
> *Prepare a boilerplate or a standard list of points to go into each e-mail, and use that boilerplate every time that type of e-mail is sent, changing such things as the item title and the total cost, depending on the situation. If you use auction-automation software, the software will coordinate those e-mails for you.*

You need to consider certain elements within each e-mail—specifically to identify cross-selling and up-selling opportunities with other products you offer.

End of Sale/Completed Transactions

Think of this e-mail as your first meeting with a buyer. The buyer has already taken the time to bid in your auction, he or she was willing to outbid everyone else who bid, and now you get to "meet" electronically. This e-mail should focus on the excitement and respect you have for this new customer, introducing them to the services your company can offer.

Start off by congratulating the buyer for winning the item, and offer a summary of the required charges, while possibly offering additional services, such as postal insurance. When eBay notifies you, the seller, at the end of the listing, you will be given the zip code of the high bidder, which helps you to calculate a proposed shipping cost for the product to present to the buyer if you did not use eBay's shipping calculator to figure these costs for you.

> TIP
>
> *Many sellers use PayPal's Winning Buyer Notification to send out that first "you've won" e-mail, which automatically includes the shipping information as well as any additional marketing information you choose to include.*

Next, present all your payment options, whether it's PayPal, money orders, checks, or other methods. Sometimes it's helpful to provide the actual Internet hyperlink addresses to take the buyer to the correct web page, whether it's your merchant credit card link or PayPal's payment page. The easier you make it for the buyer to pay you, the quicker you typically get paid.

The final part of the e-mail can be formatted in several ways, but while you have the buyer's attention, you should use this section to present other auctions or product listings that the buyer might be interested in, based on the product sold. Offer links back to your company web site when possible. For example, the payment link could sit on your web site, and that particular page could have links to other web pages within the company web site, where the customer can add on to that purchase via the company's e-commerce shopping cart program.

How to ...   Tell eBay to Generate an Invoice and Send It to the Buyer

You can have eBay send an e-mail to a buyer with the item number, description, the correct subtotal, the shipping charges you specified, and payment instructions they should follow to close the transaction.

1. Go to the eBay listing's specific web page offering the product you sold.

2. If you are not logged into eBay, click the Sign In link and follow the prompts to log in. When you're done, click the Item I Was Looking At link to go back. You should see a Send Invoice button. Click it to continue.

3. You will see a screen showing the buyer's user ID and zip code, and a list of all the listings in which that buyer bought items from you. Here you can update the shipping and handling charges, add an insurance charge, collect sales tax, and provide payment instructions and a personal message. You can also add other payment methods not specified when the auction was listed, and decide whether you want to receive an e-mail copy of the result.

Send Invoice to Buyer

Review or update the information below. When you're done, click the **Send Invoice** button and eBay will email an invoice to your buyer.

Buyer: awesomeirwin (369 ☆)

Zip Code: 98226* (for shipping calculations)
            *Please confirm with the buyer.

Enter Payment Details

Item #	Item Title	Qty.	Price	Subtotal
2241048908	Witchblade 1st edition Statue by Moore (1997)	1	$132.50	$132.50

Subtotal: **$132.50**

Shipping and Handling: Standard Delivery $ 25.00

Shipping Calculator | Add another

Shipping Insurance: Optional $ 5.00

Sales Tax: California   8.250 %

☑ Apply sales tax to subtotal + shipping and handling.

Enter Payment Instructions & Personal Message

Give clear instructions to assist buyers with payment, shipping, and returns.

4. Finally, click the Send Invoice button to send out the invoice to your buyer.

Changes in the After-Sales Process

In the early days of eBay, the after-sale process was excruciatingly slow:

1. The buyer would write a check and mail it within a few days of the listing closing.

2. The check would take a week or more to arrive at the seller's location.

3. It would take another week or more for the check to clear the seller's bank account.

4. At this point, the seller would ship the item, which took another week or more to arrive to the buyer's address.

Today, with credit card or PayPal payments, a seller can get paid within minutes of the listing closing, reducing these steps to an instantaneous process.

Use this opportunity to cross-sell or up-sell with other products. You can offer shipping discounts if the buyer purchases additional products; just be sure to keep track of that when it comes time to pack and ship the items. You can also offer your buyers a chance to receive a company newsletter.

TIP   *If your buyer was an under-bidder in any of your other listings, offer the buyer those products at or near their high bid price using a Second Chance offer or a private Buy It Now listing, perhaps with a shipping discount if the buyer purchases it immediately with the other product. Use the Search By Bidder function to see everything that the buyer bid on, including completed items and items the bidder did not win.*

Follow-up/Payment Reminder

It's easy to get that sense of accomplishment when you send out the end-of-sale e-mail. The bidding is done, the buyer has all the information he or she needs, the payment should be coming, and, once it does, you can send out the goods and move on to the next project.

If the buyer hasn't responded within several days, it's usually customary to send a reminder or follow-up e-mail regarding the payment. To do this, log into your My eBay page under your Selling section. Here you will find an option to send out a reminder e-mail to your buyers.

Shipping Notice

Once payment has been received, it's considered good etiquette for the seller to notify the buyer that the product has been shipped and offer some sort of tracking information so the buyer can follow the progress of the shipment from your location to their doorstep. Generating and sending this e-mail has several advantages:

■ You have shifted the burden from you to the shipping company in terms of completing the sale. Once the shipping company takes possession of the package and the buyer has the tracking information, any final problems can be resolved between the buyer and shipper, taking you out of the loop and saving you from dealing with "Where are my products?" questions.

■ Your responsiveness will encourage the buyer to leave positive feedback for the transaction, improving your eBay reputation, which encourages future sales.

■ This e-mail gives you one more opportunity to present other items and special deals. Perhaps at this point, you include a web site link to your eBay store, where the buyer can purchase a related product for a special price. You won't be able to offer a combined items discount, but the buyer will feel better about the sale, knowing that the package has been sent; increased trust in you may tempt the buyer to try out other offers.

Feedback

One of the pioneering changes that eBay has brought to the world of e-commerce and global trading is the idea of a feedback system, whereby buyers and sellers enter public comments about how the other party handled a sale. Small businesses are gathering reputations like big multinationals. Feedback is a highly valued and widely used tool for buyers to help decide which sellers to buy from, which listings to bid on, and how a seller handles the after-sales process. If you want to be respected and profitable on eBay, you need to understand the importance of feedback, both *about* you and *from* you. Your feedback is gold on eBay—it is your entire reputation.

While your company reputation may help you gain bids from people who trust your company, a high feedback rating ensures more bids, because it tells buyers that your company understands the eBay customer. Your reputation also helps determine the number of bids you get for an item, and it can sometimes be the difference between realizing the worst price for an item and the best price.

One of the cardinal rules of feedback is that once feedback has been entered, it cannot be removed. Therefore, think about feedback carefully before you post a comment. After all, according to eBay, "your star is your symbol of trust and experience in the eBay community." Once you leave negative feedback, the other party has every right and the ability to come back and enter a similar negative remark about you. Therefore, a number of sellers keep this in mind and treat their customers with responsiveness, courtesy, and appreciation.

> **TIP** *You can use feedback as your marketing tool, since your user ID appears right next to it. Instead of saying "buyer paid quickly, asset to eBay, AAA++++," you could say, "Thank you for the purchase & fast payment for the John Deere tractor." Now everyone viewing the feedback knows that you (your user ID) sell John Deere tractors.*

Feedback Tips

Some believe a seller should always leave positive feedback the moment the item payment is received, because this shows responsiveness and because you're usually helping out another eBay user who wants that high feedback and will reward you later with positive feedback as well.

Did you know?

Square Deal from SquareTrade

In some limited cases, the buyer and seller can file a case with a mediation service called SquareTrade (http://www.squaretrade.com), that can recommend altering a feedback comments' status in the system or removing the negative feedback point from your record. This involves you as the seller and the buyer coming to an arrangement to handle the misunderstanding and agreeing to the removal, and eBay accepting the SquareTrade recommendation.

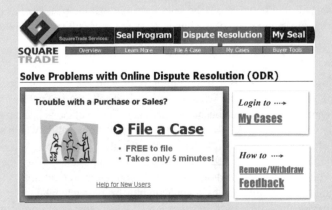

Nowadays, eBay doesn't fully remove the negative feedback; it simply removes the point from the "score card" on your feedback profile, and at the point where the negative feedback occurred, an automatic note is appended, saying that the feedback has been withdrawn but will still be present, just not in the overall summary.

However, others say that doing this neutralizes your ability to comment later, so if the other party causes trouble, you'd be powerless to respond accordingly (for example, if there is a problem with the shipment or other final details).

However, holding off on leaving feedback can irritate a user who really wants to build up his or her feedback rating. This tells the user you're not interested, and if you don't add feedback, they'll stop shopping with you and find other sellers who will leave feedback.

NOTE *A good seller usually leaves feedback after the buyer's payment is received.*

The key is to be responsive and thorough with your feedback. Once a buyer has successfully paid you for the listing, you should typically leave positive feedback saying that payment was successful. Depending on the volume of business, you can set up predefined feedback messages that you use often, or you can tailor your feedback to advertise the specific item you sold to this buyer. If you use the My eBay screen to manage your after-sale processes, find your item in the Items I've Sold section, and look for the words *Leave Feedback* in the summary line of that listing. Once you know the buyer has successfully paid for the item, you should leave feedback and thank the buyer for supporting your listing. This method is the most professional way and encourages loyalty and repeat business.

We never encourage negative feedback—we think most disputes can be worked out. The bottom line is that people really want their eBay user IDs to be clean and perfect with zero negative comments. If there's a conflict, the buyer and seller should work it out so neither party sends negative feedback and causes future buyers to doubt the seller, and vice versa. While it's important to read the feedback description for everyone you do business with, you should also take the time to read the comments and feel the excitement positive people can generate for each other.

If you do find yourself in a situation where a transaction cannot be resolved, consider leaving negative feedback. At the very least, this should be done to alert the rest of the community about this buyer. (This is tantamount to posting bad checks on the counter in a restaurant.) Also, when you leave negative feedback, stick to the facts, be professional, and do not use invective—remember that your user ID appears next to the feedback.

Immediate Payment

As eBay listings are closing faster, and people use options like the one-day listing, eBay is looking into other methods to make the after-sale processes as quick and automatic as possible. While services such as PayPal make payment lightning-quick compared to mailing and cashing a personal check, a seller still has to wait for the buyer to see that the listing closes, log into PayPal, and send the payment.

In response to sellers' requests, eBay originally implemented the Immediate Payment option for use with items that have "expiration" dates, such as tickets, holiday items, and any other short-notice type listing. Here's how Immediate Payment works:

1. A buyer clicks the Buy It Now button in your listing and is directed to pay immediately for the item using PayPal.

2. Until the buyer completes payment, the item remains available for other buyers to purchase for the duration of the listing. The first buyer to complete the PayPal payment officially wins your item.

3. Once a buyer completes payment, the listing ends and you are directed to ship the item.

4. If the listing reaches its ending time before any buyer has completed payment, no one wins the item and you can relist it.

Relisting Existing Auctions

You can spend a lot of time creating an eBay auction, and typically, you're going to offer goods that are in great supply. However, since putting all the goods up at one time could mean getting a lower price for all those items, you may decide to space out your auctions and sell a few per week to help encourage stronger bidding. eBay has created a function that makes doing this easy; it's called the Relist option.

In a relisting, eBay takes all the information you provided to list a certain item and automatically puts it back into a new listing for you. When you relist an item, you have the option to update any aspect of it, from the starting price to the description to the number of days it should be listed. If the listing is exactly as you would like it, it is not necessary to make any changes. Like a regular auction, eBay will allow you to preview your listing, and once you approve it, that new listing is uploaded to the system.

NOTE *One benefit eBay provides when you relist an auction is that it will add a web site link from your old listing that takes people to the new listing. This way, if people have searched Completed Items and found your listing, you can preserve the sale when they click the Relist link to see the current auction.*

You can access the Relist option in several ways:

- If you are logged into eBay and bring up the completed auction listing on your Internet browser, you will see a link that will take you to the Relist option.
- From the My eBay All Selling section, if you go to the Unsold Items section, one of the last options on the page is the action link for Relist, which will take you to that option.
- You can access the Relist option from the eBay Site Map page (or by bookmarking that page with your Internet browser) and enter the eBay item number you want to relist.

Once you access the option, eBay will take you to the Review page, where you can view all the details of your listing. If you want to keep everything exactly the same, including the length of auction and the starting price, you can click Confirm and instantly list your new auction.

NOTE *If you use auction-management software, you will be able to automatically relist your items.*

The Relist auction is a time-saving function that can allow you to build a library of items you keep on sale every week, with very little work for you after the initial auction creation.

NOTE *In Chapter 15, we discuss the next step in this process: creating an eBay store and keeping items up for sale for months at a time.*

Second Chance Offers

Second Chance offers provide you with a way to increase your sales without increasing your listing fees. A Second Chance offer allows you to follow up with the people who bid but did not win your item and offer them a second chance to purchase the product.

A Second Chance offer allows you to use eBay to contact the non-winning bidders in your auction and make offers to them to buy your products at their highest bid. Traditionally, this occurs under the following conditions:

- The highest bidder is unwilling to complete the transaction and you'd still like to make the sale without paying to relist the item.

- The reserve price was not met, but you are comfortable offering the item to the highest bidder.

- More than one of the items that was offered for sale exists, and you would like to sell those extra products to your non-winning bidders. These additional items must be exactly the same as the original auction—relative to color, size, condition, and every other important factor.

Odds are, most of you will be exercising the third condition, as businesses traditionally have depth of inventory to sell. The Second Chance offer allows you to capitalize when the right offer comes along.

> NOTE   *You can choose to send a Second Chance offer to only those buyers whose high bids are acceptable to you.*

You can make multiple Second Chance offers, but each bidder will pay only their highest bid amount, not the final selling price of the product. Therefore, if the highest bid was $500, the second highest bid was $490, and you make a Second Chance offer to that second highest bidder, he or she will pay only $490, not $500. You are not charged a listing fee for making a Second Chance offer, but you will pay a Final Value Fee if the bidder accepts the offer.

Once an auction listing has ended, you can access the Second Chance offer feature in several ways:

- The completed auction page—Click on Bid History to see whose bid you are willing to accept.

- My eBay—Under Items Sold, go to Action, and click on Send A Second Chance Offer.

- Closed Listing Page—Once you sign in, you will see a link in the top part of the auction that will allow you to offer a Second Chance offer to the under-bidders.

Click to start the Second Chance offer process, and you'll be asked to log in, strictly for security purposes. After that, you'll see a screen that explains the three rules for a Second Chance offer, asking you to confirm the eBay item number in question. Click the Continue button to move

10

forward. At that point, you will see a screen like the one shown in Figure 10-9, asking you to make two choices:

■ Select all the bidders to whom you'd like to extend a Second Chance offer.

■ Select how long you'd like to extend the offer. Your options are one, three, five, or seven days. After you've made the Second Chance offer, you cannot cancel it until either the bidder says yes or the offer expires, so choose your offer time appropriately.

TIP *Many sellers recommend a one-day offer. The potential winner of your Second Chance offer has already bid on this item, so you know they want it. Moreover, you don't want to keep your inventory out of stock longer than 24 hours.*

Check the appropriate checkbox if you'd like a copy of this offer to be e-mailed to your account once it's completed. After you've made your selections, click the Continue button to confirm.

Second Chance Offer

To submit this offer, please select a duration and bidder below, then click **Continue**.

Original item number:	2241048908
Title:	Witchblade 1st edition Statue by Moore (1997)
Duration:	1 day ▾

Select bidders who will receive your offer
The number of bidders you select can't be more than the number of duplicate items you have to sell. The Second Chance Offer price is a Buy It Now price determined by each bidder's maximum bid. Learn more

Select	User ID	Second Chance Offer Price
☑	**earth406** (3) ☺	US $130.00
☐	**chronobreak6919** (200 ☆)	US $78.91
☐	**dirtyharry.44** (36 ☆)	US $75.00
☐	**redhot-67** (104 ☆)	US $50.99

Bidders who have chosen not to receive Second Chance Offers or who have already been sent one will not appear above.

Receive a copy of your Second Chance Offer

☐ Send me a copy at: jelad@topcow.com
Change my email address

[Continue >]

FIGURE 10-9 Second Chance Offer setup screen

eBay will prompt you with a list of the bidders you selected and their respective high bid prices and will ask, "If you are ready to send this Second Chance Offer, select Send Offer." Clicking the Send Offer button will start the transaction, and the non-winning bidders will be sent an e-mail from eBay with a new auction URL created just for them. This auction URL includes a Buy It Now price of what the bidder originally bid on your item, asking the bidder to look at your auction again, and offering a chance to buy the product at his or her high bid price.

If the bidder decides to buy the item, you'll get an e-mail stating that the product was sold, like any other item closing on eBay. If the bidder does not respond in the offer time extended, you will get an Item Not Sold e-mail. Remember that you pay no listing fee to make a Second Chance offer, only a fee if the item sells, so there's no additional cost to try out this feature.

If you have a healthy supply of products to sell, you can reap great benefits by using the Second Chance offer process, when the bids are appropriate.

Summary

eBay has created a home base where you can monitor your eBay activity. Using My eBay, you can watch your selling activity, update your account specifics, and create favorites regarding categories, search terms, and sellers that are important for your company to monitor.

When it comes to responding to auction questions, remember two important rules:

- Answer as quickly as possible.
- Keep track of those questions.

Gaining timely feedback from your customers is very important. While your company reputation may help you gain bids from people who trust your business entity, it doesn't ensure bids, as not every company translates well to the fast-paced, intimate direct sales model that eBay brings to the table. Your reputation, in turn, helps determine the number of bids you get for an item.

Relisting your auctions allows you sell the same products over and over again without the need to create a new listing each time. Listings that are being relisted can be submitted as is or modified before they are uploaded to eBay.

Second Chance offers provide you with a way to increase your sales without increasing your listing fees and allow you to follow up with the people who bid but did not win your item, offering them a second chance to purchase the identical product.

Part III

Integrate Your eBay Business into Your Infrastructure

Chapter 11

Align eBay and Your Current Infrastructure

In this chapter...

- Work with departments to integrate eBay into the business
- Tie sales back into the books
- Examine the data structure of an eBay transaction
- Download transaction information
- Customize your PayPal transaction files

Now that you have begun implementing your business plan for the eBay component of your sales, it's time to work with the existing departments in your company to integrate eBay into their daily operations. In this first chapter of Part III, we take a look how specific departments can play a role in your company's growing eBay strategy. We then home in on the accounting/finance aspect of the integration and detail some quick ways to gather transactional data from both eBay and PayPal to automate your record-keeping and smoothen the integration.

How eBay Sales Integrate with Different Departments

In Part I, we looked at the different parts of your business and gauged how helpful these departments can be to your eBay strategy. Here we revisit that topic but focus on best practices and tips that can help ensure a successful integration of your eBay strategy into the corporate entity.

Marketing and Sales

The first key to a seamless integration of your eBay plan with other departments in the company is to maintain communication with those departments. Always make an effort to report your past, current, and future product listings to the marketing and sales staff. Particularly notable sales make excellent anecdotes for sales and marketing folks while they talk to clients to show the power of your company and its products. ("These new models are already going for over retail on eBay!") eBay successes also make excellent sidebars or feature articles in the next company-sponsored marketing newsletter. As the marketing staff plans marketing campaigns, they will know, and hopefully ask for, eBay product listings that can correlate to their regular efforts.

You should educate your marketing staff on how and why they should ask you for eBay product listings. You can be proactive in communicating listings to the marketing team in the following ways:

- Send a weekly eBay report to the marketing department.
- Have weekly meetings with marketing staff.
- With the team, develop an ongoing strategy for marketing your company's eBay products and online profile.

Just as you feed these departments information, don't be afraid to draw on the knowledge of marketing and sales folks to help make your job easier. Ask for information about product sales and experiences. The best eBay descriptions have good "usage stories" about how the product can improve a buyer's life or save buyers money. Anecdotes from current product owners can't hurt when it comes to making a big sale. If a well-known manufacturer is using your custom grinder, for example, and you're selling it on eBay, a success story from that company is an endorsement of your product when other potential buyers come calling.

A good plan here is a standard report summarizing product listings and average sale prices, highlighting unusual sales and/or enthusiastic buyers, and projecting what future listings you're looking for, perhaps with a few requests or bullet points for ideas, new items, or an offer to augment the next marketing campaign with a suggested eBay sale. The timeliness of this report should correspond with the sales and product cycles within your company and whether such information is disseminated on a weekly, monthly, or quarterly basis.

IT Department

Your IT department will play a critical role in your eBay business. This team will most likely help you in developing a couple of good HTML listing templates, and they'll be key players in helping automate your sales and create your brand identity. If possible, work with someone in IT who knows a bit about HTML and web design, and work with the management team to gain some development time to help lay out a clean, impressive HTML template.

Having a couple of good standard listing templates will definitely improve your branding efforts. It will also make your repeat customers smarter shoppers, because the consistent template interface will always guide them to the critical information each time they browse your listings. Once you have developed a couple of standard templates, you'll just need to plug in the item descriptions and links to the photos; you should be able to reuse templates over and over again. A set of standard templates is essential to standardizing the listing process and automating your eBay sales.

Here is a checklist of what a good template should include:

- Company logo
- A marketing link to bring customers to your eBay store
- Section for the name of the product being sold
- Section for the description of the product
- Section for images (you should be able to add multiple images to the template)
- Section outlining the fantastic customer service your company provides
- Section for shipping policies
- Section to display other products your company sells (perhaps a gallery of some listings with the prices and the ending times)
- Section to post feedback from previous customers

11

> TIP
>
> *If the IT folks set up and/or designed the company web site, you can suggest using the existing HTML code from a product listing page on the company site as your template, perhaps with some modifications.*

The next biggest contribution that IT can make is assistance with auction-management software. Auction-management software helps you organize your listing initiative, from describing and listing your products for sale to defining the after-sale processes of sending e-mail confirmations, collecting money, and shipping the product. These programs store a lot of information and photographs and help you keep track of sales data for use in a variety of reports that can be generated to gauge progress.

Some software must be installed on your individual computer, and this can require the approval and assistance of your IT department, depending on your computer setup. The key is to focus on the fact that after the "ramp-up" time when they install and you learn how to use this software, this tool will automate your tasks and enable your strategy to scale up and thrive, with IT as your partner along the way.

Shipping

Shipping can be one of the quickest areas of an eBay strategy to automate, depending on the variety and characteristics of the products you plan to sell. If you can ensure that your shipping partner has the supplies necessary to send your products to customers, that allows more time for you to focus on other efforts and enables you to scale effortlessly. If your company has a reliable shipping company that makes regular visits to your corporate location, consider limiting your shipping options within your auction listings to match the offerings of this company, so you can streamline your efforts. Your guide should be the expert advice of your shipping department or, lacking that, advice from your most widely used shipping partner.

First and foremost, talk with your shipping department and set up reasonable expectations and estimates for the work they'll need to process. Offer to help point your shipping staff in the right direction to get shipping supplies, and work with them to procure supplies from other eBay sellers, if necessary. If this type of system doesn't exist already, encourage the creation of a special work area where you and your eBay team have easy access to the products, shipping supplies, and a computer and printer where shipping labels are printed.

Work with one main shipping company, if possible, and organize your efforts online. Many shippers offer corporate discounts and online label creation. Not only does this provide automated tracking information for each package, but depending on the tool, it helps complete other after-sale processes. For example, PayPal currently offers tools you can use to print either UPS or US Postal Service prepaid labels and the amount is deducted from PayPal. If you use that feature, PayPal will create the tracking number and e-mail that number to your buyer automatically, so you don't have to send a separate e-mail informing a buyer of tracking information. If your shipping department focuses on using the US Postal Service for shipping, look at several online stamp options including Endicia.com, Stamps.com, USPS Click-N-Ship, and solutions from Pitney Bowes. Otherwise, a corporate account from a shipping company such as UPS or FedEx will handle all the billing, tracking number creation, and e-mail generations when you send out your products. As your needs grow, work with your shipper to add any necessary features to your operation.

One final suggestion in this area that can help save time is to make sure you notify your shipping department of any unusual items *before* you list them for sale. Let's say you find unique, old advertising posters from your company that might be of interest to collectors. You decide to list them on eBay, the listing ends, you are paid for the goods, and when you send the posters off to your shipping department for processing, they don't have the time or resources to prepare the appropriate packaging. At this point, your shipping department is scrambling for supplies while the buyer is waiting day after day for the package. It may sound like a simple problem, but it's a common one.

Accounting/Finance

Based on our recommendations so far in this book, your company should create a PayPal account in conjunction with its eBay strategy and go through the registration and verification steps. You need to make sure that the accounting staff is on board with the eBay plans either at account creation time or when the first dollars start coming in.

In the next section, we talk more specifically about how your accounting department can fully integrate your various eBay sales back into line items in the overall company ledger while retaining the ability to track, report, and summarize the contributions of the eBay strategy as part of the larger whole.

Tie Sales Back into the Books

If you've ever seen or worked on the floor of a stock exchange, you know the frenzy of a trading environment. Deals go down all day, records are kept, negotiations ebb and flow, and at the end of the day when the bidding stops and after the excitement is over, everyone works on reconciling their data to figure out how much money they've made or lost. As in any environment that involves the exchange of cash for goods or services, appropriate accounting is a must.

Data Structure of an eBay Transaction

Before you or your accountant can create invoices or develop a link between eBay sales and your company's other sales, it's important that you know what information is available from an eBay transaction. Following are some suggestions as to how eBay information can be correlated into the financial records of a typical company sale, including some of the basic data elements of every eBay transaction. Although many other pieces of information could be useful for accounting purposes—from the starting date, to the number of bids, specific fees/costs for that listing, and other information—we believe the information presented here is the primary data that will be useful for your finance department. This type of data is shown in Figure 11-1.

eBay Item Number

This unique number is created when an eBay listing is submitted to the system and is used for tracking the listing from beginning to end and beyond. This unique number would make an excellent invoice or purchase order number for your system, with one exception: If you sell multiple items

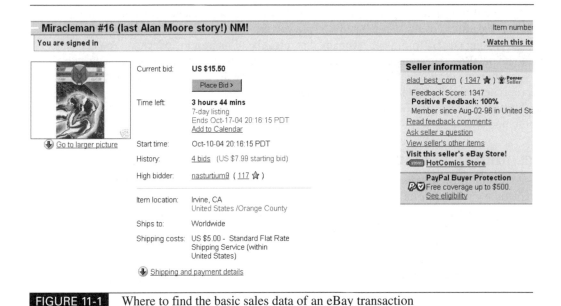

FIGURE 11-1   Where to find the basic sales data of an eBay transaction

in one listing (a Dutch auction), each item sold will reference the same eBay item number on the transaction logs. If you need a unique key for your database or spreadsheet accounting program, one option is to combine the eBay item number and the buyer's user ID or e-mail address.

> **NOTE**   *Any item sold via a Second Chance Offer (described in Chapter 9) will have a new item number created when the offer is extended. If you're using the item numbers and recording them into your systems upon item creation, be sure to make a note each time you extend a Second Chance Offer.*

Closing Date

Typically, a closing date field containing the exact date and time a listing will end (in the Pacific time zone) is calculated when you list a product for sale. This date is exactly one, three, five, seven, or ten days after the auction listing goes live on the eBay system. However, any person who exercises the Buy It Now option will change the listing closing date/time to whenever the Buy It Now option was exercised. Also, any store item will show a closing date/time of the purchase, or a multiple of 30 days since the item was listed if it goes unsold.

> **TIP**   *It's helpful to use the closing date as the "date of purchase," since officially, that is when the sale occurs, the listing ends, and the seller and high bidder have been identified.*

Final Price (Winning Bid)

This field of information, typically in your native currency (US dollars, Canadian dollars, Euros, and so on), will also be available the moment your auction listing closes. Regardless of the additional charges you levy onto the cost—such as shipping, insurance, or escrow fees—the final price should reflect the actual sale price of the product, as if you were writing it on an invoice.

Item Title

In Chapter 8, we talked about the best, most optimized title you can give your listing. This 55-character field will contain the exact spelling, punctuation, and characters that you used in your auction listing. While this title serves your listing well, it may not serve the purposes of your accounting information, invoices, and other financial needs.

You may want to consider *not* using this field as a direct corollary to the Product Title field in an invoice summary, for example. Trim out any additional keywords, and work with your accounting department in case they have a defined list of product descriptions that they already use.

Winning Bidder

eBay will always show you the user ID of the highest bidder of your listing, as well as all the under-bidders. If you are logged onto eBay and look further into the listing details, eBay will display the e-mail address of the winning bidder. In your listing summary e-mail, which eBay sends out once the listing has ended, eBay typically also provides the first initial and last name of the user, based on the winning bidder's user ID profile with eBay. By keeping that e-mail, or linking with (potential) PayPal data, you can automatically fill in the name of your buyer and his or her e-mail address in your invoice.

> **TIP** *Ask your shipping department to print out or upload a report of the daily shipments with the customers' addresses.*

Another thing to consider is the category of sale. Some companies may choose to label all their sales as eBay sales for the category. Others may include each sale depending on the product line and record just the product sale and not the channel of that sale. Work with accounting to make that decision ahead of time, or during your first conversations with the accounting folks. And to make their life (and yours) even easier, you can pull potential reams of information electronically and effortlessly from eBay and PayPal.

> **NOTE** *A seller or high bidder in a listing can request profile information from eBay in order to resolve a listing. If either the buyer or seller requests it, both parties are sent an e-mail with both sets of information. That way, each party now learns the name, phone number, and e-mail on file with eBay for that user ID.*

Downloading Transaction Information

As you begin your sales on eBay, you could keep track of all your sales via a yellow legal pad or by eyeballing the My eBay sales pages. However, as your sales volume grows, so does the number of transactions—with the various fees, ending prices, and buyers. It becomes important to find a way to automate the collection of such data. Thankfully, eBay and PayPal provide ways to download this information onto your computer to make it easy to import it to various software applications.

eBay Logs

Every month, eBay e-mails you an invoice detailing each listing you listed and a line item for each fee, whether it's an insertion fee, listing upgrade, final value fee, reserve fee, or picture fee (discussed in Chapter 8). While this invoice is thorough, an e-mail usually doesn't translate into a file you can import easily. However, eBay allows you to view these invoices online and offers the option to download your invoices into a comma-separated file for use in importing into such software applications as QuickBooks or Microsoft Excel.

To download your invoice, log onto eBay and go to My eBay. Under the last option on the left navigation bar, My Account, you should see a subtopic called Seller Account. Click that, and you should see the Account Status & Invoices page shown in Figure 11-2. From this page, you can either view your transactions by month or customize a date range. Choose the dates for which you're interested in getting the data, and click View Account Status.

In the Account Status page shown in Figure 11-3, you'll see a summary of your eBay account (your company's financial information will not be displayed). You'll also see a listing of your eBay transactions. Look for the Download link, as shown in Figure 11-3. By clicking that link, your Internet browser will prompt you to save a comma-separated file onto your computer. Rename the file as appropriate and use the file to import the data into your accounting program.

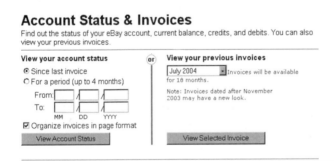

FIGURE 11-2   Account Status & Invoices page

Download link

Account Status for topcowauctions (E29883738001-USD)
Current balance: $62.63

Account State	Active
Account Name	topcowauctions
Account ID	E29883738001-USD
Billing Cycle Date	15 (day of month)
Payment Type:	eBay Direct Pay
Bank Routing Number:	122016066
Bank Account Number	xxxx xxxx xxxx 1725
Bank Info Update:	Feb-04-03 17:09:21 PST

Account Past Due	No
Amount Past Due	US $0.00
Date of Last Invoice	Jun-15-04
Last Invoice Amount	US $27.24
Last Payment Date	Jul-07-04
Last Payment Amount	-US $27.24
Total Payments This Billing Cycle	-US $73.59

Page 1 of 1

Account Status (34 transactions since last invoice)
Sort by: **date** | fee type | item number   🖶 Printer-friendly view   📄 Download

Date ▽	Title	Item	Fee Type	Amount	Balance
Jun-16-04 17:30:22 PDT	Joe Jusko Lady Pendragon Original Double Cover Painting	2248470980	Reserve Price Listing Fee	-$24.99	$48.60
Jun-16-04 17:30:22 PDT	Joe Jusko Lady Pendragon Original Double Cover Painting Final price: $2,005.00 (Second Chance Offer)	2251398366	Final Value Fee	$43.20	$91.80

FIGURE 11-3   Account Status information page

The account information is, by default, sorted by date. However, eBay gives you the option of sorting either by fee type or item number. The power of these sorts is that if you use a sort and then download the information, that file will contain subtotal information that can speed up your data integration and cost analysis.

For example, let's say that you sort by item number. eBay will group all the related fees based on one item number, and after all those individual transactions are listed, it will display a subtotal for that item number and the sum of those fees, as shown in Figure 11-4. When you download that file, some lines of data will appear with the words *Subtotal for Item #*, the item number, commas, and the sum of that item's fees. When you import this information, you can call out those lines and know your eBay costs for each product listing.

NOTE
Keep in mind that as your transaction level data increases, you may choose to consider working with your IT or MIS department to enroll in eBay's Developer Program to create software that integrates specifically with your business.

PayPal Transactions

Depending on your eBay strategy, a high number of transactions may use PayPal. If so, PayPal offers a wide range of features to help you track your transactional data in the form of monthly reports, logs, and downloadable files. These downloadable files can be customized into Quicken, QuickBooks, Excel, or comma-separated value formats for easy import into whatever accounting program you use for your company accounting.

Customize Your PayPal Transaction Files

Check out the Customize My History Download page shown in Figure 11-5. You can open this feature from the PayPal Download History page.

Account Status for topcowauctions (E29883738001-USD)

Current balance: $62.63

Account State	Active
Account Name	topcowauctions
Account ID	E29883738001-USD
Billing Cycle Date	15 (day of month)
Payment Type:	eBay Direct Pay
Bank Routing Number:	122016066
Bank Account Number	xxxx xxxx xxxx 1725
Bank Info Update:	Feb-04-03 17:09:21 PST

Account Past Due	No
Amount Past Due	US $0.00
Date of Last Invoice	Jun-15-04
Last Invoice Amount	US $27.24
Last Payment Date	Jul-07-04
Last Payment Amount	-US $27.24
Total Payments This Billing Cycle	-US $73.59

Account Status (34 transactions since last invoice)

Sort by: date | fee type | **item number**   🖨 Printer-friendly view

Date	Title	Item ▽	Fee Type
Jun-20-04 01:01:45 PDT	Direct Pay Payment -- Automatic Monthly Billing -- Thank You		
Jul-07-04 00:19:01 PDT	Direct Pay Payment -- Automatic Monthly Billing -- Thank You		
Jun-16-04 17:30:22 PDT	Joe Jusko Lady Pendragon Original Double Cover Painting	2248470980	Reserve Price Listing Fee
	Subtotal for Item# 2248470980		

FIGURE 11-4   Account status sorted by item number

FIGURE 11-5   PayPal Customize My History Download page

How to ...   **Download PayPal Information**

1. Log into PayPal and at the main screen, click the History tab near the top. You should see a Download My History link in the upper-right part of the screen. Click that link to open the page shown here:

Download History   Secure Transaction 🗎

Select your options below.   View Changes to
                                                    Download History

From: [07] / [05] / [2004]   To: [07] / [12] / [2004]
      Month Day Year   Month Day Year

Download File Types
  ⦿ Comma delimited file (for use in any spreadsheet application)
     ⦿ All Activity
     ○ Completed Payments Only

  ○ Tab delimited file
     ○ All Activity
     ○ Completed Payments Only

  ○ Quicken

  ○ QuickBooks

  ☐ Ignore previously downloaded transactions and transactions older than 30 days.

                                                    Download History

2. Choose a range of transactions based on the dates for which you're interested in getting information. While PayPal will automatically show just the last month, you're free to go back as far as to the date when the PayPal account was created.

3. Choose the format that you need for the data, whether it's comma-separated (which can be read by multiple spreadsheet programs), tab-separated, or something more specific, if you use Intuit's Quicken or QuickBooks software. Click Download History to see more information if you use PayPal as your shopping cart program on your e-commerce web site.

11

TIP *If you plan to download data often with this page, check out the option that says Ignore Previously Downloaded Transactions And Transactions Older Than 30 Days. This feature will help you keep clean data without duplication each time you update your records.*

4. After you've made your selections and clicked Download History, you'll be prompted to save the file to your computer. Follow the prompts and save it to a directory where you use your accounting information. Give it a specific name that denotes it as PayPal data for your eBay transactions.

After that file is downloaded, use your accounting or spreadsheet program to open the data file and manipulate the data any way you need for your company's records.

From here, you can choose the data fields that you want to analyze for your eBay activities. Simply check the boxes next to the fields you wish to include in the downloadable log. After you do that and click Save, your log file should contain the fields that you selected.

As a default, PayPal will always include several fields in the log, as shown in Table 11-1.

Field Name	Field Definition
Date	Date of PayPal payment
Time	Timestamp of PayPal payment
Time Zone	Time zone on which the Time field is based
Name	Name on file for other party in transaction
Type	PayPal has five types of payments: eBay Items, Auction Items, Goods, Services, and Quasi-Cash
Status	Notes status of the payment: still in progress, completed, etc.
Currency	Denotes which currency is used (USD, CAD, etc.)
Gross	Gross amount of money sent or received in the transaction
Fee	PayPal fee for the transaction (it's free to send money; Business Accounts pay to receive money)
Net	Gross amount minus PayPal fee
From Email Address	PayPal e-mail address of the person initiating the payment
To Email Address	PayPal e-mail address of the person receiving the payment
Transaction ID	Unique PayPal ID created to track this transaction
Reference Transaction ID	If a PayPal transaction depends on a previous transaction, previous transaction ID appears here
Receipt ID	Unique number used when receiving quasi-transfers
Balance	PayPal balance after this transaction occurred

TABLE 11-1 PayPal Fields

The Customize form then lets you choose from fields shown in Table 11-2, depending on whether the transactions are Website Payments, Listing Payments, or Other. For the purpose of our discussion, we'll look at the Listing Payments section, where you can select whether to include these fields in your log file.

Check the boxes for which you need the data, and uncheck the boxes (or leave the boxes unchecked) when you do *not* want that field of data to appear. If you process a large amount of transactions through PayPal, you may want to optimize your file to have only the key elements so as not to include any unnecessary information in the system. On the other hand, if these systems tie into other systems, where addresses and e-mail addresses are important, consider importing as much useful information as you can to pass along to other systems.

> **TIP** *PayPal is constantly making changes to the Downloadable Log feature to make it more useful to businesses of all sizes. Log into PayPal and then check its Update page at https://www.paypal.com/us/cgi-bin/webscr?cmd=p/acc/history-download-messages to see what new features have been added that you can take advantage of the next time you synchronize your sales data.*

Field Name	Field Definition
Item ID	The ID number used by the listing site (eBay) for the product
Item Title	The title from the auction site's listing
Shipping Amount	The amount of money specified for shipping and handling when the buyer pays the seller using PayPal
Insurance Amount	The amount of money specified for insurance when the buyer pays the seller using PayPal
Auction Site	Which auction site the listing was posted on (eBay, Yahoo!, etc.)
Buyer ID	The user ID of the buyer in this transaction
Item URL	The web page URL of the auction listing
Closing Date	Exact date when the listing bidding ended
Single Column Shipping Address	Entire shipping address of buyer in one column
Multi-column Shipping Address	Shipping address of buyer in several columns (street address, city, state, zip)
Counter Party Status	Whether the buyer is a Verified or Unverified PayPal member
Address Status	Whether the buyer's address on file has been confirmed or unconfirmed
Sales Tax	Amount of sales tax paid, if any, by the buyer

TABLE 11-2   PayPal Customize Form Fields

Summary

A focus on integrating eBay with all the appropriate departments in your company will allow you to add eBay as a revenue-generating stream into your company's existing business. Establish good communication between your eBay efforts and your marketing and sales departments. An exchange of sales information and synchronization of efforts can lead to success for everyone. Also work closely with the IT department to create the appropriate templates and setup for your Internet-based work.

Speak early and often with your shipping department and help them prepare for the task of shipping all the various products sold. Your accounting or finance department should be consulted prior to beginning your listings on eBay to set up the standards for which they require data input and money flow. Find out what they require and work with them as the money flows in. Pick the key elements from your eBay (and PayPal) transaction, and use that information to build corresponding records in your company's financial books.

Finally, take advantage of downloadable files containing your eBay transaction data, from both eBay and PayPal, when trying to reconcile sales data and automate this process.

Chapter 12

Utilizing eBay to Market Your Business

In this chapter...

- ■ Create and measure marketing objectives
- ■ Use the four Ps of marketing
- ■ Incorporate eBay in your Internet and offline presence
- ■ Make "Be Creative" your overarching principle
- ■ Use eBay to cultivate customer relationships
- ■ Respect the power of user feedback

Peter Drucker, business professor and *Wall Street Journal* columnist, once wrote that "Marketing and innovation are the two chief functions of business. You get paid for creating a customer, which is marketing. And you get paid for creating a new dimension of performance, which is innovation. Everything else is a cost center." While a little simplistic, there is a great deal of truth to this statement.

Many businesses view marketing simply as a cost center or a necessary "fee" for doing business, when in fact it should be factored into the cost of creating a sale. By adding eBay to your business as a new sales channel, you will not only complement revenues in your existing sales channels, but you will be adding a powerful new marketing channel to your business at very little cost. This important marketing channel will drive business to your eBay listings and generate more excitement and sales for your brick-and-mortar and Internet storefronts.

Create and Measure Marketing Objectives

Marketing in general is more than just sheer publicity or "buzz" about a company, and eBay as a selling platform deals with marketing with this in mind. When you develop marketing objectives for your eBay sales, remember that, first and foremost, meeting marketing objectives should lead to sales of your products. Specific marketing tools and techniques are designed to grow sales, improve sell-through ratios, and increase your net profit per item. However, your marketing objectives should take into account their contribution to the overall strategy. Just as a brick-and-mortar storefront engages in marketing to enhance the customer experience, so should your eBay strategy promote an encompassing, safe, and satisfying user experience.

NOTE   *Beware of the trap of marketing your eBay identity solely for the benefit of one or two corporate executives, or of imposing your own standards without taking into account your eBay audience's needs. This can lead to ineffective marketing and a weak overall strategy.*

When marketing your business with eBay, you should define objectives that contain the following three characteristics:

- They must be clear.
- They must be performed within a set time frame.
- They must be measurable in terms of revenue generated.

For example, some eBay marketing objectives for your business could include variations on the following:

- Create online buzz for the release of a new product on rollout so that June sales are up by 16 percent.
- Increase product visibility among eBay buyers by offering package shipping discounts, leading to a 12 percent improvement in sales over the next six months.
- Using eBay listings, inform target markets about features and benefits of your new product line, leading to a 10 percent increase in sales over the next fiscal year.
- Increase product sales at local trade shows by 30 percent by next spring by referring trade show customers to your 24/7 eBay presence and linking those sales to your trade show presence.

Use the Four Ps of Marketing

After you have decided on your marketing objectives, your next step is to decide which of the four defined areas of marketing you want to pursue. These areas, called the *Four Ps,* were originally presented by Jerome McCarthy, author of the classic business text *Basic Marketing.* The Ps stand for *Product, Place, Price,* and *Promotion.*

Which one of the four Ps you choose to emphasize as your primary focus should be determined by the nature of your product, the resources you have available, and which strategy you believe will most likely help you meet your goals.

12

TIP   *You are not limited to choosing just one of the four Ps in your marketing strategy. The best marketing plans incorporate elements of all four. However, it's rare to have a product that's so unique or a company willing to put resources behind a push that's big enough to encompass each area. By and large, focusing on one primary area with a strong secondary is the best bet: for example, marketing your product's unique features along with its competitive price tag.*

Product

Product means any individual goods, product lines, or services that your company offers. If you decide to make this your primary area, your product must offer clear, distinct, and non-arguable value to the buyer. For example, let's say your company sells DVD players. If the DVD players include features, accessories, service, warranty, or packaging that is unique or superior to that of the competition, this would be an ideal area to emphasize in your marketing.

Remember that your eBay product listing is a billboard to the world, where you can precisely control the presentation of your product details, guide people to your particular items without talking to them in person, and differentiate your product while demonstrating value to the consumer. Conversely, your eBay listing has to be strong to stand apart from others, because that web page has to convince the buyer to go with you instead of another seller. You may interact with potential buyers if they ask questions, but the best sellers get ahead because their product description and listing presentations are convincing enough to make the sale on their own.

Ask yourself the following questions: Do you run a business in which a personal touch sets you apart? Are you more focused on services than tangible, boxed products? If the answers are yes, offering occasional specials on eBay can bring an interesting twist to how your company markets its services.

Place

Place refers to your product's distribution channels—where the product is located in a store, the placement of an online or newspaper ad, or the fulfillment and shipping system you use. As outlined in earlier chapters in this book, one of the natural strengths of adding eBay to your sales channels is that it places your product in a huge targeted marketplace. Buyers come to eBay for the sole purpose of purchasing products. By placing well-written listings, driving traffic to your listings and your eBay store, and generating excitement about your products, you can use eBay to improve your product's placement in any market.

If one of your goals is to build up the excitement of your company's listings within the eBay channel, one way to improve a particular product's place is to offer it only on eBay.

Price

Price points, or the price that clients are willing to pay to purchase a given product from you, tend to vary depending on the degree of innovation in marketing your product. In general, the more unique, rare, or cutting-edge your product, the higher the unit price you can realistically charge versus the price you receive for a basic model. Tickets to a sold-out event or tickets in a particularly great seat, like those offered in Figure 12-1, qualify.

NOTE
The "degree of innovation" price structure tends to be time-based. Consider software sales, for example: Your product may be the only one with a feature that sends data to a digital scanner, but it's only a matter of time before that feature is duplicated by another company's product. So you can garner premium price points now but perhaps not do so later. Another example might be the concert tickets shown in Figure 12-1. The innovative element might be the rare, desirable front-row seats. But as these are sold and the standard seats remain, it's unlikely the price premium will hold up.

eBay marketing can offer you several options if you pursue a price-based strategy. As discussed in Chapter 4, you can use eBay as the channel in which you roll out your most up-to-date items, allowing you to charge a premium for a user being the first on the block to get the latest product. You can also add value to your product's price by creating special product bundles. This unique

Front Row Tickets to upcoming REM Concert!   Item number

You are signed in   · Watch this ite

	Starting bid:	**US $9.99**	**Seller information**
		Place Bid >	elad_best_com (1349 ★) Power Seller
	Time left:	**4 days 22 hours**	Feedback Score: 1349
		5-day listing	**Positive Feedback: 100%**
		Ends Oct-23-04 19:04:34 PDT	Member since Aug-02-96 in United St
		Add to Calendar	Read feedback comments
Go to larger picture	Start time:	Oct-18-04 19:04:34 PDT	Ask seller a question
			View seller's other items
	History:	0 bids	**Visit this seller's eBay Store!**
	Buy It Now Price:	**US $499.99**	HotComics Store
		Buy It Now >	**PayPal Buyer Protection**
			Free coverage up to $500.
	Item location:	Irvine, CA	See eligibility
		United States	
			Financing available NEW!
	Ships to:	Worldwide	**Only $21 per month**
	Shipping costs:	US $5.00 - Standard Flat Rate	if you use PayPal Buyer Credit. Subject
		Shipping Service (within	approval. US residents only. See repay:
		United States)	See details	**Apply now**
	Shipping and payment details		

FIGURE 12-1   This hard-to-get item commands a premium price point.

approach can position your products in a way that is unmatched by the competition. Additionally, eBay allows you to up-sell and cross-sell add-on products to your product line staples.

Conversely, eBay attracts a lot of bargain hunters. If your product is a simple mass-market commodity, you can use eBay to showcase how you can offer the product below the price a user would find it in a local store.

Promotion

Promotion means that you are communicating desirable information about your product with the customer. Promotion in this context includes both the public relations side of the business and the customer fulfillment/feedback area. In other words, if you successfully raise customer awareness and gain a sale, you still haven't succeeded in your marketing strategy if the client receives poor treatment when trying to return the item, gets unsatisfactory warranty coverage, or gets little or no company feedback about a problem.

The opportunity to communicate effectively with your customer is one of eBay's greatest strengths. Not only does eBay allow you to promote your product and provide added value by steering customers to your online store, it also provides near-instant and public feedback, like that shown in Figure 12-2, as to how you are doing in fulfilling orders. Since the feedback mechanism is transparent, sellers are encouraged to work with buyers to smooth out problems and perform better.

12

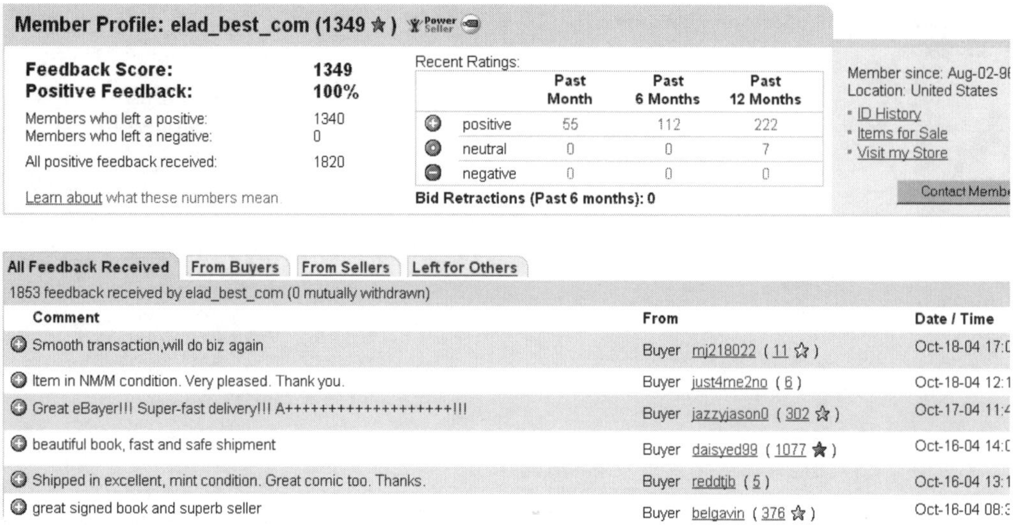

Member Profile: elad_best_com (1349 ★) 🏆 Power Seller

| Feedback Score: | 1349 |
| Positive Feedback: | 100% |

Members who left a positive:	1340
Members who left a negative:	0
All positive feedback received:	1820

Learn about what these numbers mean

Recent Ratings:

		Past Month	Past 6 Months	Past 12 Months
⊕	positive	55	112	222
⊕	neutral	0	0	7
⊖	negative	0	0	0

Bid Retractions (Past 6 months): 0

Member since: Aug-02-9?
Location: United States
• ID History
• Items for Sale
• Visit my Store

Contact Membe?

All Feedback Received   From Buyers   From Sellers   Left for Others

1853 feedback received by elad_best_com (0 mutually withdrawn)

Comment	From	Date / Time
⊕ Smooth transaction,will do biz again	Buyer mj218022 (11 ☆)	Oct-18-04 17:0
⊕ Item in NM/M condition. Very pleased. Thank you.	Buyer just4me2no (6)	Oct-18-04 12:1
⊕ Great eBayer!!! Super-fast delivery!!! A++++++++++++++++++!!!	Buyer jazzyjason0 (302 ☆)	Oct-17-04 11:4
⊕ beautiful book, fast and safe shipment	Buyer daisyed99 (1077 ★)	Oct-16-04 14:0
⊕ Shipped in excellent, mint condition. Great comic too. Thanks.	Buyer reddtjb (5)	Oct-16-04 13:1
⊕ great signed book and superb seller	Buyer belgavin (376 ☆)	Oct-16-04 08:3

FIGURE 12-2   eBay's feedback mechanism in action

eBay
Success Story

Building Excitement and Promoting Loyalty over the Miles

Continental Airlines has taken an innovative approach to its eBay listings to emphasize *product* in an industry where *price* is normally the main marketing factor to travelers. Since the actual business of flying to major destinations such as Los Angeles or New York is not inherently unique, Continental's approach has been to make the trip itself part of a unique selling proposition.

The company's strategy has been to auction off special travel experiences in conjunction with eBay, such as a pair of tickets to the Grammy Awards in Los Angeles. Another popular bonus was a pair of tickets to see the Chicago Bulls—with opportunities to meet the players. As an even more innovative twist, Continental allowed the bidders to pay for these listings with their earned frequent flyer mileage, thereby getting double-duty out of this marketing effort: generating excitement and increasing customer loyalty at the same time.

Incorporate eBay in Your Internet and Offline Presence

After you've determined your goals and decided which of the four areas you want to present, you can choose from among many options to bring these ideas to your target eBay audience. eBay can help you raise customer awareness of your brand, your company, and individual product lines both over the Internet and offline. Just as you've learned to think of eBay as a complementary channel for your sales, you can continue to view eBay as a method of expanding and enhancing your present marketing efforts.

Harness eBay in Your Internet Presence

One often overlooked area of synergy lies with the integration of your eBay strategy into the corporate web site. Typically, companies separate web site services into the IT group or outsource their efforts to a separate web content group run by web gurus who focus on security issues and user requests rather than adding a new sales or marketing channel to the company web page. Thankfully, many companies have added marketing personnel dedicated to or responsible for the company web site and Internet, and these people are the first ones you should contact.

eBay Success Story

Integrate eBay and Your Brick-and-Mortar Storefront

Janelle Elms, one of the authors of this book, has repeatedly demonstrated how eBay should be used by Internet-savvy entrepreneurs. She's also shown store owners that there should be no difference in the way they market merchandise between eBay and their brick-and-mortar store presence.

"I once had a client who ran a shop selling all kinds of antiques," Janelle related at one of her eBay University classes. "One day I walked in and asked her where all of her items were that were for sale on eBay. She stated that she had put them in back so that no one could buy them! I immediately told her to get those items out in the store for sale." With Janelle's help, the owner placed signs on all the items that read, "This item isn't available for purchase in this store, but it IS available on eBay. Let me show you how to shop from us 24 hours a day, 7 days a week."

By displaying these items in this manner and not hiding them out of view of the browsing buyer, the owner maximized the items' visibility. Additionally, by displaying the items but pointing out that they were for sale only to eBay buyers, she conveyed the idea that these items were special and therefore more valuable than other, similar items.

12

The development of multiple management staff influencing what needs to be done in the IT area is part of the reason it's best to have one person tasked to set up and run your eBay channel development, to keep that singular focus. We've discussed this at length earlier in the book, but it's important enough that we wanted to remind you of this again here.

Some of the tools you'll want to use to augment your online marketing efforts with eBay include the following.

A Link to the eBay Listings on Your Web Site

At minimum, you'll want to include a hyperlink on your web site that allows the user to go directly to your listings on eBay. A better solution would be to have your web content developers create special eBay buttons or icons on your web site that do the same thing. eBay provides sample buttons and banners that your web designers can use or enhance. Since these items are more visual and user friendly than a simple text link, they'll call attention to themselves much more readily. eBay can help you with creating these linkable buttons. Log in and go to http://cgi3.ebay.com/aw-cgi/eBayISAPI.dll?LinkButtons.

Examples of how the text and graphical methods might look on your web site are shown in Figure 12-3.

The best option is to list your eBay listings directly on your web site by using the eBay Merchant Kit. eBay allows you to add a few lines of specific code to your web page to display your eBay listings within another web page, as demonstrated in Figure 12-4. This method does double duty: not only does it call attention to your eBay presence, it provides visibility to your potential customers to the items that you sell on eBay.

FIGURE 12-3   Examples of using a simple hypertext link to your eBay listings (left), and a graphics-oriented approach (right)

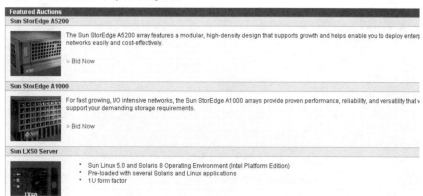

SUN MICROSYSTEMS AUTHORIZED AUCTIONS

Sun Auctions
» Warranty
» Frequently Asked Questions
» Subscribe to Sun's Dynamic Pricing Bulletin
» Questions/Feedback

eBay: New and Remanufactured Product

eBay is the world's largest personal online trading community. eBay created a new market: efficient one-to-one trading in on the Web. eBay users buy and sell items in more than 4,320 categories. Users can find the unique and the interesting everything from IT Solutions products (workstations, servers and networking products) to portable devices: PDA, laptops Each day, eBay hosts over 4 million listings, with over 450,000 new items joining the "for sale" list every 24 hours.

→ FAQ → View All Auctions → Dynamic Pricing Bulletin

Featured Auctions
Sun StorEdge A5200

The Sun StorEdge A5200 array features a modular, high-density design that supports growth and helps enable you to deploy enterp networks easily and cost-effectively.

» Bid Now

Sun StorEdge A1000

For fast growing, I/O intensive networks, the Sun StorEdge A1000 arrays provide proven performance, reliability, and versatility that v support your demanding storage requirements.

» Bid Now

Sun LX50 Server

* Sun Linux 5.0 and Solaris 8 Operating Environment (Intel Platform Edition)
* Pre-loaded with several Solaris and Linux applications
* 1U form factor

FIGURE 12-4 List items for sale on eBay with a link from a company web site, as with this example from Sun Microsystems.

TIP *You can find out more information about the eBay Merchant Kit at http://pages.ebay.com/ api/merchantkit.html. We go into further detail about this feature in Part IV.*

When using this method of marketing your eBay links on your web site, consider adding a Buy It Now option to the current listing price, as shown in Figure 12-5. If your client base is used to purchasing directly from you as opposed to waiting for a listing to close, this may be the excuse they need to purchase the item at the reasonable Buy It Now price before a bidding war commences that might allow someone else to win the item.

Internet Message Boards and Forums

One way to get the word out regarding specific product listings is to announce a sale on appropriate Internet message boards and forums. By going to specific for-sale or listing forums, you can create a post that describes the product or sale and provides a direct link to the listing.

TIP *Be aware that advertising products in irrelevant message boards or forum areas is considered spamming, which can negatively affect your corporate and eBay presence. Instead, consider adding a link to your listings in the signature you use on the forum. That way, every time you answer a question or post ideas with other people, they will see a link to your products for sale.*

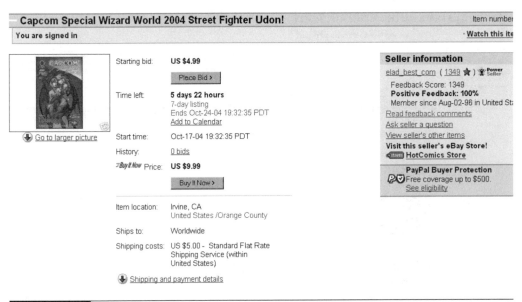

FIGURE 12-5 A listing with the Buy It Now option displayed

Opt-in Newsletters

One last item you might want to add to your online presence is to offer a free subscription to your business's online newsletter. Either as a link posted in your auction listing or in e-mails that you send to your customer to complete an eBay transaction, you can allow customers to opt-in to receiving your free newsletter. By getting your customers' e-mail addresses when they sign up, you have the opportunity to build customer loyalty and retention through frequent e-mail communications of your company's newest products and special sales.

CAUTION *Within e-mail, you can offer customers the option to be included on your newsletter list during the course of a normal business transaction. You cannot e-mail all of your pre-existing customers and market to them without their permission, however.*

We strongly recommend not using an opt-out strategy, as people who neglect to make the opt-out selection will assume that you're spamming them when you send e-mail information—which will give your company an extremely negative image. More important, this violates eBay policy and will most certainly put your account into jeopardy. Communities of online customers have been known to boycott unofficially or discourage others from buying at companies that are suspected of spamming or selling customer information to marketing companies that generate spam.

TIP *One of the best ways to encourage sign-ups on a mailing list is if you offer a special deal, such as the chance to be notified prior to the general public about a one-of-a-kind piece or sale items, or perhaps to receive a free shipping coupon.*

Harness eBay in Your Offline Presence

As we discussed earlier, your company's printed materials should tout your eBay presence. Work with your company's marketing department to integrate the eBay portion of the business into all of its marketing materials.

You need to understand that with any change, such as adding an eBay sales channel, it's important that you work closely with other departments. For example, make sure the human resources department is notified and receives the correct spelling of the company eBay sites so this information can be added to business cards. Talk to your administrative staff so they have the correct information to update the company letterhead. Getting everyone on the eBay bandwagon should lead to a strong integration.

In general, make sure that you mention eBay as one of your sales channels in one or more of the following:

- Company letterhead
- Business cards
- Stationery
- Flyers
- E-mail signature files—the tags that are automatically appended to the bottom of e-mails sent out by anyone from your company
- Invoices
- Shipping labels

Be Creative to Stand Apart from the Rest

Your overall objective when it comes to using eBay to market your business both on and offline should be to generate interest in your company in a way that makes you stand out from the rest of the market. You can use eBay for creative marketing efforts in many ways. For example, you could offer company coupons, like the offer shown in Figure 12-6. You can present your potential customers with special package deals that they can buy only on eBay, bundle products together in a unique and creative way, or offer company collectibles that cannot be purchased in any other venue.

eBay offers you a new area to tout extended warranties on your product or to offer specials on group rates, package deals, or combination items that simply can't be found in stores. In addition, you can market your products by offering special options. For example, you might offer a 100 percent money-back guarantee to your clientele, which studies have shown will encourage up to 6 percent more bids on your items.

Offering company collectibles or other unique items is a strategy that is common on eBay, but it is common because it works to generate interest. Be creative in offering value to your target market, and don't be afraid to think outside the box!

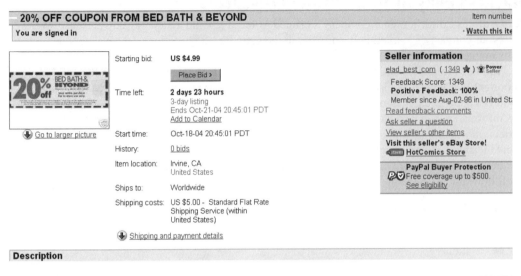

20% OFF COUPON FROM BED BATH & BEYOND		Item number
You are signed in		· Watch this ite

Seller information

elad_best_com (1349 ⭐) 🏆Power Seller

Feedback Score: 1349
Positive Feedback: 100%
Member since Aug-02-96 in United Sta

Read feedback comments
Ask seller a question
View seller's other items
Visit this seller's eBay Store!
🏪 HotComics Store

PayPal Buyer Protection
Free coverage up to $500.
See eligibility

Starting bid: **US $4.99**

Place Bid >

Time left: **2 days 23 hours**
3-day listing
Ends Oct-21-04 20:45:01 PDT
Add to Calendar

Start time: Oct-18-04 20:45:01 PDT
History: 0 bids
Item location: Irvine, CA
United States
Ships to: Worldwide
Shipping costs: US $5.00 - Standard Flat Rate
Shipping Service (within
United States)

Shipping and payment details

Description

Go to larger picture

FIGURE 12-6   eBay allows to you offer coupons in a whole new way.

eBay Success Story

FOX Benefits from Paying Columnists

One of the most interesting marketing treatments using eBay has been the auctioning of temporary employment with FOXSports. In 2003, the sports division of the FOX network ran several listings on eBay, offering the opportunity to write a column for its web site about an upcoming NASCAR race.

At first glance, this might have appeared a little odd. After all, would people really pay for the opportunity to get a "job" with FOXSports? As it turned out, it was an excellent marketing tool, and a lot of buzz was generated by word of mouth. Many NASCAR fans couldn't wait to have their names in a byline under the network's banner. Best of all, the network actually made a profit on its marketing expenditures. Recognition-hungry fans paid an average of $300 each to join the FOX team for their one-column stint.

Use eBay to Cultivate Customer Relationships

As the use of the Internet to market, sell, and distribute goods continues to develop, the lack of face-to-face customer interaction has led some companies to conclude that customer relationships are of secondary importance. However, you should continue to make customer relationship development a primary objective. The lack of face-to-face interaction may change the *nature* of the communication with your clientele, but not its *importance*.

Respect the Power of User Feedback

If anything else, the nature of the Internet unites users from around the globe who might never meet, but they certainly will share a poor experience they had with a company over the Web. Furthermore, one of eBay's legendary strengths has been its feedback system and involved user community. Bad reputations travel fast on eBay and can cripple your sales efforts no matter what deals you offer or items you display.

If you're still not convinced that user opinions hold a great deal of power on the Web, do a search with Google or Yahoo! to find people's recollections of bad experiences with particular companies. Users who are really angry share their views with everyone on the Web, and sometimes they're moved to do so with a web site that catalogs each misstep of a poor experience. Feedback does not stop with the eBay Feedback Forum, as eBay users have been known to use the community bulletin boards and direct e-mails to warn other users of certain sellers. Thankfully, the converse is true, and excellent feedback can only enhance and further your eBay identity as your buyers become ambassadors and can tell others about their positive experience with you.

Online Response Time

Instead of the telephone, the majority of your customer contact will be via e-mail. Many of the same customer service rules apply to both methods. Companies who provide top-notch service have a policy to answer the phone by the third ring, or, if this is impractical, they'll keep customer hold times to an absolute minimum.

Similarly, e-mail should be answered promptly, preferably within the same business day. At the very least, your business should make an iron-clad policy to follow up with customer queries and complaints within 24 hours or less. Inadequate response times discourage potential clients from bidding on an item that they cannot get information about.

E-mail should also be answered in a professional, courteous manner, just as you would want your company to answer the customer on the phone. Most important, be honest in what you tell your customer.

Often, customers inquire "Have you shipped my item yet?" If you haven't provided a tracking number for the package, be honest if the item has met with a delay in shipping; apologize and promise that the order will be shipped as promptly as possible. (Ideally, of course, you'd notify your customers in advance if any potential shipping delays occur.) And, of course, if the transaction becomes unworkable for any reason that you cannot straighten out, provide a refund promptly and politely. Such excellent customer service will ensure a growing, profitable business on eBay.

12

Examples of Providing—and Not Providing—Customer Service

Author Janelle Elms has been on the customer side of the business with eBay as well as on the seller's side. "I've seen both wonderful—and disappointing—levels of service from sellers," she related. "And believe me, it makes a difference as to whether one will proceed with a transaction. I actually received the following e-mail response to my question about a reserve auction:

> I'm not tellin you nothin. You type of people just askme [sic] all sorts of questions and take up my time and never bid. Go find someone else to bother.

To this day, I'm not sure of what this lady's motivation was to be selling online, but the result was the important part: I did not bid on that item or any of that seller's other listings." Now, compare that response to a professional business that understands how to deal with potential customers:

> Thank you very much for taking the time to look at my auction and write. Yes, the painting includes the frame that you see in the picture. The frame is made out of maple wood that has been stained with a red color. The red stain highlights the color of the roses beautifully. It is triple-matted with acid free mats. I have attached a picture of the authenticity that I found on the back of the frame. I also have the matching sconces up for sale on eBay. You can find them at the following link: www.ebay.com. If you are interested in them, I would be happy to save you money by combining the shipping charges. This painting would be a breath-taking centerpiece for any room. Good luck with your bid and thank you again for your time.

"This seller quickly answered my question and made me feel comfortable about my purchase. Better yet, the seller also redirected me back to her listings. This is how great customer service also acts as a free and effective way to market your products."

Charity Events

One final way to deepen your relationships with clients and your local customer base is to participate in charity events. eBay is a great way to auction your services for a charity event. The buzz around the listing will help drum up excitement for your business.

Even though eBay is a global site, it works well for local listings. Include a link to the listing in the signature of your e-mail so everyone with whom you communicate during the 10-day listing is aware of it.

TIP *Be sure to notify your local newspapers about your charity listings—the media loves to report on unique uses of eBay, at the local or national level.*

eBay Online Community, DOUA, Empowers Individuals

The Disabled Online Users Association (DOUA) has established the Helping Hand Program to help disabled individuals achieve steps toward financial independence as online auction sellers. Given the flexibility of online hours, eBay has opened a whole new sales channel for individuals to empower themselves.

Marjie Smith, founder and executive director of DOUA, says, "Our goal at DOUA is to help the differently-abled become self-sufficient and independent. If you're disabled and would like to start your own online business, we can help."

DOUA is available at 1-888-703-9542 or at http://www.doua.info, shown next. DOUA's one-on-one mentoring program is the best in the world for teaching people with disabilities how to become online sellers.

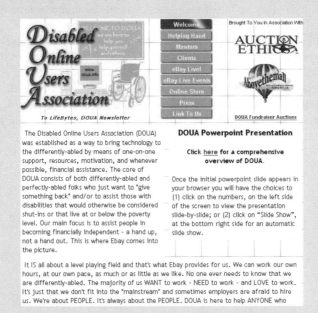

Qualified participants, who include legally disabled persons already registered at eBay.com but who have not yet listed more than five listings, receive the following materials and services, at no cost to the client:

- Five products to list on eBay

- Available support from an assigned mentor, via telephone and e-mail

- Loaner cameras and postage scales for clients that wouldn't be able to begin any other way

12

Summary

Marketing objectives should lead to sales of your product. If that's not the case, you need to look at your marketing plans and methods. Your company's marketing objectives should be clear, measurable, and performed within a set time period.

Once you have decided on your eBay marketing objectives, your next step is to decide which of the Four Ps you want to pursue: Product, Place, Price, or Promotion. Your choice should be determined by the nature of your product, the resources you have available, and which objective will help you meet your goals.

eBay can help you raise customer awareness of your brand, your company, and individual product lines both over the Internet and offline. Just as you've learned to think of eBay as a complementary channel for your sales, continue to view eBay as a method to promote and enhance your present marketing efforts.

Develop an integrated strategy so that eBay and your company's web site complement each other. Your printed marketing materials should also showcase your eBay presence. As a start, make sure that you mention eBay as one of your sales channels in company letterhead, business cards, stationery, flyers, and e-mail signatures.

As the use of the Internet to market, sell, and distribute goods continues to develop, you should continue to focus on good customer relationships. Make customer service one of the priorities of your online eBay presence.

Use eBay to market creatively and think out of the box. eBay provides you with a phenomenal opportunity to test creative sales and marketing ideas. For only the cost of a listing fee, you can try out a variety of creative marketing ideas to find the one that will explode your product's sales.

Chapter 13

Leverage Your Brand Online

In this chapter...

■ Integrate eBay sales into your marketing and sales information

■ Create your company's eBay home page

■ Use eBay Merchant and Editor Kits

■ Time your listings with release of marketing material

■ Create cross-promotional events between eBay and other sales channels

■ Utilize the eBay Exclusives program and Merchandising Calendar

■ Set up charity listings

As you continue to grow your business with eBay, keep in mind that your eBay sales do not exist in a vacuum. Instead, they are just one piece of your company's overall sales picture. Because of this, eBay product marketing and sales promotion should not be limited to the eBay site; this information should branch out and be incorporated into the general marketing and sales information your company provides to the public and your customers.

Earlier in the book, we discussed the topic of incorporating your eBay identity into overall marketing vehicles, from your company stationery to your corporate web site. In this chapter, we focus on the actual product sales you plan to generate and how those specific sales can be tied to existing and new efforts by your company to increase revenue, profits, and your customer base.

Create a Company eBay Page

While each eBay product listing has its own unique eBay item number and URL on the Internet, your company should offer one consistent web page, an eBay home page, that customers can visit as a starting point to find all your eBay sales. If you decide to set up an eBay store (which more and more sellers are doing—see Part IV), this will be your eBay store's home page. If your company chooses not to open an eBay store, the most likely home page would be your eBay About Me page. Another alternative would be to have an internal page on your corporate web site designed to be your company's eBay home page. Whatever you choose as the launching pad for your customer's Internet visits, remember that it's vital that your company have a strong and consistent presence on eBay. Your home page will go a long way toward establishing this presence.

The beauty of a home page is that regardless of how many products you list in a week, you are pointing your customers to the "right" place every time they visit. This can, in effect, condition customers to come back to check out your new product listings or buy more of their favorite items.

We've already discussed the About Me page and how to create it in Part II of this book. This page, an example of which is shown in Figure 13-1, is a free and easy way to make sure your company description, auction listings, and feedback are presented to your customers in a clear format that's easy for you to set up through eBay.

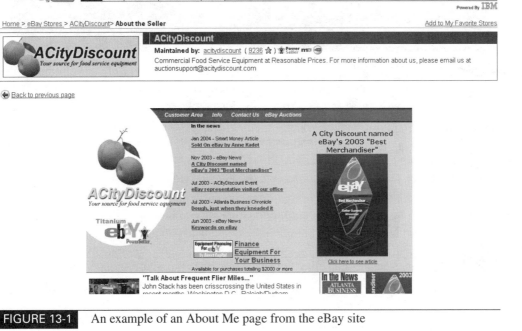

FIGURE 13-1   An example of an About Me page from the eBay site

An eBay store page, such as the one shown in Figure 13-2, is more dynamic and consistent with the look and feel of an e-commerce shopping site. An eBay store allows your business to present both auction listings and fixed-price store inventory items that are available all the time.

NOTE *A complete evaluation of the eBay store can be found in Part IV. Read through those chapters and then decide whether an eBay store is right for your business.*

Your last option is to create an internal web page on your corporate web site and set it up to contain all the vital information your customers would need regarding your eBay identity and sales. An example is shown in Figure 13-3.

eBay understands that your company needs to promote its eBay sales internally to your employees and provides several tools that can help you achieve a dynamic, up-to-date web page for customers without them having to leave your company Internet site. Companies that use a secure, private intranet for their employees and/or customers would require a page on the intranet if it contains information that's not available to the general public.

Speak with your IT department to gain necessary access and permissions to include a new page within the company web site; IT folks can also provide the technical expertise needed to build this eBay web page. You or your IT staff can also use some eBay-sponsored tools while constructing this page.

13

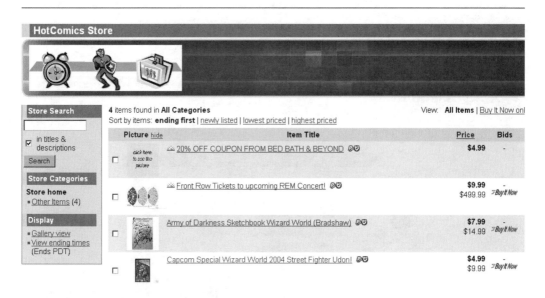

FIGURE 13-2   An example of an eBay store page from the eBay site

NewComix.Com Store on eBay!

NewComix.Com operates an eBay based storefront (not an auction site) to sell specialized comics directly to the public. If, for any reason, you have troubles using eBay to purchase any of these comics, please e-mail me at elad@newcomix.com.

To see the listings, click on the following link and you will be taken to the store:

Enter the NewComix storefront

Home
Online
 Shopping
Promotions
Resources
Gallery
FAQ
Awards
About Us

FIGURE 13-3   This page from a company's Internet site acts as a launching pad to the company's eBay listings.

The eBay Merchant Kit

The eBay Merchant Kit, shown in Figure 13-4, is a free sales tool that lets you display your eBay items on your own web site with a minimum of technical know-how. Using the Merchant Kit, you can simply add a line of code to the HTML on a page of your site. Your listings are displayed using the Merchant Kit template. The advantage to using this eBay product is that it allows you to keep your customers on your site longer, while simultaneously showcasing your merchandise on two separate online sales channels: your company's web site and your auction listings on eBay. To check out the kit, go to http://www.ebay.com/api/merchantkit.html.

The Editor Kit

eBay also offers an Editor Kit, shown in Figure 13-5, that allows you to add real-time eBay listings to your company's web site. The links to the information on this product are available at http://affiliates.ebay.com/tools/editor-kit/.

The difference between the Merchant and Editor Kits is that while the Merchant Kit lists your auctions, the Editor Kit will dynamically show pertinent eBay listings and listing details, including product information, gallery images, bidding prices, and ending times. Each specification is completely customizable. For example, a company online newsletter focusing on a product could use the Editor Kit to add a box with that product's current eBay listings next to the article.

FIGURE 13-4   Click the link to set up your own merchant page using the Merchant Kit.

FIGURE 13-5   The eBay site Editor Kit links

NOTE   *Based on eBay's tracking, the Editor Kit produces click-through rates two times greater than traditional banners. This alone makes the product well worth your time to investigate.*

Time Your Listings with the Release of Marketing Materials

If your company uses specific printed marketing materials, such as direct mail, brochures, sell sheets, or similar advertising that is timed to coordinate with a specific event or campaign, consider augmenting that initiative by including pertinent eBay listings as part of the campaign. Select the products you want to sell as you plan the campaign, share photos used in these marketing materials among the various pieces, and create your item listings in advance and include specific URLs in the other media devices. Figure 13-6 shows an example of a company that uses this strategy.

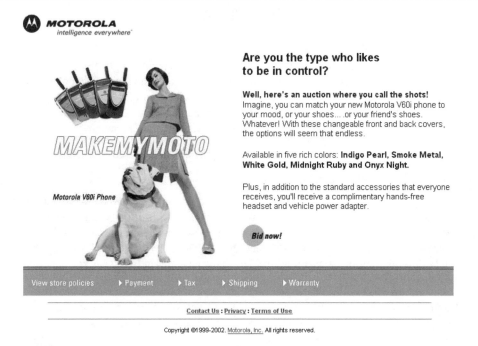

FIGURE 13-6   Motorola allows customers to bid on customized phones on eBay by connecting marketing pages from the company web page with its eBay identity.

Did you know?

Schedule a Listing in Advance

To ensure that your listings will be ready for the release of your marketing materials, or if you want to use a specific listing URL in your campaign, eBay's scheduled listing feature allows you to create your listing up to 21 days in advance. For 10 cents per listing, you can indicate the exact day and time (in 15-minute increments) when your listing will be listed; upon creating this listing, you'll get the valid auction number and URL that eBay will use once the item goes up on the site. For more information on scheduled listings, visit http://pages.ebay.com/help/sell/schedule.html.

Create Cross-Promotional Events with eBay and Other Sales Channels

To achieve your goal of seamlessly integrating your eBay sales channel with your company's other sales channels, you can create some cross-promotional events among the channels. Cross-promotional events will tie together your regular customers with your eBay customers, and they encourage those customers to purchase your company's products from multiple venues. eBay has created several programs to help you coordinate these efforts while taking advantage of eBay's advertising muscle.

eBay Exclusives Program

In 2004, eBay launched a program to create more brand equity among manufacturers and their customers, while promoting a method for these manufacturers to specifically target the ever-growing eBay audience. The eBay Exclusives program allows manufacturers, distributors, and retailers to create special editions of their product, dubbed an "eBay Exclusive," and sell that product solely through their presence on eBay's site. This provides at least four key benefits to participating businesses:

- **Customer acquisition** By providing an eBay Exclusive item, you are unveiling this new product line to eBay's 125 million registered users across the globe. This kind of exposure dwarfs most conventional media outlets.

- **Distribution enhancement** Any manufacturer understands the value of a good distribution channel, and eBay provides a highly liquid, higher margin channel than some of the retail channels used today. Using an eBay Exclusive can provide the differentiation needed to keep existing channels happy while exposing at least one product to the eBay community.

- **Competitive advantage** Companies that provide an eBay Exclusive product are still extending and promoting their unique brands, with eBay's assistance. Additionally, these companies extend their online presence, guaranteeing future revenue streams.

- **Proven concept** By using different avenues to reach new and continued customers, certain manufacturers understand the value of reaching the customer. An eBay Exclusive product allows you to promote your presence on eBay, build up demand for the exclusive product, and position yourself to attract more interest in the eBay Exclusive product as well as your company's other merchandise.

Here's how the eBay Exclusives program works: Companies create and sign an agreement with eBay that specifies exactly what their eBay Exclusives item will be, including descriptions of the item, quantities to be produced, and sale prices. eBay will include that information when it promotes all of its eBay Exclusives, both online and offline, and the company can use either its eBay store or About Me page to host the description and link to the item sale page.

During an exclusive time period, all the eBay Exclusives products will be available for sale, and eBay will support this with heavy promotion on its site. For example, as many items were being prepared for the 2004 holiday shopping season, the eBay Exclusives launched November 15,

Did you know?

CDs Sell as eBay Exclusives

Universal Music Group has produced sets of 100 signed, numbered CDs of the top albums that they sell on eBay as eBay Exclusives. Under the company's eBay ID, universalmusicgroup, the company has branded the Universal Collector's Edition and marketed it as exclusively on eBay. As shown, the CDs are sold individually, with detailed descriptions and CD cover pictures, and certificates of authenticity are offered to the winning bidder of each listing.

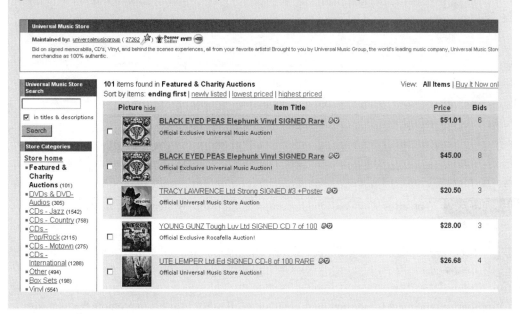

giving companies 30 days to sell their exclusives on eBay. After that time period expired, companies were able to use their other existing channels to move remaining inventory.

eBay offers several marketing efforts with the Exclusives campaign:

- eBay will build and promote a unique Exclusives hub page to direct traffic only to various eBay Exclusives.

- eBay will implement a holiday press relations and marketing outreach campaign, employing advertising on eBay's main home page, an e-mail outreach to eBay users, and press releases to the general media.

- eBay will offer each participant $150 in credit toward its Keywords Advertising Program, whereby companies can pay for specific ads served up when users enter specific keywords into their eBay searches. As shown in Figure 13-7, eBay has structured this feature to be as "turnkey" as possible so that your business can concentrate on selling its product, not trying to place ads in places where companies won't create new business.

13

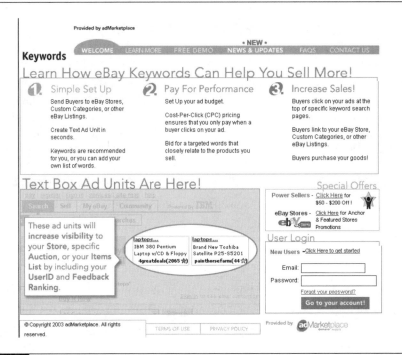

FIGURE 13-7   The eBay Keywords page, complete with step-by-step online instructions

NOTE *Go to http://ebay.admarketplace.net for more information on the Keywords Advertising Program.*

A primary requirement for the company creating an eBay Exclusive is to promote the exclusive item through at least one company-managed marketing vehicle, whether it's the corporate web site, a direct mail piece from the corporation, inclusion in a newsletter, a specific press release or community announcement, or an announcement to a specific network of partners.

NOTE *Any participating company needs to have either an eBay store or an established About Me page, carry a positive feedback rating of at least 10, and state its policies clearly in the listing, such as shipping, returns, and taxes. In addition, all company marketing information regarding the eBay Exclusive must be approved by eBay, especially since companies will be allowed to use a special eBay Exclusives logo for this promotion.*

Selling an eBay Exclusive is accomplished via a standard eBay sale, the same as any other listing or eBay store listing your company would create. Each listing comes with the standard listing and final value fees, and you can choose between auction-style bidding, fixed price, or reserve listings to sell products. All post-sale processes for eBay Exclusives items are the same as those for a regular listing item.

Collectibles Manufacturers Profit from Customer Exposure via eBay

When eBay launched its Exclusives Program in January 2004, the initial rollout was designed to help expand businesses and grow the collectibles market. Dan Neary, director of eBay Collectibles, said, "eBay works to develop innovative programs that help contribute to the growth of the collectibles industry. The Exclusives program gives manufacturers exposure to the world's largest community of collectors, while rewarding those collectors with the opportunity to purchase an exclusive limited edition from their favorite manufacturer."

Three leading collectibles manufacturers, Goebel, Enesco and Disney, each offered exclusive products. Enesco, producer of Precious Moments and Cherished, was joined by several other smaller crafts-oriented collectible companies such as Fenton Art Glass to produce items available only on eBay.

The approach taken by each manufacturer was slightly different. For example, a smaller manufacturer such as Fenton offered a small number of artist-signed items using eBay's traditional listing format, while the mainstream, non-exclusive pieces were offered at a fixed price. Goebel and Enesco offered a unique, eBay-only coupon that could be redeemed at participating retailers to purchase products.

The program was a resounding success. Five months after the launch, Goebel, Enesco, and Disney sold a combined value of more than $2.6 million in eBay Exclusive collectibles. "The [eBay Exclusives] promotion helped Enesco reach a broader audience of Precious Moments collectors and gift buyers," says Dan Dallemolle, president and CEO of the Enesco Group. "And the certificate drove traffic to our traditional retail stores, making this a positive promotion for everyone," he continued. "We see eBay as an ally to the world of collecting and to collectibles companies. As shown by this type of promotion, collectibles companies can use eBay's audience to generate the thrill of the hunt, which is so tremendously vital to the success of this industry."

13

eBay Exclusives provide excellent options for any company to generate market interest in its product and accelerate product demand.

eBay's Merchandising Calendar

Studies have shown that eBay's home page is among the top 10 visited web sites on the Internet. eBay understands the value of its real estate and has organized its home page to capitalize on the attention it receives. Every time you visit the eBay home page, you will notice that a different set of products are featured, as shown in the two examples in Figure 13-8. eBay decides in advance what themes to promote and the length of time they will be promoted. These marketing decisions make up the eBay Merchandising Calendar.

FIGURE 13-8 Two eBay home pages feature different themes that eBay is promoting; these themes can change even between reloads of the eBay home page.

The eBay Merchandising Calendar gives users, especially sellers, advance notice of what themes eBay plans to promote on its home page in the next few months. By arming sellers with this information, eBay encourages them to list more items related to these themes, since sellers know that eBay will deliver more traffic to their listings through the promotion. By plotting out Merchandising Calendars to cover months at a time, eBay gives sellers time to stock up on upcoming "hot" items and allows them to prepare to add appropriate listings during a particular time period.

NOTE   *eBay does reserve the right to change any of the promotions, dates, or featured categories on this calendar. eBay updates the calendar to reflect any changes that have occurred as soon as possible. You should check the site often if you are planning to capitalize on these promotions.*

Figure 13-9 shows the Merchandising Calendar for July 2004. While the obvious theme of Americana is featured because of the American Independence Day holiday on July 4, eBay also chose to highlight its Apparel category with a "Summer Fashion Brand Blowout" as well as its commodity items with a "Summer Dollar Days" promotion that spanned multiple categories. Similar themes are proposed by eBay category managers and approved by several groups, including category marketing, management, and overall eBay marketing managers.

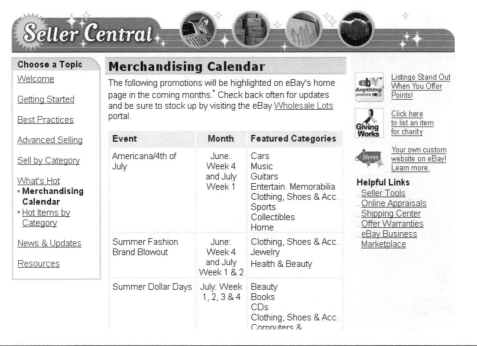

FIGURE 13-9 eBay's Merchandising Calendar for July 2004

Make a note of this calendar, and try to align your listings with promotions that fit the categories in which you are selling items. Make sure that you time your listings to fall in the designated weeks of the month specified. Also check to ensure the appropriate categories are being used for these listings, and perhaps consider adding a new category to your listing to capitalize on this promotion. And, of course, follow up after the listing is over to see whether your products got better visibility and bidding improved during this time period compared to previous listings.

Charity Listings

Sometimes companies can generate more than just company profits in an eBay listing; companies can use eBay listings to give back to the community. Various organizations have worked with eBay to create a new sales venue—eBay Giving Works. This function, which partners with an organization called MissionFish, allows businesses to come together with nonprofit organizations and individual eBay users to "build a marketplace for change." Companies who use the Giving Works program, shown in Figure 13-10, can support their communities while building their businesses.

13

FIGURE 13-10   The Giving Works program

Giving Works is simple. When your company lists an item for sale, you can choose from a long list of approved and validated nonprofit organizations who will benefit from all or part of the proceeds. Then you set a percentage of the sale amount that you would like donated to the specified charity. Your listing will be denoted with a special Giving Works icon, letting every shopper know that the listing will benefit a nonprofit organization. eBay's search engine allows buyers to search based on whether a purchase benefits nonprofits, so your items can be easily found by those people wishing to shop and support charities. Finally, since the percentage and charity information are built into the listing by eBay, the program provides the buyer with a clear idea of how your listing's sale will benefit the charity and lead to higher sales of your products.

MissionFish is the organization powering Giving Works. It provides the nonprofit verification to charities who wish to benefit from the program and creates a listing tool for charity items to be placed on eBay, tracks and gives receipts for the donations that come from these listings, and offers some customer service assistance.

When creating a Giving Works listing, you'll want to market the listing so it gains maximum exposure and bids to benefit your designated nonprofit organization in the best way. One free method of promotion is to submit your listing to eBay Giving Works, and based on space and availability, an editorial board will review your submission and decide whether it will be included on the web page.

How to ... **Create Charity Listings on eBay**

1. Log into http://www.missionfish.org/seller_regintro.jsp, and register with MissionFish as a seller, as shown here:

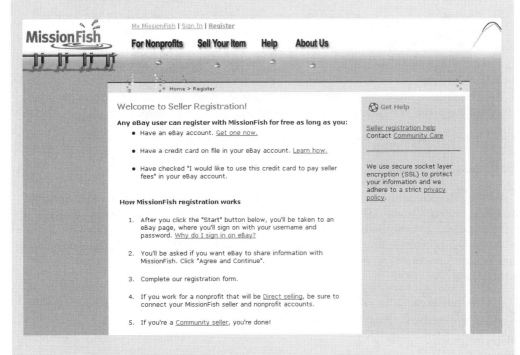

2. From the MissionFish directory, select the designated charity you wish to assist.

3. Select the percentage that you'd like to donate, from 10 to 100 percent. A $10 minimum donation is recommended for each successful Giving Works listing.

4. Create your auction listing as you would on eBay.

MissionFish will submit your listing to the designated charity to be approved. After that nonprofit approves the listing, it will be submitted to eBay, you will be notified, and you will manage the listing just like any other eBay listing. MissionFish will process your donations via your credit card filed with eBay and then deliver those proceeds, minus their processing fees, to the nonprofit, providing you or your company with a tax receipt.

When you are ready to market your listings, send the following information to givingworks@ebay.com:

- Your company's eBay user ID and contact information
- A brief description of the sales event, including dates, estimated number of items, and value of merchandise to be listed; the designated charity; and any planned media outreach efforts you'll use to promote this event
- The URL for either your About Me page, your eBay store home page, or MissionFish's home page
- A graphical image (specific requirements for the image can be found at http://pages.ebay.com/sell/givingworks/marketing_your_event.html)

Additionally, don't forget to use the free tools available on eBay, such as your About Me page, to promote this event, as well as paid programs such as the eBay Keywords program.

> **NOTE** *If you're planning a large-scale event and want to ensure excellent placement on specific eBay web pages, consider contacting eBay's Strategic Partnerships team at mediaplanning@ebay.com to set up a meeting and discuss other options.*

Finally, eBay has created a specific calendar within the Giving Works program called Spotlight on a Cause. In this calendar, eBay pools a number of events under themes that speak out to the diversity of the community and create a larger platform to generate awareness, promotion, and merchandising opportunities, giving the participating sellers increased traffic and greater branding opportunities. Some events for the calendar may include such issues as education, women's issues, and holiday giving.

> **TIP** *Be sure to check the eBay Giving Works home page for more information on Spotlights. You can find this page at http://givingworks.ebay.com/.*

Summary

Successfully integrating your eBay sales and marketing materials with your other corporate promotional materials will give your eBay sales channel a cohesive fit within your company's overall sales promotions. Whether you're adding eBay URLs into your marketing materials, adding information about eBay listings to your company web site or newsletter, or providing updates to your sales force about upcoming listings, endeavors to integrate your sales venues will result in increased sales in each channel.

Create a consistent eBay home page where your eBay and traditional customers can visit to get up-to-date information on what eBay events you are planning. Your options here include an eBay store page, your About Me page, or a special page on your corporate web site.

Time your listings with the release of upcoming marketing materials, such as direct mail pieces or media advertisements. Always coordinate launch events to include an eBay presence.

The eBay Merchant Kit sales tool gives you the ability to display your eBay items on your own web site, with a minimum of technical know-how. eBay also offers an Editor Kit that allows you to add real-time eBay listings to your company's web site.

You can use the eBay Exclusives program to create specially branded merchandise that is sold through the eBay Exclusives hub page, promoted by eBay, but available only through your eBay listings for a given time period.

Using eBay's Merchandising Calendar, you can plan events to match up with specific advertising periods on eBay's home page, highlight the categories in which you wish to sell products, and benefit from additional free exposure to your category.

Companies can sponsor charity listings and promote these on eBay using the eBay Giving Works program, sponsored by MissionFish. These special listings contain information about the benefiting charity, the percentage of listing proceeds to go to the charity, and special icons that alert consumers to the charitable aspect of the sale.

13

Chapter 14

Track and Evaluate Your eBay Sales

In this chapter...

- Define which data needs to be reviewed
- Analyze eBay data
- Mine new connections from your data
- Go deep with HammerTap's DeepAnalysis
- Determine costs of eBay sales
- Separate initial startup costs from recurring costs

After you've opened your eBay sales channel for business and you're conducting transactions, you're ready to evaluate your sales process and improve your listings, marketing techniques, and eBay business strategies. To do this, you'll need to analyze your sales data and make adjustments based on your findings.

Define Data That Needs to be Reviewed

A variety of checkpoints in the eBay selling process will provide you with invaluable data from which to draw:

- The average selling price of your items or categories of items
- The list of all of your current and/or past auction items
- The average number of bids per item
- The categories utilized in listing your products
- The success rate of your listings
- The success rate depending on the keywords or categories used

Monitoring the effectiveness of your sell-through rate as well as the traffic to your listings and your final sales price will help you determine whether you are positioning your products in a way that maximizes sales. Tracking your sales data will allow you to spot trends in buyers, assess your product pricing strategy, and forecast upcoming sales price and volume.

Analyze eBay Data

eBay processes millions of transactions every week. *Data mining* (see the section "Mine New Connections from Your Data," later in this chapter) pours through millions of transactions to pick out the key sales factors for any given product you wish to study and compares the data to your own listings. Several overall factors will affect every seller who reads this book, regardless of product category, and data mining can help identify room for improvement.

Get the Highest Number of Bidders on Your Listings

To get the highest number of bidders on your listings, you must maximize the traffic or number of potential bidders who view your listings. To assess the number of people who have visited your listing, you can use an auction *counter*. (For more on counters, see "Web Counter— A Basic Data Mining Tool," later in this chapter.)

By comparing the number of visitors who access your listings versus the number of bids on your auctions, you can determine whether or not your site content is effectively converting visitors to buyers. A high number of visitors to your listing in conjunction with a low number of bids suggests that you should look at what you can do to improve your listing parameters and listing description.

Compare Your Starting Price to the Average Price

If your starting price is significantly higher than the average selling price achieved on eBay for this product, you may be pricing your product out of the market. Do your research on completed listings to determine not only the average selling price, but the starting price of successful listings. Pricing strategies are a key metric you should consider when evaluating your sales data.

Use the Correct Keywords in the Title

As we have already mentioned, it is crucial to continually do your research using the data and marketing off the eBay site. The 55 characters that appear in your product title are the most valuable real estate in your entire listing. Getting your listings into the "hands" of potential buyers is the key to maximizing your sales. Ninety percent of buyers on eBay search for a product using keywords. This means that your 55-character title must be jam-packed with searchable keywords. Review the most successful listings of products similar to yours and see how their keywords compare to the keywords you have selected for your listing title.

Evaluate Your Item Description

Did you lay out a complete, detailed description of your item, with a photo, for buyers to consider? If not, find the most successful listings and learn from their style, descriptions, and graphics.

Define Products in Your Category that Move the Fastest

Once your items start selling, you'll be looking to "scale up"—that is, move a larger quantity quicker without a huge drop in average sales price. Data mining can help you identify which products are the most popular in their category, which have the highest sell-through ratio, and which have the highest total sales. This information can in turn help you position your company to sell larger quantities of items or to limit availability to build up product demand.

eBay's Seller Central feature provides two free reports that can help you sort out these details:

- **Hot by Category report** Lists the hottest growing subcategories in each main category; available as a downloadable PDF file at http://pages.ebay.com/sellercentral/whatshot.html.
- **In Demand reports** List the top 10 picks and the top 10 buyer searches for a category; available at http://pages.ebay.com/sellercentral/sellbycategory.html. Shown in Figure 14-1, this page provides data and also access to discussion boards with other successful and beginning vendors in your categories, no matter what you're involved in.

14

FIGURE 14-1   The Seller Central main page

If you want to access the Hot by Category report, it's free of charge, but you'll first need to download the latest Adobe Acrobat Reader to open the file. Free copies of Adobe Acrobat are available at http://www.adobe.com. (This download will also allow you to read any other file with the .pdf suffix.)

After you've identified some of these key factors, compare them to your listings and consider the following information:

Match Your Activity Level to What's Popular   If a category is gaining heat, perhaps due to a seasonal or cultural event, make sure to prioritize the listing of that category's products ahead of products in categories that are a little "cooler." Speed up your listings where it counts; slow down the listings where it doesn't.

List Multiple Listings Within One Time Frame   If you've set up a system in which you list items once per week, consider multiple single-item listings in that week if the items are hot or popular. This way, you can experiment with different listing description styles, ending times, and other factors, and compare sales against your base listings.

Evaluate Whether Your Company Sells Below or Above Average Prices

Evaluating your final sales prices by comparing them to those of your competitors will help you determine whether you are presenting your products in the best manner to command the highest final sales price. Use data mining to determine the average sales price and average bids per item, and compare the numbers and the corresponding listing pages to your listing results and listings. Then think about the following concepts.

Listings of the Highest Priced Items

If 67 product listings appear within one week for a given product, but one listing or one particular seller seems to get closing prices that are higher than everyone else's, that seller is doing a better job. Study the seller's listing and look for common themes. Evaluate the listing description, customer service policies, and any extra services the seller provides. Additionally, check to see whether services or sales are lacking in any categories or areas—if you find a need in a product category that is not being filled, you have an opportunity to provide that service or product configuration to your customers as an added value.

NOTE   *Sometimes the same seller with the same item listing will get different prices every week, due to fluctuating buyer demand. You can determine the average prices in such cases.*

Average Number of Bids

If your items are getting fewer bidders than most other listings for similar products, you need to figure out what is driving buyers to bid up the price on the other listings.

TIP   *Buy It Now auction bids can skew your averages. When someone uses Buy It Now to purchase an item, the listing ends with only that single bid. If a high amount of sales show up with only a single bid, and the sale amount is above average, chances are those listings were Buy It Now auctions. The key in this case is to find a price that makes you money but stops a potential bidder from searching further, so they buy your item.*

14

Mine New Connections from Your Data

If you've been in business for a while (and if you've been paying attention as you read this chapter), you've heard about *data mining* as the hot topic among the database programming set. However, contrary to popular belief, data mining is only subtly different than typical data analysis. Data analysis usually involves very straightforward issues—such as how many hours or days it takes to move a lot of widgets, for example. Data mining is the process of finding correlations or patterns among different pieces of data or from different perspectives and turning them into information that can be used to increase your company's revenue, cut your cost of doing business, or both.

Here's an example of how you might use data mining to move beyond a typical data analysis. Let's say that your company sells women's accessories and perfume. A casual analysis of your sales data might show that 75 percent of your items are sold to Saturday evening shoppers. However, you mine your sales data and find out that of these Saturday sales, the majority of the purchases were made by buyers who purchased more than one item. More important, you discover that these buyers almost always purchased an accessory (such as a silk scarf, handbag, or a mascara case) together with a bottle of perfume.

Your company could use this newly discovered information in various ways to increase revenue. For example, you could make sure that complementary items show up in your "See More Great Items" section: so if the buyer is looking at perfume, you can point her to accessories for more purchasing opportunities. You could offer a special discount on shipping a perfume and accessory purchase made on Saturday. You can also ensure that you have plenty of listings available of both fragrances and accessories with the same end date and time—Saturday evening.

Web Counter—A Basic Data Mining Tool

A very low-tech way to gain some basic data to mine is to use a web counter, also known as a hit counter. A counter appears as an indicator on a web page that graphically displays the number of users that have accessed, or hit, your site.

> TIP   *The free web counter that eBay offers you is a valuable marketing tool. If your item does not sell and your counter shows that only three people visited your listing, you need to rethink your title—clearly no one was able to find you utilizing the keywords in your current title. On the other hand, if the counter shows hundreds of people found your auction but still no one bid, you'll want to revisit your pricing strategy, description, or pictures.*

As Figure 14-2 shows, counters can display numbers in many fonts or graphical styles. Web counters range from very simple Java-based scripts that run in the background to more sophisticated types. Some companies offer counters as a service: they place the counter on your page and monitor the information collected for you.

Web counters typically provide very basic information, such as the number of hits on a page and the time the hits occurred. Suppose, for example, that you determine that your eBay store page or company web page has experienced a large number of hits compared to the number of purchases. Armed with this data, you might be able to conclude that something is generating interest but discouraging sales.

More sophisticated counters also tell you from which web domain your visitors are coming when visiting your site. Again, you can mine this simple data for information. For example, if your company sells lab supplies, and the majority of your hits are from domains that belong to local universities but not research facilities, you might consider tailoring product, sale prices, and listing times around a university student clientele and academic schedules.

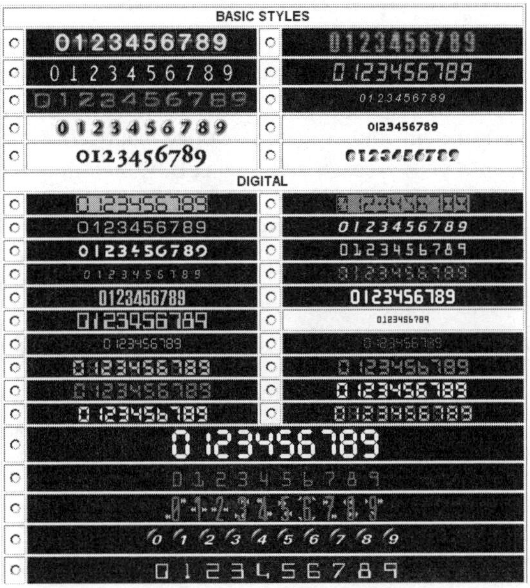

FIGURE 14-2   Different styles of web counters

Did you know?

Don't Rely Solely on Web Counters

We don't recommend that you rely solely—or even strongly—on a web counter for information to supplement your sales data. All web counters are prone to recording misleading statistics by under- or over-counting the number of visitors to a given page. At best, web usage statistics produced by these programs should be used only to make informed guesses about the number of people who have visited a web site or web page.

For example, you shouldn't rely on a counter that relies on Java or JavaScript. The numbers from such counters will greatly underestimate the number of times your page has been viewed and the variety of browsers that your visitors are using. This occurs because many people run web browsers that cannot use Java or JavaScript, or they have turned off the Java features to reduce the amount of visual "clutter" that Java animations can produce when used in online ads.

14

Go Deep with HammerTap's DeepAnalysis

If you plan to get into more involved areas of data mining, one of the most effective tools in the area of data research is HammerTap's DeepAnalysis software. The software can be purchased and downloaded from http://hammertap.com/deepanalysis/. DeepAnalysis analyzes sell-through rates, average number of bids per item, and average sale price in any eBay category or subcategory to provide valuable insights into your areas of selling on eBay, including the following:

- The most popular products and product groups
- The best categories in which to list your items by viewing bid data, sell-through rates, and average sales
- Sales trends by product title, seller, and category

HammerTap's software is stable and compatible with Microsoft products. It allows you to download and export sales data about all listings in your category to a database such as Microsoft Access (Figure 14-3).

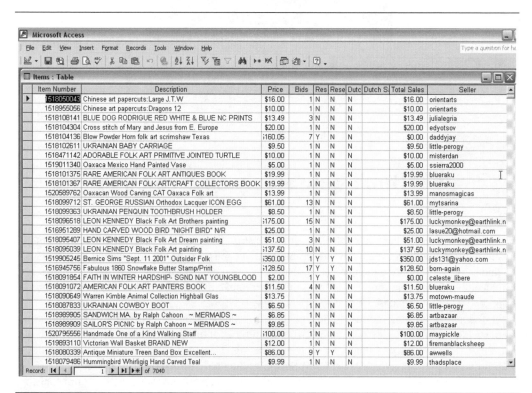

FIGURE 14-3   Viewing DeepAnalysis in Microsoft Access

Adapting to Rapid Market Change

Marketing studies of companies selling on eBay agree that constantly seeking categories in which to place product is a positive strategy. "eBay is a dynamic marketplace where sales follow the laws of supply and demand in real time," says eBay spokesperson Chris Donlay. "We find that individuals and small businesses are often in the best position to react quickly and take advantage of these changes."

Entrepreneur Dan Kasal, who sells phones on eBay, has managed to make these trends work for his business. For example, four years ago he bought 50 Ericsson Bluetooth-enabled phones at $350 apiece. Since no other eBay seller had these phones in stock, he was able to sell each for about $1000.

Today, the cell-phone market is saturated with sellers offering the latest gizmo. By studying the market to lower price while maintaining profitability, speeding up inventory turnover, and boosting customer service, Kasal not only held his own but prospered, grossing $6 million in 2003 to remain one of the top cell-phone sellers on eBay.

Determine Cost of eBay Sales

A vital piece of data that is key to the success of any company that wants to create and maintain eBay as a profitable sales channel is determining the ultimate cost of eBay sales. Despite the fact that this data directly impacts your company's profitability, many eBay sellers rely only on "best guess" estimates. But to be useful, your sales figures must be determined accurately. With accurate figures, you can take steps to improve your sales operations and ultimately improve your bottom line. While each company's operation will be different, you can follow a couple general guidelines to get the data you need:

Work Within a Set Time Frame   It is critical that the elements of the cost calculation (sales, inventories, and purchases) are representative of a set time period. Products are always moving through the sales channel—from initial placement of the product, to the time spent waiting for the listing to finish, to the time between payment and shipping—so it's best to pick a time frame to take a "snapshot" of your company's process.

Work with your company accountant or sales manager to set up a regular time frame in which to do cost analysis. Depending on the nature of your company, you will want to analyze your eBay sales channel data in accordance with the parameters that you use to review other sales channel data for your company.

Isolate the Correct Data   If your company has an accounting department, make sure that you see the data shown on the accounts receivable reports as opposed to seeing only a rough estimate from your sales division. If you want to determine the expense of setting up and automating eBay sales from your webmaster, ask to see a timesheet or list showing the exact number of hours per week spent setting up your company storefront or listing items.

14

TIP *Reference sales generated or costs allocated only within the allotted time frame you've selected. This way, you can properly correlate the actual costs incurred in that time frame toward appropriate revenues, to generate an accurate profit realization for that specific time frame.*

Capital Invested When Selling on eBay

Luckily, investing company capital in your eBay sales channel isn't as weighty an investment as opening up a new office branch, nor is it as risky as putting money into research and development. Two of eBay's most positive traits have been its dedication to a moderate fee structure, which is designed to encourage multiple listings, and absolute transparency as to what investment is required. eBay does not believe in hiding costs or fees to prospective sellers, making your calculations relatively easy.

eBay fees for sellers come in five categories:

- Insertion fees
- Picture services
- Final value fees
- Listing upgrades fees
- PayPal fees

All fee pricing is located at http://pages.ebay.com/help/sell/fees.html.

NOTE *If your company is going to open an eBay store, remember to reference the eBay Store Fees page, located at http://pages.ebay.com/storefronts/pricing.html.*

PayPal Costs

When determining costs involved in selling through your eBay channel, be sure to include costs that may not be directly levied by eBay but that are definitely related to the sales of your auctioned items. For example, you'll want to include the costs of working through PayPal with your calculations. Much like eBay, PayPal has shown a dedication to keeping its fees low and provides sellers with an easy-to-understand fee structure. PayPal costs are shown in Table 14-1.

Action	Account Fee
Open an account	Free
Send money	Free
Withdraw funds	Free for US bank accounts; fees for other banks
Add funds	Free
Receive funds	2.2% + $0.30 USD to 2.9% + $0.30 USD
Conduct multiple currency transactions	Exchange rate includes a 2.5% fee

TABLE 14-1   Costs Associated with PayPal

Note that while withdrawing funds may be free for bank accounts in the United States, this is not the case for overseas banks. Figure 14-4 details the fees that are specific to each country.

Credit Cards Costs

As a business, you probably already have a credit card or credit line as part of a merchant account. Today's credit card providers offer you several processing options. Which one you choose depends on the emphasis you put on specific sales channels—whether through eBay, your company web site, mail or phone orders, or a retail storefront.

If you're just moving your business into the online world of eBay and company web portals, make sure that the credit card provider you choose provides Internet processing for online businesses. Do not remain with your provider if it charges a fee to add this feature—many services today are more than willing to compete for your business and offer better deals. Choose a site that prominently displays all of its merchant account rates and fees, as shown in Figure 14-5, to ensure that you're getting the best deal.

PayPal®

Sign Up | Log In | Help

| Welcome | Send Money | Request Money | Merchant Tools | Auction Tools |

Withdrawal Fees

Bank Location	Currency	Withdrawal Fee	Return Fee
Australia	Australian Dollar	$1.00 AUD	$20.00 AUD
Austria	Euro	€1.00 EUR	€20.00 EUR
Belgium	Euro	€1.00 EUR	€6.00 EUR
Canada	Canadian Dollar	$0.50 CAD	$30.00 CAD
Denmark	Danish Krone	5.00 DKK	42.00 DKK
Finland	Euro	€1.00 EUR	€6.00 EUR
France	Euro	€1.00 EUR	€23.00 EUR
Germany	Euro	Free	€23.00 EUR
Hong Kong	Hong Kong Dollar	$3.50 HKD	$40.00 HKD
Italy	Euro	€1.00 EUR	€6.00 EUR
Japan	Yen	¥500 JPY	¥620 JPY
Mexico	Mexican Peso	20.00 MXN	180.00 MXN
Netherlands	Euro	€1.00 EUR	€23.00 EUR
New Zealand	New Zealand Dollar	$1.00 NZD	$23.00 NZD
Norway	Norwegian Krone	5.50 NOK	45.00 NOK
Singapore	Singapore Dollar	$1.00 SGD	$9.00 SGD
South Korea	Korean Won	1,500 KRW	6,500 KRW
Spain	Euro	€1.00 EUR	€6.00 EUR
Sweden	Swedish Krona	7.00 SEK	53.00 SEK
Switzerland	Swiss Franc	0.50 CHF	8.00 CHF
Taiwan	New Taiwan Dollar	35 TWD	70 TWD
United Kingdom	Pound Sterling	Free for £50.00 GBP or more	£14.00 GBP

FIGURE 14-4   Withdrawal fees for PayPal, listed by country

14

Already Processing Credit Cards? <u>CLICK HERE</u> and take advantage of our special CONVERSION program!

Merchant Account Rates and Fees	
Discount Rate Retail (Swiped)	1.59-1.61% 1.71% after 4/1/04 (see note)
Discount Rate Mail Order/Phone Order/Internet	2.17% 2.28% after 4/1/04 (see note)
Transaction Fee Retail (Swiped)	$.20
Transaction Fee Mail Order/Phone Order/Internet	$.25
AVS (Address Verification) Fee	$.05
Monthly Service/Support/Statement	$9.95
Application Fee	FREE
Annual Fee	FREE
Programming	FREE
Batch Fee	FREE
AMEX Setup	FREE
Shopping Cart	FREE

FIGURE 14-5   A good open fee disclosure page

The fees for accepting Visa and MasterCard range on average from 1.5 to 3.0 percent, depending on the volume of your company's sales. The Discover card offers similar rates depending on the promotion being offered. American Express and Diners' Club tend to be higher and range between 4 and 5 percent. When considering merchant account fees, do not forget to include your account opening cost as well as your monthly account fee.

Shipping and Insurance Costs

One of the advantages of using eBay as your sales channel is that the buyer typically pays the shipping costs—and insurance if they want it. If you charge for shipping, you might also include a reasonable handling charge in the shipping fee to cover the cost of an employee packing, labeling, and shipping out products.

Your shipping department and/or accounting department should have the data you need regarding the amount spent on shipping and insurance for each package within your selected time frame. If you can't get this data, another option if the items you ship are relatively constant in size and weight is to extrapolate costs based on eBay's shipping calculator (http://pages.ebay.com/services/buyandsell/shippingcenter7.html). At present, eBay can calculate shipping and insurance rates for the following services:

- US Postal Service Priority Mail

- US Postal Service First Class Mail

- US Postal Service Parcel Post

- US Postal Service Media Mail

- UPS Ground

- UPS 3-Day Select

- UPS 2nd-Day Air

- UPS Next-Day Air Saver

Separate Startup Costs from Recurring Costs

While it may take you an hour to lay out, develop, and spell out a given auction listing, if you plan to sell the same item every week, you'll spend an hour the first time but only a minute every week thereafter, by relisting the same item and keeping all that formatting information. The drop in the cost of recurring listings should be factored in to your listing cost evaluations.

Summary

Tracking your listing sales data and analyzing it accordingly is a key factor in establishing a successful eBay sales channel. Data mining can help you identify which products are the most popular in their category, which have the highest sell-through ratio, and which have the highest total sales.

eBay's Seller Central feature gives two free reports: the Hot by Category report listing out the hottest growing subcategories in each main category, and the In Demand reports that list the top 10 picks and the top 10 buyer searches for each category. This information is useful in helping you position your products.

A very low-tech way to gain some basic data to mine is to use a web counter. These indicators on a web page display the number of previous users that have accessed your page.

If you plan to get into more involved areas of data mining, one of the most effective tools in the area of data research is HammerTap's DeepAnalysis software. The software will analyze sell-through rates, average number of bids per item, and average sale price in any eBay category or subcategory.

A vital piece of data is determining the ultimate cost of eBay sales. It is critical that the elements of the cost calculation (sales, inventories, and purchases) are representative of a set time period.

While it may take you an hour to lay out, develop, and spell out an auction listing, you will need to average in the cost of relisting an item to get a true picture of the expense incurred to run a listing.

14

Part IV

Grow Your eBay Business

Chapter 15

Grow from Auctions to a Storefront

In this chapter...

- ■ Expand your presence with an eBay store
- ■ Consider the top reasons for opening an eBay store
- ■ Design a store layout
- ■ Identify cross-promotional items
- ■ Set up a store
- ■ List a store item
- ■ Use eBay tools to track sellers and traffic

At this point, you've seen myriad eBay listings, whether they were auction-style, fixed-price, or reserve-price goods. Regular eBay listings last at most 10 days, but you may plan to post a set of merchandise regularly for which you want to control flow onto the market to get better prices and then release slowly to generate a steady stream of income.

As the amount of inventory you dedicate to eBay sales grows, you may find that some items are always in stock or that such a healthy quantity of other items exists that you're looking at every avenue possible to move them. eBay has created a powerful mechanism to make inventory readily available to the eBay user community—24 hours a day, 7 days a week—in a dynamic, interactive format that allows you to sell items steadily by the month alongside your regular auction listings. It's called an eBay store, and it allows any eBay seller, big or small, to create a virtual presence on the World Wide Web.

An eBay store is simply an eBay seller's online storefront, where every product listed for auction can be showcased along with your store inventory. As a seller, you post items in your eBay store with a fixed price; you can set the length of the listings for a period of 30, 60, 90, or 120 days, or simply until the good is sold—which means the product will be listed indefinitely until the quantity reaches zero.

The power provided by an eBay store is more than the ability to sell fixed-price goods. It provides a complete platform you can use to present and sell your goods where *you* have the power to offer cross-selling and up-selling, to reduce your costs of selling on eBay, and to gain additional exposure through marketing your store to the top search engines on the Internet.

Expand Your Presence with an eBay Store

By creating an eBay store, your company can create its own portal into its eBay sales, beyond an About Me page or a list of open listings. Your eBay store can feature custom categories and a search engine dedicated to your store listings only. Most important, you can create a constant set of inventory that you promote to anyone who bids or wins a regular auction listing, all while capitalizing on the familiarity of the eBay environment.

Creating the layout of your eBay store means creating an unlimited amount of virtual shelves, where merchandise is displayed online and sold as buyers come through and take a look. You can specify exactly how the items are pitched to your customers and have eBay recommend other products with each potential sale. Best of all, eBay can provide you, the store owner, with detailed reports each month on store activity—even information on how your shoppers look through your store.

By using an eBay store, your company has a central location and a fixed web address that you can give to anybody, anytime to find your eBay items for sale. eBay provides you with the tools necessary to customize and organize a storefront so it can be up in minutes. An eBay store has no initial setup fee and a low monthly cost that can easily be recouped, due to extremely low listing fees per item.

Once you build your store, you can focus on getting people through its doors, as you would in any retail operation, by marketing and promoting your eBay store at every opportunity. eBay is helping its stores get placed on all the top search engines, including Google.

Top Reasons for Opening an eBay Store

If you're simply looking to sell more items, eBay's infrastructure allows you to insert as many auction listings as you'd like, using the Sell Your Item form or auction-management software. For a powerful eBay strategy, however, you should consider your entire presence, not just the

eBay Success Story

What the Tool King of Denver and Home Depot Have in Common

Even the most "commodified" of industries have begun to arrive on eBay, with retailers in the lumber, tool, and hardware businesses joining in eBay's ever-growing success story. From a local supplier like the Tool King of Denver to retail giants like Home Depot, Sears, and Wickes Lumber, traditional brick-and-mortar retailers are setting up eBay stores.

These retailers are selling both familiar name brands of hardware and lumber and no-name equipment of more obscure origins within their eBay stores. Bob Hebeler, eBay vice president for category development, tells buyers that eBay is "the place to check out before you buy. It depends on the item, but on average, you'll see prices 10 to 20 percent below retail. We [the community of eBay sellers] carry every brand…and every product from a collectible planer to a new one. Need a new chuck for an older version of a drill? We have those! Type in any tool and you'll get an amazing list of items that are both fun and something you need."

Hebeler also notes that when it comes to businesses moving to eBay, "there's no doubt that brand-name stores add credibility. Someone making their first transaction on the site might be more comfortable with a well-known retailer." Building on that brand name and established customer trust has allowed businesses such as Home Depot to prosper on eBay alongside smaller stores.

15

specific number of listings per week, and that is why you should open an eBay store. The features listed here are some of the top reasons why adding an eBay store can dramatically increase your sales and expand your business both on eBay and offline, including your average sales per customer and sales bottom line.

Enjoy Bigger Profits

Studies by eBay have shown that store sellers see on average a 25 percent incremental increase in sales in the three months after opening their stores. This is, of course, dependent upon factors such as an active store strategy and a well-stocked and well-promoted storefront. The key is that an eBay store can provide a higher velocity of sales through the eBay channel, which should lead to bigger profits.

Experience Longer Product Shelf Life

Your eBay store product listings run in 30-day increments, as opposed to the 1- to 10-day increments of regular eBay listings. This results in fewer relistings and time saved monitoring the active inventory of your eBay products. After all, with store items, you can set a multiple quantity in advance, and eBay will keep track of available inventory after each individual purchase is made.

Enjoy Discounted Listing and Gallery Fees

As a store seller, you'll save on listings fees—paying just 2 cents for each 30-day period and 1 cent for the Gallery feature. This feature alone allows you to increase the volume of goods for sale dramatically via eBay without large, up-front listing fees. It allows you to consider expanding into goods with smaller profit margins or to conduct special promotional sales with minimal expense.

Establish Credibility as an Online Retailer

When you create an eBay store, you are not only providing your buyers an easier way to shop with you, but you are helping them gain a sense of confidence in your business. An eBay store shows potential buyers who you are as a company and your commitment to the eBay platform. A store also allows you to provide the best selection and value to the consumer.

Create a Permanent Web Address

Unlike the dynamic nature of an eBay listing URL, an eBay store provides a fixed URL that never changes and that allows you to advertise one URL across your company. Your store address will be short and easy to read: www.stores.ebay.com/*yourcompanyname*. This permanent URL can be used for marketing in printed materials, on your company's web site, on company promotional items, in your e-mail signature, on your product labels, in conjunction with your logo, and much more.

Create a Unified Storefront

Organizing your products with an eBay store unifies your eBay sales into a businesslike e-commerce storefront that makes shopping easier for your intended customers. You can group, control, and maintain all your sales from one mechanism.

Establish Solid Branding

Your eBay store gives you a platform to create solid, recognizable branding of your products in addition to providing a vehicle to market your value. Your eBay store helps differentiate you from the competition and gives your customers a recognizable, renewable experience each time they shop with you.

Create Your Own Categories

An eBay store allows you to create up to 19 customizable category names to organize and merchandise your listings so that your customers can easily find them. Even more beneficial is that eBay submits the names of each of your categories (and your store title and description) to major search engines such as Google. Your product's exposure is not limited to eBay but can traverse this trading platform to reach the entire online world. Best of all, eBay provides you with search engine advertising as part of your store subscription.

Create Custom Stores Easily

With easy-to-use online tools and "how to" tutorials, eBay gives you the power to customize your store quickly and easily. You will control the design of your storefront, which allows you to build a brand and encourage repeat business with your customers. You can use either the templates that eBay provides or upload your company templates into your eBay store for a look and feel that is unique to your business.

Cross-Promote Your Store Inventory

As an eBay store seller, you can show prospective buyers a list of complementary items as they are shopping in your store; the eBay store cross-promotional tool allows you to designate which products are cross-promoted to your customers. Additionally, your eBay store allows you to drive targeted traffic from your listings or your marketing directly to your store. You can effectively market items of differing profit margins by using a combination of eBay listings and your eBay store.

Get Free Monthly Reports

As an eBay Store owner, you will receive monthly sales reports that outline your store's activity and organize this activity into different categories, such as monthly gross sales, number of buyers, shopper conversion rates, store traffic or specific keyword search results. If you own a Featured and Anchor store, you'll receive additional data on the entire eBay marketplace, which will allow you to benchmark your store relative to other eBay sellers.

Get a Store-Specific Search Engine

Your eBay storefront comes with a search box that, when accessed by your customers, displays only items that you are selling as opposed to the standard eBay search that returns search results of items listed by every seller. With a store-specific search engine, your customers are shopping from your product selection only, with no outside competition.

How to ... Find a Store

You can find the eBay store listings in one of two ways:

■ Click the eBay Stores link in the upper left corner of the eBay home page.

■ Go directly either to http://www.stores.ebay.com or http://www.ebaystores.com.

If you want to identify whether a specific seller has an eBay store, you can look for a red Stores icon next to that seller's user ID, look for links that direct you to a seller's eBay store on their View Item pages, or look for their store name in the eBay Stores directory.

Get Free Advertising

eBay will advertise your store and funnel customers to your store listings through several mechanisms:

■ The eBay Stores pages at http://www.stores.eBay.com

■ The Shop eBay Stores search box on all search and listings pages on eBay.com

■ The Stores merchandising section on the eBay.com home page

■ If 10 or more listings show up in a general search, eBay will include a link at the bottom to additional products in the eBay stores

■ If less than 10 listings show up in a general search, eBay will fill in the search with items from the stores

■ Submission of your store description and title to Google, in which you control the search keywords when you write the description of your eBay store. Once eBay submits your store description to Google, your store listings will show up in the search engine query based on the keywords that you choose. (Note that search engine position is relative to the keywords you have used.)

■ As with the submission of your store description, eBay will also submit your store categories to Google. Using searchable keywords to describe your store's categories will enable you to get the most exposure for your products throughout the Internet.

Store Design and Features

One of the most useful services that eBay offers a businessperson new to the site is the ability to use predesigned layouts or customize the design of your eBay store. Much like a brick-and-mortar storefront, you can create a distinct presence on eBay simply by creating a visual theme that distinguishes your store from other sellers in your general category.

For example, if you're in the business of selling fresh-cut flowers, you may find that competing companies use graphics that show off the pastel colors and fresh quality of their products. One way to hold your business apart from theirs could be to design your storefront with graphics emphasizing the speed of your delivery. Or it could display the exotic plants that you carry that no other florist does. Whatever features you choose to make your business stand apart from the crowd can be referenced in your store design.

Predesigned or Custom Layouts

When creating your storefront, you might start with one of eBay's predesigned page layouts. These layouts have predetermined locations and sizes of pictures and text on the page—all you have to do is decide which order and orientation you want on the page and fill in the appropriate spaces. While this might limit some of your creativity, the advantage is that you don't need any technical expertise or design sense to get a professional-looking result.

On the other hand, if you are comfortable using HTML or you have a web-savvy IT or graphics person handy, you may want to start with a completely customizable page layout. This lets you break out of the predesigned layouts to create a unique look that could set you apart from other stores and help create a distinct brand for your products.

Store Inventory

In store inventory listings, your product appears in your eBay store next to your auction and/or your fixed-price listings. What sets the store inventory listings apart is that they also appear in a distinct place on the Search Results pages. For example, when a buyer searches for an item and fewer than 10 results appear in the auction or fixed-price formats, they will see additional store inventory listings that match their search. This means you get more visibility for your store's listings, more traffic is generated to your store, and you benefit from higher sales volumes.

Store listings have the added advantage of lasting for a long time: 30, 60, 90, or 120 days—or even "good 'til cancelled." This enables you to give maximum exposure time to your product listings. Additionally, when listing a product in your eBay store, you can list a quantity of more than one for each listing. Whenever you sell an item in your store that has multiple quantities in one listing, eBay will automatically adjust the number of items available in the listing.

Store inventory listings require less monetary outlay than regular eBay listings. Store inventory listings are the lowest priced type of listing on eBay, at a mere 2 cents for 30 days. The Gallery feature is also available for a penny more.

15

> **TIP** *Store inventory listings are one flat price, regardless of the quantity of goods you're selling. Whether you list a single grinder, 10,000 grinders with the same sku, or an entire machine shop in one listing, the price is 2 cents for 30 days.*

Establish Cross-Promotions with eBay Stores

A cross-promotional item is an item that complements another item that a buyer is bidding on or purchasing. When you utilize eBay's cross-promotions feature, up to four of your related items will be displayed at the bottom of a listing page. You will see the cross-promotional items in both your regular listings and your eBay store listings. eBay sets up a store with default cross-promotional relationships for each custom store category. Cross-promotions are automatically selected based on these default relationships, though you can alter these rules if you wish.

The items selected for cross-promotion can vary in several ways. For example, let's say that your business sells sets of kitchen knives on eBay. Complementary items that could be displayed as a cross-sell could involve any of the following:

- Similar items (the same knife set, but with different color handles)
- Accessories (a sharpener or holder)
- Items for an up-sell (the deluxe meat cleaver set for only $100 more)
- Directly related items (an additional fruit paring knife)
- Items that are more distantly related (a wire whisk or pasta strainer, made by the same company that made the knives)
- Complementary sale items (off-season items, such as holiday kitchen towels)

> **TIP** *To set up cross-marketed items, log into your eBay store, select Manage Your Store, and then select the Cross Promotion Link from the Promotions section of that page.*

Identify Cross-Promotional Items

Customers like to minimize the number of separate purchases they make so they can save time shopping and spend more time enjoying or using their products. Therefore, box-store or super store retailers often provide "one-stop shopping" for their customers. The idea of cross-promotion has been around in business a very long time. One of the benefits of an eBay store is the power to cross-sell complementary items at the exact moment your customers are looking at or buying other products.

Consider the following to help you identify cross-selling items for one of your products:

- What other goods will my customers need when they buy product X?
- What products do I offer that enhance or promote the benefits of product X?
- What products have a buyer target market similar to that of product X?

By thinking about these characteristics and looking at the nature of your products, you will be able to identify several opportunities to cross-sell your products. While some combinations may be obvious (someone who buys a laser printer will need to buy toner), be aware of some combinations that fit your typical buyer markets that may not fit the general population.

Many new eBay sellers don't realize how powerful it can be to use their regular auction-type listings to cross-promote store inventory. Wording at the top of a listing description could include, "Don't want to wait for this auction to end? Click Here to Buy It Now in my eBay Store," or "Looking to save money? We will gladly combine your shipping on multiple item purchases. Click Here to see our entire inventory in our eBay Store." The Stores discussion group offers many cross-marketing ideas. You can locate this informative site at http://forums.ebay.com/db2/forum.jsp?forum=21.

eBay Store Ownership Levels and Fees

eBay store ownership comes in three levels: a basic store, a featured store, and an anchored store. Each comes with its own set of features and capabilities, and, of course, its own price tag. Table 15-1 offers a comparison of the three types of stores.

Basic

The basic store level is well-suited for lower volume sellers or for those on a limited marketing budget. It's also an excellent entry point for companies that require a demonstration of effectiveness before upgrading to a featured or anchored store. The basic store comes with the power of the store platform and a pricing structure that benefits a small number of transactions. As your eBay strategy becomes more aggressive, an upgrade to a higher level will benefit you due to lower overall costs and increased features.

NOTE   *Even if you opt for the basic store, as your business expands, the option to upgrade to a featured or anchored store level is always available.*

Featured

The featured level offers a more comprehensive solution, since it includes more eBay-generated reports such as traffic and sales reporting. Even better, your store enjoys improved placement when eBay returns the results of buyer searches. The eBay Selling Manager Pro software, normally $15.99 per month, is also available for no extra charge to featured store owners.

This level's enhanced features can be grouped into three areas:

- **Customization and brand control**   Up to 10 fully customizable pages are available in your store, and the eBay header can be minimized on all your store pages.

- **Advanced business intelligence**   Relevant marketplace data is included in your monthly sales reports, and sophisticated traffic reporting monitors buyer pathways through your store.

- **Increased exposure and branding opportunities**   Your store gets priority placement in eBay's onsite promotions, and your company gets a $20 credit (per month) toward eBay's Keywords program for advertising.

15

Type of Service	Basic	Featured	Anchored
Additional fully customizable pages in your store	5 pages	10 pages	15 pages
Free subscription to Selling Manager Pro	No	Yes	Yes
Advanced store traffic reporting	No	Yes	Yes
Advanced store sales reports	No	Yes	Yes
Increased exposure on eBay	No	Yes	Yes
24-hour dedicated live customer support	No	No	Yes
Monthly subscription fee	$9.95	$49.95	$499.95

TABLE 15-1   Comparison of Store Subscription Levels

Anchored

Finally, the anchored level offers an effective solution for sellers who want maximum exposure to generate a higher volume of sales to support their business investment. Much as with a large anchored store at your local shopping mall, an eBay anchored level store will give you maximum visibility in searches for a particular category and within the category's pages.

NOTE *For more information about how to sign up for an anchored store, contact eBay at anchorstores@eBay.com.*

Store Inventory Listing Fees

While your monthly store subscription fee covers the basic setup of your store, other fees are related to listings of each individual store item. The main thing to note for store inventory listings, however, is that the costs are minor compared to normal auction listing fees. For example, Store Inventory Listings cost 2 cents per item for each 30-day listing period, and adding a gallery picture for that item is only another penny. Of course, these items also have a Final Value Fee if the item sells successfully, just like in an auction listing.

Insertion Fee Listings

The insertion fees, shown in Table 15-2, cover any quantity of items with a single listing. The fees vary based only on the duration of your listing.

Final Value Fees

Final Value Fees are paid on the final sale price of your item. The fee structure (shown in Table 15-3) is the same for all listing formats.

TIP *eBay has developed a program to help store sellers get 50 percent of their Final Value Fee credited as they promote their eBay store to outside sources. The program details can be found at http://pages.ebay.com/storefronts/referral-credit-steps.html.*

Type of Fee	Insertion Fee	Surcharge	Total
30 days	2 cents	N/A	2 cents
60 days	2 cents	2 cents	4 cents
90 days	2 cents	4 cents	6 cents
120 days	2 cents	6 cents	8 cents
Good 'til cancelled	2 cents/30 days	N/A	2 cents/30 days

TABLE 15-2   Store Inventory Format Insertion Fees

Closing Value	Final Value Fee
$0–$25	5.25 percent of the closing value
$25–$1000	5.25 percent of the initial $25 ($1.31), plus 2.75 percent of the remaining closing value balance
Over $1000	5.25 percent of the initial $25 ($1.31), plus 2.75 percent of the initial $25–$1000 ($26.81), plus 1.50 percent of the remaining closing value balance

TABLE 15-3   Final Value Fees

Set Up a Store

In this section, we'll walk through the steps required to establish your online eBay store. It's important that you remember that your design is flexible, and you do not have to have every item you want to sell on your desk when you create a store. However, be sure that you have your eBay user ID and password available. Also, keep in mind the products that you would like to place in your store and an idea of how many categories of products you hope to move through your eBay store on a regular basis.

To set up your store, complete the following steps:

1. Go to the eBay home page (http://www.ebay.com).

2. Click the eBay Stores link on the left side of the page, as shown here:

> **Specialty Sites**
> **eBay Motors**
> **eBay Stores**
> **Half.com by eBay**
> **PayPal**

3. On the eBay Stores home page, shown in Figure 15-1, click the Open A Store button.

4. Review the eBay User Agreement, and if you're interested, click the Features And Benefits link. When you are ready, click the I Accept The eBay User Agreement button.

Build Your Store: User Agreement

Your eBay Store is subject to the eBay User Agreement and its related policies. This is the same agreement you accepted when you registered on eBay.

To begin building your eBay Store, please reconfirm your acceptance of the eBay User Agreement by clicking the button below. Or, click on a link for more

- Review the eBay User Agreement
- Learn more about eBay Stores features and benefits or about eBay Stores fees.

[I Accept the eBay User Agreement >]   Cancel

15

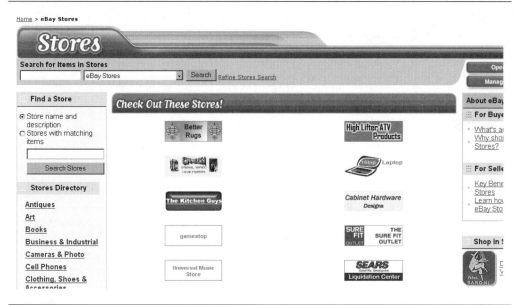

The eBay Stores home page

5. In the Build Your Store: Select Theme page shown in Figure 15-2, choose from dozens of predesigned themes or go for a classic or minimal header layout for your store in a wide variety of color schemes. After choosing a store theme, scroll down to the bottom of the screen and click the Continue button.

NOTE   *Some say that the classic theme focuses on your products more than the look of one of the more complex store designs. On the other hand, some predesigned themes can be more appealing to the average consumer. These are strictly subjective opinions, and which layout options you use is totally up to you.*

TIP   *If you click the pictures displayed in Figure 15-2, a separate window showing a close-up of the store layout will be presented. This may make it easier to visualize how your store will look.*

6. In the Build Your Store: Provide Basic Information page shown in Figure 15-3, you're asked for two key pieces of information:

■ **Store Name**   A maximum store name length of 35 characters will determine your eBay's store's web site address. For example, if your company's eBay store name is International Graphics, your eBay store URL will be http://stores.ebay.com/international_graphics/.

■ **Store Description**   A 300 character paragraph summary describes the products you plan to sell and what your store is all about. When creating your store description, use keywords your customers will use in searches. Using searchable keywords will give you a huge advantage in your search engine rankings. So, for example, a description for International Graphics could be something like this: "We provide many graphics needs, including business cards, official letterhead, printing supplies, and industry-specific custom printing machines."

7. Choose a logo for your store from one of three options:

   ■ Choose from one of 28 predesigned logos relating to various categories on eBay.

   ■ Provide your own logo, which should be on your company web server. Enter the exact URL of the logo in the box provided.

   ■ Do not display a logo for your store if you want to free up some screen space on your storefront.

   Once you've made a choice, click Continue to move on to the next page.

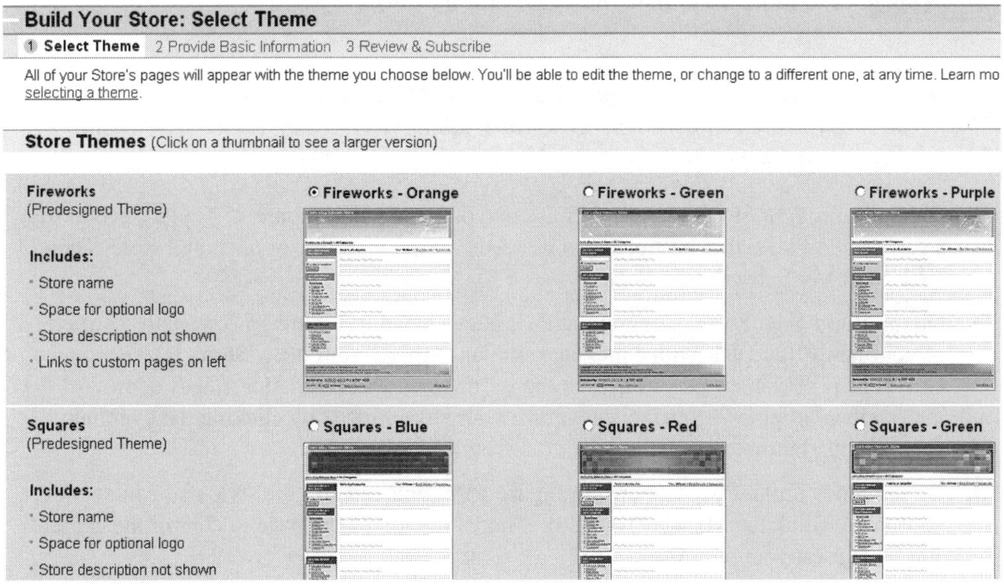

Build Your Store: Select Theme

① **Select Theme** 2 Provide Basic Information 3 Review & Subscribe

All of your Store's pages will appear with the theme you choose below. You'll be able to edit the theme, or change to a different one, at any time. Learn mo selecting a theme.

Store Themes (Click on a thumbnail to see a larger version)

Fireworks
(Predesigned Theme)

Includes:
· Store name
· Space for optional logo
· Store description not shown
· Links to custom pages on left

○ **Fireworks - Orange**   ○ **Fireworks - Green**   ○ **Fireworks - Purple**

Squares
(Predesigned Theme)

Includes:
· Store name
· Space for optional logo
· Store description not shown

○ **Squares - Blue**   ○ **Squares - Red**   ○ **Squares - Green**

FIGURE 15-2   The Build Your Store: Select Theme page

15

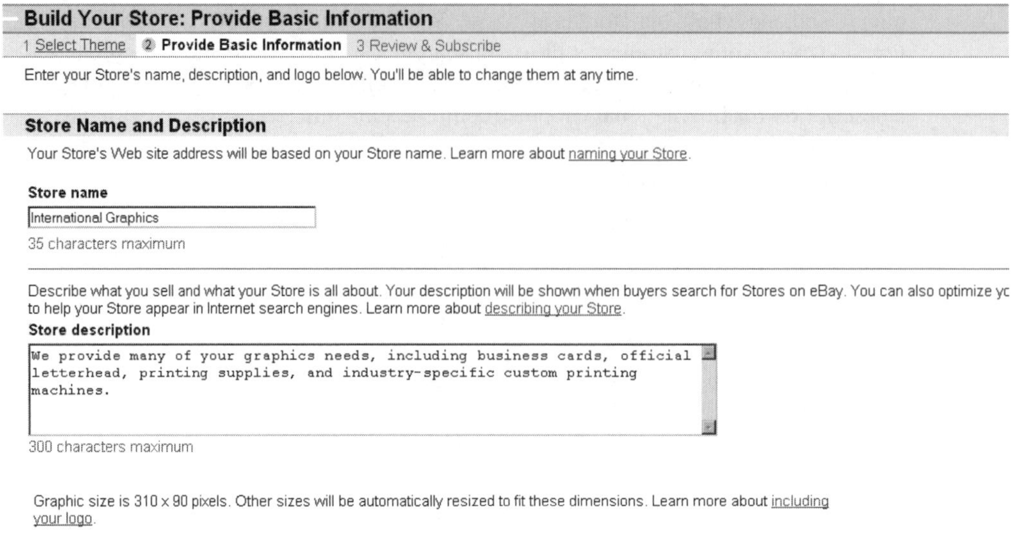

Build Your Store: Provide Basic Information

1 Select Theme   ② **Provide Basic Information**   3 Review & Subscribe

Enter your Store's name, description, and logo below. You'll be able to change them at any time.

Store Name and Description

Your Store's Web site address will be based on your Store name. Learn more about naming your Store.

Store name

International Graphics

35 characters maximum

Describe what you sell and what your Store is all about. Your description will be shown when buyers search for Stores on eBay. You can also optimize yc to help your Store appear in Internet search engines. Learn more about describing your Store.

Store description

We provide many of your graphics needs, including business cards, official letterhead, printing supplies, and industry-specific custom printing machines.

300 characters maximum

Graphic size is 310 x 90 pixels. Other sizes will be automatically resized to fit these dimensions. Learn more about including your logo.

FIGURE 15-3   The Build Your Store: Provide Basic Information page

CAUTION   *The exact URL of your logo is not the same as the URL of your company's home page. To be sure you are using the correct address, after you type it in, click the Preview link under the text box and your logo should appear.*

   8. On the Build Your Store: Review & Subscribe page shown in Figure 15-4, you can choose a subscription level that best meets your needs: basic, featured, or anchored store. Then click Start My Subscription Now.

   9. On the Build Your Store: Congratulations! page shown in Figure 15-5, you are notified of your new eBay URL with a message similar to this: "Your eBay Store, International Graphics, is now open for business at the following URL: http://stores.ebay.com/ internationalgraphics." You can customize your store further by clicking the Continue Customizing button.

   10. On the Store Builder page, shown in Figure 15-6, you can edit the style and content of your store. Click the Manage Your Store link at the top of the page to control the content and listings on your storefront.

   11. On the Manage Your Store page, shown in Figure 15-7, you can manage your listings, account settings, and your store's traffic reports. From this page, you'll be able to create, edit, delete, or reorder pages, or change their active/inactive status.

Build Your Store: Review & Subscribe

1 Select Theme   2 Provide Basic Information   ③ **Review & Subscribe**

Selected Theme:

Once you choose a subscription level below and click **Start My Subscription Now**, your Store will be open for t Internet. In addition, you'll be able to continue customizing your Store:

• Add new pages with all your own content
• Create and edit categories to organize your listings
• Change the layout of item lists and search results
• Edit your Store's theme

Customize as much as you like to develop your brand and create a unique shopping experience for buyers – it's Learn more about how you can customize your Store.

Subscription Level

Choose a subscription level that best meets your needs. Learn more about the benefits of each subscription level.

○ **Basic Store** ($9.95/month)

A Basic Store is an ideal solution for businesses that are just starting out and want an affordable and easy-to-use platform to sell online.

○ **Featured Store** ($49.95/month)

A Featured Store is a more comprehensive solution for small-to-medium sized sellers who want to aggressively grow their online business.

Anchor Store ($499.95/month)

An Anchor Store is an advanced solution for higher-volume businesses that want maximum exposure on eBay. To become an Anchor Store, contact anchorstores@ebay.com. One of our representatives will personally assist you with your subscription.

FIGURE 15-4	The Build Your Store: Review & Subscribe page

Build Your Store: Congratulations!

Your eBay Store, International Graphics, is now open for business at the following URL: http://stores.ebay.com/internationalgraphics

Your current eBay listings will be included in your Store within 24 hours. Any new items you list will also be included automatically.

Customize your Store further by clicking the **Continue Customizing** button.

What would you like to do next?
• See my Store's home page
• Explore other aspects of managing my Store
• Learn more about the benefits and features of my Store

Continue Customizing >

FIGURE 15-5	The Build Your Store: Congratulations! page

15

Store Builder

Use this page to edit the style and content of your Store. Learn more about using the Store Builder.
To manage other aspects of your Store, use the Manage Your Store page.

Basic Information   Edit

Store name: International Graphics

Store URL: http://stores.ebay.com/internationalgraphics

Logo:

Store description:

We provide many of your graphics needs, including business cards, official letterhead, printing supplies, and industry-specific custom printing machines.

Store Theme   Edit this theme | Change to another theme

Store theme:

FIGURE 15-6   The Store Builder page

Manage Your Store

Use this page to manage the various aspects of owning and operating your Store.

Did you know you can save 50% off Final Value Fees? Learn More   2004 Best in Stores Winners!

Store Editing / Branding

Store Builder
  Custom pages
  Custom categories
Custom listing header

Account Settings

View Your Store Traffic Report
  Learn more about this report
Change Store subscription
Subscribe to Selling Manager or Selling Manager Pro

Manage Your Items

Listing Activities
  List an item
  Revise a listing
  End a Good 'Til Cancelled listing

Promotions

Cross-promotions
  Default category settings
  Preferences
Setup Shipping Discounts
Export listings
Buy eBay Keywords
Register your domain name

FIGURE 15-7   The Manage Your Store page

List a Store Item

In a sense, a Store Inventory Listing is simply a Buy It Now item in a seller's eBay store that buyers can purchase immediately for a fixed price. Here's how to list a store item:

1. You can click on the Sell button on eBay's home page, or log into your eBay store, select Manage Your Store, and then select the List An Item link from the Manage Your Items section of that page.

2. Select a selling format from those listed on the Choose a Selling Format page shown in Figure 15-8. Select the third option, Sell In Store Inventory, since this will allow you to add an item directly to you store. Then click Continue.

3. From this point on, the process for inserting an item for sale in your eBay store is exactly the same process you'd use to insert an individual item for sale, except for the pictures and details page. To review the process for inserting an item, see Chapter 8.

In a few areas, the options differ between inserting an item via the eBay store versus inserting a single item for listing. In the Sell Your Item: Enter Pictures & Item Details page shown in Figure 15-9, note that you first have to assign each store item to a specific store category.

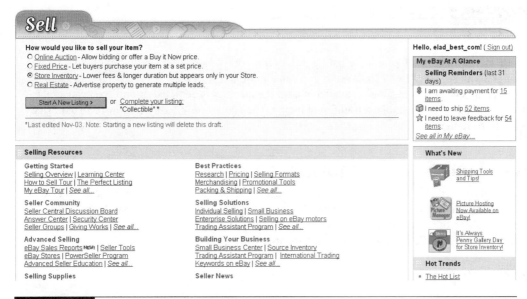

FIGURE 15-8 Select a selling format

15

Sell Your Item: Enter Pictures & Item Details

1. Category 2. Title & Description 3 **Pictures & Details** 4. Payment & Shipping 5. Review & Submit

Title
Graphic Novels

Subtitle
Graphics

Store Category ✶ Required
[Other ⏷]
Edit Store Categories in the Store Builder.

Pricing and duration

Buy It Now price ✶
$ [   ]
Sell to the first buyer who meets your Buy It Now price.

Duration ✶
[Good 'Til Cancelled ($0.02 / 30 days) ⏷]

Start time
⦿ Start listing when submitted
○ Schedule start time ($0.10) [Select a date... ⏷] [Select a time... ⏷] PDT
   Learn more about scheduled listings.

FIGURE 15-9	Setting pricing and duration information

Also, the duration of your store listing differs from that of a regular single-item listing. Store listings allow 30, 60, 90, or 120 days, or you can choose to list as item as Good 'Til Cancelled. This option lets your item show as available until the quantity is depleted or until you cancel the listing. As for the price, unlike a traditional listing, you can set only a Buy It Now or Fixed Price for your store items.

Analyze Your Store Performance

After you have created your eBay store, you'll need to be able to see data to help measure your store's performance. eBay has done a superb job of assisting you in this endeavor by providing you with a pair of tools you can use to monitor the sales activity of your stores that will assist you in making specific changes to generate and improve sales.

Seller Report

The Seller Report provides a monthly metric on the performance of your eBay store. Available for free to all store sellers, regardless of subscription level, the report breaks out the data by listing format and category for all of your auction listings that ended within the stated month. An example of this breakdown is shown in Figure 15-10.

Stores Seller Reporting Detailed Definitions

YOUR AUCTIONS THAT ENDED THIS MONTH - DATA
This section includes data by category for all of your Auction listings that ended within the stated month.

COLUMN NAME	DEFINITION
Category	The category that the listings were in. This is the category that is 4 levels deep in our category structure. For example, if you listed in a number of Auctions in Sports > Sporting Goods > Golf > Putters > Callaway, the category that you will see shown here is "Putters".
# of Listings	Your total number of Auction listings that ended within the stated month.
# of Successful Listings	Your total number of Auction listings that sold.
Quantity of Items Listed	The total quantity of items that you listed in Auctions
Quantity of Items Sold	The total quantity of items that you sold in Auctions
# of Bids	Total number of bids on your Auctions
Gross Sales ($)	Total dollar amount sold in your Auction listings
# of Unique Buyers	The number of buyers who bought from one of your Auctions in this category. For example, if you had 10 putters sell via Auction, but one buyer

FIGURE 15-10   How store report data is broken down

> TIP
>
> *While all store sellers get the free monthly report on their sales, anchored and featured store sellers also receive eBay Marketplace data so that they can benchmark their own performance.*

Traffic Reports

Traffic Reports for store sellers are the same reports used by eBay to monitor its own traffic. Even more exciting is the fact that eBay has made this technology available to all store sellers for free, regardless of their subscription level.

eBay Traffic Reports offer all store sellers real-time reporting on the following data:

- Page views for each listing and store page
- Display of the most popular pages
- Keywords entered by prospective buyers to find listings

Additionally, store owners who have subscribed at the featured and anchored levels get the following functionality:

- Path analysis showing how visitors move within your store
- Bid/BIN tracking to help you optimize your store for bidders and buyers

15

Summary

When creating an eBay store, your company can create its own portal into its eBay sales and offer a coordinated, visible presence with maximum exposure. Your eBay store provides a fixed, central location where you can promote your products and provide a controlled environment to keep repeat customers coming back for more. Most importantly, you can create a constant set of inventory that you can promote to anyone who bids or wins a regular auction listing, all while capitalizing on the familiarity of the eBay environment.

Opening an eBay store for your business gives you a dozen key advantages. Utilizing these benefits will not only give you the competitive edge, but it will have a direct impact on your company's profits.

You can choose from three levels of eBay Store ownership: basic, featured, and anchored store. Each comes with its own set of features and capabilities and can be customized to meet the needs of your business.

eBay stores provide you with the opportunity to cross-sell and up-sell merchandise based on product sales. Be sure to investigate these methods and provide plenty of options for cross-selling when adding new items to your store.

eBay provides several tools that you can use to monitor the sales activity of your stores and make specific changes to improve sales. Seller Reports and Traffic Reports can provide insight into buyer activity at your eBay store and provide key metrics to measure your success.

Chapter 16

Create New Markets

In this chapter…

- ■ Determine potential products to introduce exclusively via eBay
- ■ Use your brand name and expertise to help others
- ■ Create a pre-sale eBay policy
- ■ Create a rollout strategy
- ■ Use existing listings to market other items
- ■ Use delayed listing timing

After you have established your product and brand name presence on eBay, you should evaluate the possibility of moving into other eBay markets for two reasons: First, opening up new markets via a different marketing strategy or by introducing new products can create lucrative opportunities. This can be especially true if you have a unique selling position that has not been used or a product or product line that you can actively sell in an underserved market. Second, as you create and dominate your eBay niche, your competitors will be actively seeking other product categories in which they can establish market share. Because of this, it is important to be proactive and seek new products to offer and new arenas to move into when it comes to eBay.

The average PowerSeller always has at least three or four new products or product lines in the pipeline. This strategy allows them to move quickly when integrating new products into their line. Adding new products or marketing strategies also allows the successful seller the opportunity to hedge against normal market sales fluctuations.

Choose Products for Exclusive eBay Sales

One of the best ways to introduce new products or services into the marketplace is to use your company's natural strengths and business relationships to create new product or service packages. For example, if your company is in the travel industry, you have the opportunity to leverage the connections you have established in the brick-and-mortar world to create unique offerings on eBay. You can put together a special "eBay only" package for your customers that includes airfare, hotel, and tickets to a special event.

Use Your Brand Name and Expertise to Help Others

Sometimes, a new product doesn't have to be a physical commodity; it can be a service supplied by your company. One successful example of this strategy is the Agilent Advantage Assurance program. Agilent Technologies, a division of Hewlett-Packard that was spun off into its own company in 1999, concentrates on the development and manufacture of equipment and services with a focus on such industries as communications, electronics, life sciences, and chemical analysis.

eBay Success Story

Motorola Offers Exclusive eBay Promotion

When Motorola was planning its HELLOMOTO marketing campaign a while back, the company set up a strategy to offer an exclusive promotional package on eBay.

First, it established an eBay account and opened an eBay store to sell products. Then the company worked with eBay to launch several charity listings that featured its brand-new v70 wireless phone. These new phones would not be available anywhere else on the market—not through established retail channels or e-commerce efforts—only through the eBay charity listings. Motorola supported these listings with extensive advertising and promotion through its web site and online advertising, among other methods.

When the bidding was over, Motorola knew that the promotion was a hit. The successful listings generated tremendous interest in the phones. In addition to the creation of an online marketing buzz, Motorola gained better insight into potential demand as well as lucrative price points when the phones went out through other channels.

Agilent noticed that its equipment was being listed and sold on eBay, as shown in Figure 16-1. However, like any industry involving delicate equipment, the issue of reliability of a used product concerned the company. The best example of this is the auto industry; because used cars are notorious for having hidden problems, automobile manufacturers have stepped in to offer precertified programs, in which dealers buy back used cars, conduct extensive testing, and certify the car with a new, shorter warranty to encourage consumers to buy used cars.

Agilent took a page from this idea and created the Agilent Advantage Assurance program (Figure 16-2). This program allows sellers to submit their used equipment to Agilent to be certified. Agilent will then

- Perform an evaluation of the hardware to determine whether it will qualify for this program
- Assuming the equipment is viable to continue, fully calibrate the equipment to its proper settings
- Test the equipment to make sure its performance meets Agilent's standards
- Provide a one-year warranty that covers the buyer in the case of unexpected repairs that are not the fault of the buyer, including free calibration for one year with each repair

After the seller successfully finds a buyer for the equipment, Agilent will ship the equipment to the buyer. The seller will collect the money and handle all the after-sale processes, except for the actual shipment of the product. The buyer will enjoy 12 months of free access to the Agilent Technical Support service, and Agilent engineers will answer questions about the product. Finally, buyers of this equipment will be able to renew this support and warranty every year as part of the Assurance program.

16

EB0118 - HP Agilent 432A Power Meter Uses 478A Sensor   Item number

You are signed in   · Watch this ite

Go to larger picture

Starting bid:	**US $99.99**
	Place Bid >
Time left:	**6 days 23 hours**
	7-day listing
	Ends Oct-25-04 21:45:03 PDT
	Add to Calendar
Start time:	Oct-18-04 21:45:03 PDT
History:	0 bids
Item location:	Irvine, CA
	United States
Ships to:	Worldwide
Shipping costs:	US $50.00 - Standard Flat Rate
	Shipping Service (within
	United States)

 Shipping and payment details

Seller information

elad_best_com (1349) Power Seller

Feedback Score: 1349
Positive Feedback: 100%
Member since Aug-02-96 in United St:

Read feedback comments
Ask seller a question
View seller's other items
Visit this seller's eBay Store!
stores **HotComics Store**

PayPal Buyer Protection
Free coverage up to $500.
See eligibility

FIGURE 16-1   An Agilent power meter offered on eBay

About Me: agilentadvantageassurance

 Agilent Technologies

Search for **Agilent Advantage Assurance** products   GO

Settle for more
Agilent's promise that you won't pay the price for unknown quality

 if you're a **SELLER** **Would a guarantee that equipment will perform to specifications bring in more bidders and leave you with more satisfied customers?** Learn about the benefits of Agilent Advantage Assurance for sellers and sign up for the program.

Sellers, Sign Up Today >

if you're a **BUYER** **FREE SHIPPING**
until 7/19/2004

Get Agilent's guarantee that your Agilent (formerly HP) instrument performs to specifications – plus get protection against the cost of repair for a full year!

By bidding only on used equipment with Agilent Advantage Assurance, you still pay far less and get equipment that Agilent guarantees will perform to specifications. We evaluate and fully calibrate each instrument, verify that it meets our performance specifications, and protect you against unexpected repair costs for a full year.

FIGURE 16-2   The Agilent Advantage Assurance program

One of the extra bonuses for the seller is that Agilent helps guide buyers to their products by offering a special Search For Agilent Advantage Assurance Products button on the company's eBay About Me page and the Agilent web site. By offering this program, Agilent is building a network of Agilent-authorized equipment dealers that they promote, and by ensuring the quality of the items that are sold on eBay, Agilent protects its own reputation and encourages continued usage of its brand, as well as a new revenue stream by offering warranty and repair services for its already-sold equipment.

Talk with Your Partners

New products don't have to come solely from within your company. Working with business partners to combine products and services will allow you to create special packages to sell on eBay. For example, a movie studio could use its relationships with various venues to put together packages on eBay that offer airfare, hotel, and exclusive tickets to shows such as the Grammys or a high-profile movie premiere.

Combination deals offer several advantages:

Sets Your Company Apart   Special offerings help set you apart from others selling your product. Your company's package can allow you to offer the eBay buyer a unique and full experience.

Increases Exposure   Joint ventures allow you to increase the exposure of all participating parties. Perhaps some of your partners are interested in eBay but haven't yet developed their strategies. They can gain exposure to eBay by partnering with you, while you enjoy their support and complementary products in your listings.

Provides Customer Incentive   Special offers give buyers an incentive to check back with your listings often. By creating different packages, you encourage your customers to come back to see what new unique items you're offering this month. By generating repeat business, you have the advantage of marketing and selling to existing customers, which will in turn increase your sales volume.

Pre-sale Policy on eBay

Many companies like to offer a pre-sale of new items, enabling those customers who really want an item to buy it before it goes on sale to the general public. The pre-sale customer commits to buying the item, which gives the manufacturer an idea of demand and whether the price point is appealing, and typically ensures a guaranteed sale when the item eventually ships out to that customer.

eBay has some specific rules regarding pre-sales, to ensure that the buyer receives the merchandise in a specific amount of time:

- ■ You, as the seller, can offer pre-sales items on a limited basis, as long as you guarantee that the item will be ready for shipment within 30 days from the date a buyer purchases the product, whether it's an eBay store purchase or an eBay listing.

- ■ Within the auction listing, you must clearly indicate that the product in that listing is being sold on a pre-sale basis and provide a delivery date that meets the 30-day requirement.

- ■ The text size used for these indications must be at least the same size as eBay's normal text size within the Sell Your Item form (in HTML terms, font size 3).

16

If you do not comply with these rules, eBay reserves the right to end the listing early and not provide a refund to the seller for listing fees. If you continue to violate these policies, eBay can suspend you as a seller and revoke your account. For more information and the most up-to-date information regarding pre-sale rules on eBay, visit http://pages.ebay.com/help/policies/pre-sale.html.

> **NOTE** *For special promotional events, eBay may approve a first-party manufacturer to sell an item outside of the 30-day pre-sale guidelines so long as the first-party manufacturer is supplying the actual item for sale. These exceptions will be made for certain promotions and must be approved prior to listing items for sale on eBay.*

Create a Rollout Strategy

In general, introducing a new product on eBay involves a great deal more than simply posting a new product online and relying on traditional marketing efforts to reach the end consumer. To succeed, you'll need to involve many areas of your business, beyond the group handling the marketing issues. Ideally, your strategy needs to include your distribution channel, sales, and operations employees. A launch of a new product or an existing product line into a new area using eBay will have the most success when all the appropriate departments in your company are involved.

Market Segmentation

Segmentation is the process by which you narrow down the field of potential customers to those most likely to buy your product. Defining your target market is critical to creating your sales and marketing strategies successfully on eBay. Your target market can be divided into segments based on such factors as age, gender, household income, education, and spending patterns. For example, let's say that you're thinking about entering your new digital camera into a new eBay product category like DVDs & Movies. Before rolling out a product into the category, you should review information on what types of people purchase these kinds of products to determine whether this product is being successfully sold on eBay and help you position the product.

Market Positioning

Positioning your product on eBay means creating the desired perception and branding for your product. A correctly positioned product will experience greater visibility, higher sales, and consumer acceptance in the e-commerce realm. To position your product correctly, you must evaluate your target market, analyze the strategies of any similar products being sold by your competitors, and have a strong and creative focus when branding your product or product line.

> **TIP** *If you've followed the 4 Ps of Marketing (discussed in Chapter 12), you should have already determined whether you are going to roll out a product based on price, promotion, or other areas.*

Above all, your marketing message in your rollout must be clear and consistent, reflecting your overall strategy. The message can be expressed in two ways:

■ **The unique selling proposition** What about your product or service presentation sets it apart from similar products being sold on eBay?

■ **Product branding** Does your product and listing present a strong and professional image? Are you selling your product to your customers by telling them exactly why they should buy from you?

Timing Your Product Launch

Once you've determined your market segment and selling position, you'll need to set a time frame for placing the product on the market and stick to it. A delay in a product launch can cause your company to miss critical points in the business cycle or in the buying habits of the consumer market. Either event could severely impact your sales. Create a schedule that reflects the time needed for each element of the launch.

For example, if your product line consists of romantic, heart-shaped chocolates, it's a good bet that you stand to gain at least 50 percent more sales if you coordinate the launch of the product on eBay with a listing cycle that ends just before Valentine's Day. In fact, an intelligently tailored rollout will ensure that auctioned items that come with a special overnight delivery option will close the night before February 14.

Fine-Tuning Your Approach

The progress of your launch program should be tracked as it unfolds, not six weeks after the launch has been completed. The best product managers tend to be those who are most involved with their launches. You should be able to fine-tune as you go, devoting more resources to one area that is

Prepare for Setbacks, but Anticipate Success

While it's common sense to prepare for potential setbacks in sales of your product on a launch, few managers prepare for the opposite circumstance. What happens when your product successfully penetrates a new market, starts selling like the proverbial hotcakes, and you don't have enough production capacity to keep pace with the orders? Worse yet, you could have enough product on hand but insufficient shipping capacity to fulfill the orders.

You lose much more than sales in this scenario—you also lose credibility in the eBay marketplace. This is especially critical for eBay, where negative feedback is fast in coming when sales are delayed and potentially a real handicap when others consider purchasing from you.

16

generating sales and pulling back on others. You can also plan more accurately for both expenditures for marketing, and for anticipating your shipping needs. Additionally, if the product is selling well, you can utilize this information by playing up its success in your company's promotional materials.

Use Existing Listings to Market Other Products

One of the most powerful mechanisms you have for reaching out to your eBay customers is right in front of you, in the form of your existing eBay listings. Cross-selling and up-selling products with your listing is an excellent way to increase your efforts. A simple, well-placed blurb in all of your listings can direct your customers to your eBay store to see your other merchandise.

> **NOTE** *Although eBay does not allow you to link directly to your company's web site from your listings, it does allow you to promote and link to your web site from your About Me page.*

You should also prominently display any special promotions or shipping discounts you offer; tout your company's strengths in product, experience, or speed; and let your customers know that you value their business.

As discussed in Chapter 12, your marketing efforts should never end with the close of the listing. The after-sale processes, including the e-mails sent to the buyer and literature included with the product shipment, can also include information about upcoming listings or new product availability.

Time-Delayed Listings

The Scheduled Auction listing is a feature that eBay offers when you create a product listing. For 10 cents per listing, eBay will allow you to choose a starting date up to 21 days in the future and the starting time, in 15-minute blocks, at any time of the day. You provide all of the information up front, review your auction listing just as you would with a regular listing, and then submit your delayed listing to eBay.

eBay will then give you the URL and item number of your new listing and store the information in its database until the designated start time. You, as the seller, can revisit that link at any time before the listing start time and change or update any of the details. You can either bookmark the link when the listing is created or use My eBay to check on scheduled listings to access the listing.

Once you've created your listing in advance, you can use that link to advertise the listing within Internet message boards and forums, on marketing literature, or as a link tied into banner advertising on other Internet web sites.

Summary

Exclusive packages sold only on eBay can provide excellent visibility for a new product launch as well as generate market demand for your product. Partnering with other companies to develop a unique product bundle or service can be a lucrative way to offer exclusive product packages on eBay.

Many companies offer a pre-sale of new items, so those eBay customers who really want an item can buy it before it goes on sale to the general public. If you are planning to offer a product for pre-sale, make sure that you follow the eBay regulations regarding this selling technique.

By creating a new rollout strategy, you can maximize the impact of your product's introduction on eBay. Market timing and market positioning are the keys to a successful product launch.

The progress of your launch program should be tracked as it unfolds so that you can fine-tune as you go, devoting more resources to one area that is generating sales and pulling back on others.

One way to generate more sales on eBay is to cross-market your products. By directing your customers to your eBay store from within your eBay listings, you are leveraging your existing eBay traffic into the potential of multiple sales.

For 10 cents per listing, eBay will allow you to choose an listing starting date up to 21 days in the future. The Scheduled Auction listing option allows you to begin and end your listings during the time that is optimal for your target buying audience.

16

Chapter 17

Expand Your Capabilities

In this chapter...

- ■ Investigate vendors in eBay's Solutions Directory Program
- ■ Work with Marketworks and ChannelAdvisor programs
- ■ Find help with the eBay Developer Program
- ■ Add people, products, and processing power to your existing infrastructure
- ■ Find and use the Trading Assistant and Trading Post Solutions programs
- ■ Get help from eLance

By this point, you've laid a solid foundation and defined a clear eBay presence for your company. You've gained experience through your continuing sales efforts, refined your marketing techniques, and updated your business strategy to maximize profit and gain exposure through your eBay identity. Now it's time to achieve the next level.

This final chapter discusses several ways you can expand your eBay business through technology and the addition of services designed to assist your business in a variety of areas. By using strategies, systems, and services designed both to integrate eBay into your business and assist you in performing several functions of your business, you will have the tools you need to take your ever-growing eBay sales channel to the next level.

Whether you're using eBay tools or you've adopted some form of auction-management software, you should have a team and system in place that helps you list new and recurring products for sale, monitor the sales activity of those products, handle all the post-sale events, and link back to your corporate infrastructure in terms of accounting, inventory management, and marketing. This chapter focuses on adding onto that structure, enhancing and scaling your capabilities to enhance your efforts.

Find Tools from Vendors in eBay's Solutions Directory

As eBay grew to prominence, many of the larger sellers and companies who saw its potential early on wanted an easier way to take advantage of eBay's powerful platform and let the tools within that platform help them better manage their eBay sales. Dozens of software companies began creating tools and programs to use in conjunction with eBay, but eBay recognized the value of properly integrating third-party software with its own growing software platform. To that end, eBay began a program of certifying software developed by certain third-party software vendors; eBay helps those vendors understand all the specific computer language tools that make up the eBay software platform. This way, eBay is able to maintain control and security over integrating software, so it can protect business standards and site integrity by ensuring that only serious companies with proper software development practices use the platform to expand sales without jeopardizing the health and security of that computer network. Of course, this expansion of sales didn't come directly from these vendors, but rather through a new market, whereby software vendors sold their tools to full-time eBay sellers to help these sellers achieve higher sales.

This program, called the eBay Solutions Directory, offers solutions to support your eBay trading activity. You can find out more about the program at http://solutions.ebay.com. You'll see a directory listing of the certified software tools, grouped into selling and buying solutions, as shown in Figure 17-1.

Whether you're looking for a total auction-management solution or a software program that helps solve one piece of the listing process puzzle, every tool listed in the Solutions Directory has been certified by eBay. Browse through the options and use the links provided to check out the software provider behind the tool and get a detailed description of its services and all associated fees.

Naturally, as your eBay business grows, your goal will be to automate as much as possible so you can scale your eBay business, much like you've scaled (or plan to scale) your current business. To help you navigate through the dozens of options presented for solutions in optimizing and augmenting your entire eBay business, we'll focus on some previously mentioned popular and tested solutions that current eBay PowerSellers and corporations are using for their eBay businesses.

Marketworks

Marketworks (at http://www.marketworks.com, previously known as AuctionWorks) is a provider of marketplace management software for online sales and caters specifically to small, midsize, and large business clients using online trading platforms such as eBay; it also works with high-end eBay sellers who wish to automate and grow their businesses. The company was founded in 1999 and quickly convinced many of eBay's early successful sellers to join the company or help

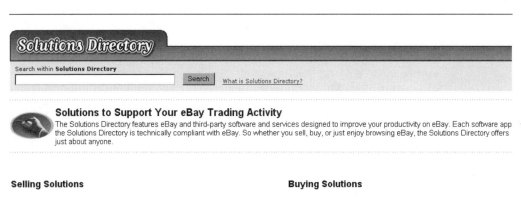

Solutions to Support Your eBay Trading Activity
The Solutions Directory features eBay and third-party software and services designed to improve your productivity on eBay. Each software app the Solutions Directory is technically compliant with eBay. So whether you sell, buy, or just enjoy browsing eBay, the Solutions Directory offers just about anyone.

Selling Solutions

- Complete Selling Solutions
  Manage all aspects of selling on eBay.

- Listing Management
  Help launch and manage your listings.

- Inventory Management
  Manage large amounts of product inventory.

Buying Solutions

- Search
  Search the eBay marketplace using customized interfaces.

- Auction Monitoring
  Find alternate versions of My eBay built for different needs and i

- Payment
  Manage all of your purchases, payments and feedback using a

FIGURE 17-1   The eBay Solutions Directory home page

17

Elite eBay Sellers Are Shooting Stars

Highest rated sellers on eBay are known as *Shooting Stars*, in response to the large amount of positive feedback that they have received over the time they have been in business. The ranking system for stars can be found on eBay's site under the Feedback area of the Help menu, as shown next. Becoming a Shooting Star means that you've entered the realm of eBay's elite sellers.

Stars

The feedback rating system is easy. You receive:
- +1 point for each positive comment
- 0 points for each neutral comment
- -1 point for each negative comment
- A star icon ☆ for 10 or more comments.

Stars are awarded to eBay members for achieving 10 or more feedback points. Here's what the different stars mean:

Yellow Star (☆) = 10 to 49 points

Blue Star (★) = 50 to 99 points

Turquoise Star (☆) = 100 to 499 points

Purple Star (★) = 500 to 999 points

Red Star (★) = 1,000 to 4,999 points

Green Star (☆) = 5,000 to 9,999 points

Yellow Shooting Star (🌠) = 10,000 to 24,999 points

Turquoise Shooting Star (🌠) = 25,000 to 49,999 points

Purple Shooting Star (🌠) = 50,000 to 99,999 points

Red Shooting Star (🌠) = 100,000 or higher

---

with developing its software platform. Because the input was very specific and detailed, Marketworks' products are geared toward the eBay high-volume seller, while the company continues to be an eBay Preferred Solution Provider.

Some of Marketworks' most notable corporate clients include Disney Auctions, Hewlett-Packard, Olympus, and Vodafone. According to its web site, Marketworks clients include 10 large corporations and more than 3000 small to medium-sized businesses. The company also works with some of eBay's highest rated sellers, known as Shooting Stars, to automate their sales, and these sellers' businesses continue to grow every year. In fact, the name change from AuctionWorks to Marketworks signifies the company's focus on the online marketplace that businesses create, not just the eBay auction marketplace.

Marketworks uses an extensive strategy when dealing with its corporate clients. As you can see from its Enterprise home page, shown in Figure 17-2, Marketworks uses strategies tailored to both the retailers and catalogers sector of businesses, as well as the manufacturers, distributors, and wholesalers sector of companies. They work with each company's systems to integrate all operational, market, and international processes seamlessly between the client's systems and eBay's business systems. You can choose one or multiple areas of services geared and customized to your business needs.

ChannelAdvisor

ChannelAdvisor (http://www.channeladvisor.com) focuses on both marketplace and auction-management solutions and services for companies large and small. It counts companies such as IBM, Best Buy, Sears, Motorola, and Dell on its list of corporate clients and offers tiered solutions to expand a company's sales potential online. Through public and private marketplaces, as well as a catalog-synchronization product that helps coordinate pricing data among numerous online shopping sites, ChannelAdvisor offers a complete solution for businesses that can cover the entire life cycle of products, as shown in Figure 17-3.

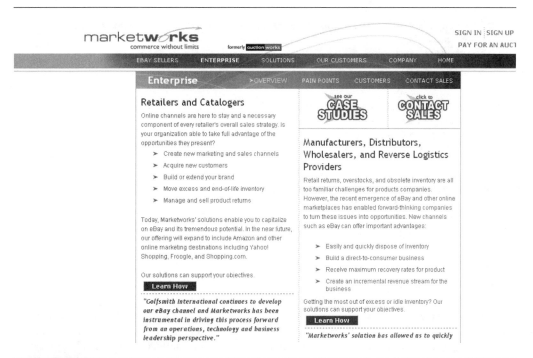

FIGURE 17-2   Marketworks' Enterprise home page

17

How to ... Get Help Selecting Services

ChannelAdvisor offers a Solution Wizard for companies that are unsure about which products they need. Go to http://www.channeladvisor.com/solution_wizard/wizard.htm and answer the questions on the form shown here. The Solution Wizard will analyze your needs and recommend an appropriate product from ChannelAdvisor's suite of services.

.: Solution Wizard

1) I would consider selling the following types of product via marketplaces and auctions:
☐ New
☐ B-stock, refurbished, used, off-lease, open box returns
☐ Single units
☐ Large lots
☐ Wholesale
☐ Not sure what would work best

2) My company's total ANNUAL sales through all sales channels (including eBay) are:
○ Greater than $200 million
○ $50 million to $200 million
○ $1 million to $50 million
○ Less than $1 million

3) My MONTHLY online auction or marketplace sales will probably average:
○ $100,000 or more per month
○ $50,000-100,000 per month
○ Less than $50,000 per month
○ Not sure

4) My corporate financial and fulfillment systems are:
○ Large and complex (SAP, JD Edwards, Peoplesoft, etc.)
○ Moderate, with standard data (Great Plains, QuickBooks, Oracle Small Business, etc.)
○ Very simple (Excel spreadsheets)

An eBay Preferred Solution Provider since 2001, ChannelAdvisor creates its enterprise solutions by adopting best practice standards among eBay sellers, automating and integrating technology to increase sales capacity, and writing new software applications to handle the varied tasks required in this setting. It also offers two prepackaged software suites: ChannelAdvisor Merchant, which focuses on the medium-sized business and high-volume individual sellers, and ChannelAdvisor Pro, which focuses on the small business and eBay PowerSeller.

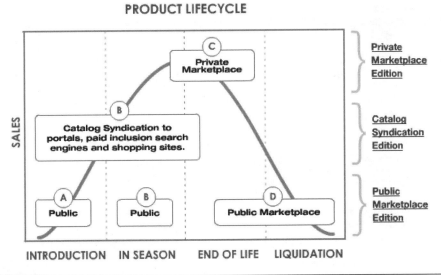

FIGURE 17-3   ChannelAdvisor services along a product life cycle

Use the eBay Developers Program

As we mentioned in Chapter 9, software tools are essential for companies to do business, but sometimes a third-party solution isn't enough. Many companies are using complex yet personalized business systems that respond to the individual needs of the company. These systems, which are often proprietary, usually cannot integrate with an "off-the-shelf" prepackaged software program. If this is the case with your business systems, you should consider the next step: the eBay Developers Program.

The eBay Developers Program was created to help third-party developers integrate their businesses with the eBay platform. As a member of the Developers Program, a developer can create custom applications that effectively and efficiently handle all types of business transactions on eBay. The Developers Program is designed to promote innovation and ideas created by developers. As part of the program, eBay provides the technology and resources to help developers fully leverage the functionality of eBay's platform. This way, developers can properly use the eBay system to streamline their software designs and response times while taking advantage of the established software platform, while eBay can ensure that everyone using the system has been trained using a central focus.

If your company needs to integrate its software with eBay's systems, you can work with your MIS or IT department to let them know about the options available with the eBay Developers Program. Either your IT department or your company's systems programmers can find a wealth of information about the eBay Developers Program at http://developer.ebay.com, shown in Figure 17-4.

17

Developers Program

Home

Business Benefits
  eBay Platform
  Success Stories
  White Papers
  Business FAQs

Developer Technology
  eBay API
  SDK
  Documentation
  Technical FAQs

Membership
  Overview
  Services / Fees
  Join
  Membership FAQs

News & Events

Developer Education

Customer Solutions
  eBay Tools

Tap into the eBay Platform

Looking for a way to escalate your eBay business? The eBay Developers Program gives you access to the eBay marketplace through Web services so you can create solutions to make trading on eBay even easier.

Grow my business ⊙
Membership highlights ⊙

Spotlight

Announcing a New Online Directory of Software and Services

The new eBay Solutions Directory gives you an online vehicle for promoting the software and services you offer to eBay buyers and sellers. "Our goal is to increase the awareness of the many innovative third-party solutions among the entire eBay community," explains Randy Ching, vice president, eBay Platform Solutions. Read the release.

New Educational and Marketing Resources for Service and Solution Providers

The goal of the new eBay Certified Provider Program is to validate and provide visibility for companies that provide eBay services to the eBay community. Check out the valuable educational and marketing resources available to companies that provide services.

Honorees Receive Star Developer Awards at Developers Conference

Distinguished members of the eBay Developers Program accepted Star Developer Awards for Early Adoption, Service to the Community and Innovative Application at the eBay Developers Conference in New Orleans on

Updates

- Get the la
  events fro
  the Devel
  via our we
- Java S
  available
  individual
- eBay fo
  Omidyar
  eBay
  Conferen
- Read suc
  to learn
  developer
  power of tl

Display the

FIGURE 17-4   The eBay Developers Program home page

TIP   *Even if you don't plan to join the program just yet, it's worth bookmarking and regularly checking this web page. The Updates section contains both breaking news in the development arena plus events of interest, such as the planned times and guest speakers at the annual eBay Developer's Conference.*

If you're looking to automate only your own business processes through this program, it's free to join and get an individual license to the application program interface (API). If, in the future, you plan to resell any tools you create for eBay automation, you would be required to upgrade to a commercial license, where pricing would depend on usage.

NOTE   *While the "individual license" title may not seem appropriate for a company's usage, this type of license grants a corporation the right to use eBay's programming interface, provided that corporation is not reselling this new software to anyone else. See the eBay Developers Business FAQ at http://developer.ebay.com/DevProgram/business/faq.asp for more information and clear definitions on all their functions.*

Some of the benefits of using the eBay API include heavy communication between eBay developers and your developers, advance information on new features, dedicated technical support, online documentation, member forums, and, most important, information on automated ways that your company software can perform the following tasks on eBay:

- List products for sale
- Search the eBay database
- Find and leave feedback on eBay
- Get the list of bidders for a certain item
- Get the list of items being sold by a particular eBay user
- Automatically relist products that don't sell initially
- Update an item's description with new information
- Access catalog information for commodity products that you sell
- Receive notifications of certain events by other users

TIP *One of the benefits of joining the Developers Program and becoming an eBay Certified Developer is that once your company creates an interesting tool, you can turn around and use eBay to resell that tool to other companies who need it. This creates a brand-new stream of revenue for your company and allows you to recoup your research and development costs or even turn a profit on your work.*

Add People, Products, and Processing Power to Your Existing Infrastructure

Regardless of the auction-management software your business chooses, there is always room for improvement when it comes to your eBay strategies. Perhaps you'd like to ramp up your internal support quickly with knowledgeable, online-savvy professionals. Perhaps you've already achieved your first goal of moving out your entire excess inventory, for example, but you've built up a great feedback rating and selling system and you've created a new goal and business plan to start acquiring goods just for eBay resale. To accomplish your goals, you may need to add more resources to the eBay segment of your business or possibly just outsource one particular piece of the puzzle while retaining control of the primary processes. Let's take a look at different functions within and outside eBay that can help you to increase your sales and provide options for enlisting resources.

Trading Assistants Program

The backbone of eBay's success has been the hundreds of thousands of professional sellers who have posted tens, hundreds, thousands, or even millions of items on eBay. These sellers have acquired many skills (and usually a high feedback rating) that are hard to describe on a résumé but are real to anyone posting the right listing on eBay. While they enjoy selling products on eBay, they may not choose to purchase new inventory for resale. In other words, they have the skill but not the goods. Conversely, some product owners don't have the time, skill, patience, or feedback rating to sell the item properly by themselves. The eBay Trading Assistants program was created to help these sellers.

17

If your eBay business is such that one person cannot manage the eBay sales volume alone, or even for those who are just launching the eBay sales channel within their company's environment, the services of a trading assistant may be a valuable solution. Created several years ago, the eBay Trading Assistants program is for people who need to hire an experienced eBay seller to help sell products.

Experienced sellers can register to be a trading assistant, and interested buyers can search from the Trading Assistants Directory (Figure 17-5) to find a person to help them sell items on eBay. The directory is organized by the trading assistant's zip code, telephone area code, and feedback rating. A buyer hires a trading assistant, who will perform some or all of the functions of posting and managing an eBay sale in exchange for a flat fee or a predetermined percentage of the sale amount.

Each trading assistant is free to create his or her own rules and conditions to provide assistance, and each user is free to choose from among the thousands of eBay trading assistants, based on their individual requirements. This free program helps connect the trading assistants who may specialize in certain product categories with item owners who have merchandise in that genre to sell and gives these experienced sellers a way to capitalize on the success and feedback rating they've accumulated through eBay over the years.

Finding a Trading Assistant for Your eBay Business

Typically, a trading assistant will work out of his or her home or office and will come to you, the interested party, to go over the details of the job, look at the merchandise, review the terms of a contract, and set up a plan to go forward. The first step is to research the various trading assistants

FIGURE 17-5   eBay Trading Assistants information page

and the services they offer. In the eBay Trading Assistants Directory, you will find not only the contact information for each assistant, but also a brief description of the selling area of expertise and some basic information about his or her services. You can select a trading assistant based on areas of experience and also location. Most assistants work locally; however, some very specialized assistants will travel to your site.

To locate a trading assistant in your local area, go to the Trading Assistants search page shown in Figure 17-6. Once you enter the requested information, you will be shown a list of assistants who are located within your zip code area.

This list is sorted by the assistant's feedback rating, so those with the highest amount of feedback show up first on the list. Go through this list, examine the terms of each assistant carefully, and find a couple with terms that you consider acceptable. Call each assistant and set up an appointment to meet and discuss your needs.

It's recommended that you start with a few items at first, to test the assistant's service level and working relationship. Additionally, you should always require a signature on a written contract that clearly spells out the services of the trading assistant. In fact, most professional trading assistants will not work without a contract in place. Once the first few eBay sales go smoothly, you will be in a position to add the eBay trading assistant to your resources for expanding your eBay business. Typically, these assistants will be happy to renegotiate terms if they see a sizable amount of future business coming their way. So don't be afraid to ask for terms that are best suited for your company's needs.

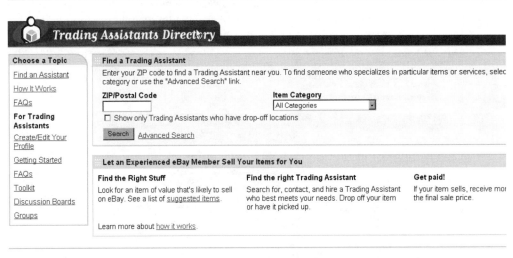

FIGURE 17-6   eBay Trading Assistants search page

Trading Post Solutions

While you can have a trading assistant come to you to help increase your eBay business, you can also sell your merchandise through one of the newest venues of eBay selling, the auction drop-off location, called a trading post. You deliver your merchandise to the trading post, where it will be cataloged, photographed, and listed for sale on eBay. The trading post will also handle all the payment, packaging, shipping, and customer service issues. Most drop-off stores require that your merchandise have a certain dollar value on eBay before it will be accepted for sale. Once your item has sold and payment has been received, the trading post will take a percentage of the amount of the final sale and send a check to your company for the balance of the profit.

eBay
Success Story

AuctionDrop Sees Green After Its One-Year Anniversary

In March 2004, AuctionDrop, the first eBay drop-off store company, marked the first year of its operation. AuctionDrop provides a simple, fast, and convenient way for consumers to sell goods on eBay. It was started by Randy Adams and Bill Rollinson, who also founded the first online retailer on the Web, the Internet Shopping Network, in 1994.

Since its introduction, AuctionDrop has expanded to five locations around the San Francisco Bay Area and 3500 locations nationwide. In one year, AuctionDrop sold more than 18,000 unique items on eBay, earning a profit of $1.3 million for its customers and establishing itself as the top-performing eBay drop-off service.

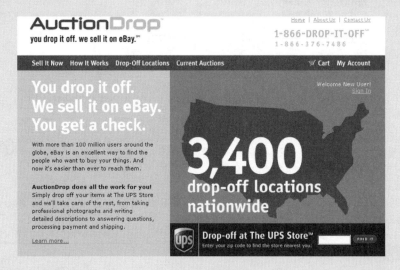

"This has been an incredibly successful first year for us," said Adams. "As we've grown, we've made adjustments where necessary to improve our business for our customers."

Several versions of the trading post system exist, from small and locally owned drop-off stores to nationwide franchises that have merchandise transportation agreements (both receipt of new merchandise and delivery of sold merchandise) in place, using nationally-known shippers. Companies such as AuctionDrop, iSold It, and QuikDrop are just a few of the franchisers attempting to go nationwide with their eBay drop-off stores.

These nationwide companies offer a backbone software solution to their franchisees to help with pricing and listing the goods, and they leave it up to the franchisee to find a location, hire employees, and train those employees on the business of selling on eBay. eBay has recently signed an agreement with PostNet, an international franchiser of retail business center packing, shipping, and mailbox services; PostNet can offer the trading post for eBay service to people dropping off goods at any PostNet location worldwide.

If you want to sell goods that are completely outside the main focus of your eBay business— products for which you don't need to recoup a specific amount or that would be too time consuming for your company to sell on eBay—you may consider using one of these drop-off stores to handle those products. You can find out more information about specific locations at the following web sites:

- **PostNet**   http://www.postnet.com
- **AuctionDrop**   http://www.auctiondrop.com
- **iSold It**   http://www.isoldit.com
- **QuikDrop**   http://www.quikdrop.com
- **bidadoo**   http://www.bidadoo.com

Help Is a Click Away with eLance

Sometimes you don't need a steady, full-time person to handle certain areas of your eBay sales implementation or expansion; rather, you need a qualified specialist to perform a particular task. This calls for a person who is a professional in the area of expertise required and will need very little training from you to get the job done. An excellent resource for hiring independent contractors to perform a variety of business-related tasks is eLance. eLance lets businesses outsource projects—including web development, graphic design, software, writing, and more. eLance is based on a bidding system; the eLance professionals will bid for the job you have posted. All this and more can be found at the eLance web site (http://www.elance.com) shown in Figure 17-7.

The eLance Online system lets you search through an extensive database of tens of thousands of registered, skilled freelancers who have signed up through the site. The web site allows you to post a project request form. The registered service providers on the site will see your project request and submit competitive bids for their services to complete that project. You review all the incoming bids and select the provider that you believe is best for your company. The site provides extensive ratings and verification services to help ensure the trust between you and the independent contractor.

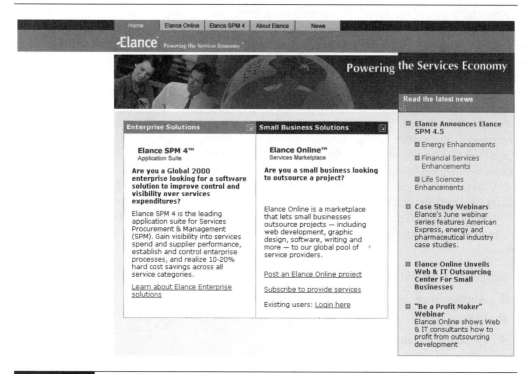

FIGURE 17-7   The eLance web site

Summary

Using any of the exciting options presented in this chapter, you can turn your eBay identity into a money-making stand-alone division or a brand-new company focused on harnessing the power of 125 million users worldwide who are dedicated to trading goods and connecting with their fellow shoppers. Legions of experts, companies, and software applications are ready to assist you as you expand your efforts. Just remember that the best lessons to be learned will be done in the field, as your customers respond to your efforts and reward you accordingly.

The eBay Solutions Directory offers a myriad of software solutions to assist you in fully integrating your business with eBay's systems. Every tool listed in the Solutions Directory has been certified by eBay.

Marketworks provides marketplace management software for online sales that can partner with your company to help you integrate your company's operations with eBay's systems.

An eBay Preferred Solution Provider since 2001, ChannelAdvisor creates its enterprise solution by adopting best practice standards among eBay sellers, automating and integrating technology to increase sales capacity, and writing new software applications to handle the varied tasks required in an online auction setting. ChannelAdvisor also offers a Solution Wizard for companies that will assist them in selecting the services that are best suited to their business.

The eBay Developers Program is designed to promote innovation and ideas created by third-party developers and gives companies a vehicle with which to integrate their businesses into the eBay platform.

The eBay Trading Assistants program is an excellent option for your business if you need assistance with managing your eBay listings. An eBay trading assistant is an alternative to hiring a full-time employee when building your eBay sales channel. Trading assistants should be selected on the basis of their area of expertise as well as their experience in dealing with corporate product sales. An alternative to selling your merchandise with in-house staff or hiring a trading assistant is the use of the auction drop-off store or trading post, which allows you to deliver your merchandise to the store where it will be cataloged, photographed, and listed for sale on eBay. The trading post will also handle all the payment, packaging, shipping, and customer service issues.

The eLance Online system lets you search through an extensive database of tens of thousands of registered, skilled service providers to use as a resource for your business in the completion of project-driven tasks. The eLance web site allows you to post a project request form on the site, and registered freelancers submit competitive bids for their services to complete that project.

Conclusion

Our goal throughout this book has been to introduce you and your company's products, reputation, and processes to the exciting and profitable world of eBay and to create a successful strategy. We hope that you look into the wealth of information and profit potential that eBay has to offer, do your research, and find that winning product mix that allows you to compete effectively with sellers around the world and grow your business at the same time.

The key is to be flexible and responsive to the ever changing environment that eBay produces. This is specifically why we gave an overview of the key concepts, as those stay constant throughout the numerous web site upgrades and design changes you will encounter. Don't be afraid to use your business sense as you develop your eBay strategy–after all, you know your products better than most people.

So, try new strategies, form new partnerships, and experiment with everything this new Internet phenomenon has to offer. Take a look at the various resources we mention, and take advantage of them. Remember, eBay is the World's Largest Marketplace because it's open for *everyone* to do business with, including your company. Jump into the action, and achieve your eBay potential!

Appendix A

Important Web Links

Y ou'll find many important web pages that can help you fulfill your eBay strategy. We have highlighted some of the major functions and companies that will assist you in your efforts. Organized into categories, these web links will guide you to important information.

eBay's Specialty Sites

http://www.half.com   At Half.com, you can buy and sell books, music, computers, electronics, DVDs, and other items at fixed buy-it-now prices.

http://www.ebayliveauctions.com   eBay Live Auctions allows you to bid in real-time on live auctions happening on the floor of well-known auction houses.

http://www.ebaymotors.com   At eBay Motors, a step-by-step method moves you through the automobile buying or selling process.

http://pages.ebay.com/realestate/   eBay Real Estate is the perfect portal page for learning about selling your home, timeshare, commercial property, or business on eBay.

http://stores.ebay.com   eBay Stores allows you to find an endless variety of items from favorite eBay sellers, at a fixed buy-it-now price.

Information on Online Selling, Tips, and Trends

http://auctionbytes.com/   AuctionBytes is a premier resource for online auction users.

http://www.channeladvisor.com   ChannelAdvisor offers multiple solutions, ranging from self-service auction management software to full-service, outsourced marketplace management solutions.

http://www.cniper.com, http://www.auctionsniper.com/, and http://www.auctionstealer.com   These three sites—cniper, Auction Sniper, and Auction Stealer, respectively—automate the process of placing your bid in the closing seconds of an eBay auction, dramatically increasing your chances of winning.

http://www.marketworks.com   Marketworks develops fixed-price storefronts with integrated eBay item checkout, automatic cross-sell at checkout, and combined shipping services.

http://solutions.ebay.com   eBay Solutions Directory recognizes companies that offer support products or services and have met certain scalability and customer service requirements. Their products and services are tailored to meet the needs of small, medium, and large eBay businesses.

http://www.vendio.com/   Vendio's main selling point is in helping commercial sellers bring auctioned material to the Web.

Trading Assistants and Trading Post Sellers

http://www.auctiondrop.com/   AuctionDrop, an official eBay trading post, offers 3500 drop-off locations nationwide, with more than 24,000 things listed on eBay. AuctionDrop is a Titanium PowerSeller.

http://www.bidadoo.com   Bidadoo Auctions, an official eBay trading post with $1 million in first-year sales, is a leading eBay consignment business in the Northwest. This unique trading post model incorporates a charity section in addition to its commercial feature and business-to-business model.

http://www.ebay.com/ta   The Trading Assistant portal page allows you to find qualified people from the eBay community who will list your items on eBay. Trading posts, a brick-and-mortar drop-off location, can also be located at this site.

Help with eBay Sales

http://forums.ebay.com/forum.jsp?forum=5   In the Business and Industrial Discussion Board, talk with other eBay sellers and buyers who use the Business and Industrial category. Ask questions, get answers, learn some new tools, and gain valuable contacts.

http://developer.ebay.com/DevProgram/   eBay Developers Program works with IT departments and third-party vendors to write software to integrate eBay functionality into a company's system. The eBay Developers Program can provide detailed information on how to hook into eBay's software functionality in a customized function to fit your needs.

http://www.elance.com   Elance lets you hire professionals for help with the service areas, such as logos, branding, and store development, when devising your online strategy. Post project proposals, collect bids, review performance histories, and hire your independent contractor here.

http://pages.ebay.com/education   The eBay Learning Center is an excellent place to take self-directed online courses to familiarize yourself with the various functions of eBay.

http://www.ebay.com/sellercentral   The Seller Central page is where you can find all the eBay functions for sellers.

http://forums.ebay.com/forum.jsp?forum=93   The eBay Workshops Board allows you to enroll in various online workshops to expand your knowledge of eBay and its ever-increasing list of functions and tools.

General eBay Help

http://www.ebay.com/help   eBay offers an all-comprehensive Help Guide here.

http://www.blackmagik.com/elister.html   Black Magik's e-Lister tool is for Mac users and is comparable to using eBay's Turbo Lister for PC users.

A

Appendix B

Glossary of eBay Abbreviations

Abbreviation	Definition
1st	First Edition
ABM	Automatic Bottle Machine
ACC	Accumulation (stamps)
ACL	Applied Color Label (wine or decorative bottles)
ADV	Adventure (books/movies)
AG	About Good (coins)
AIR	Air Mail (stamps)
AKA	Also Known As
ANTH	Anthology (books)
AO	All Original
AOL	America Online
ARC	Advance Reader's Copy, usually a paperback edition of a book released for publicity purposes before the trade edition release
AU	About Uncirculated (coins)
AUTO	Autographed
BA	Bronze Age
BB	BB-sized hole drilled through record label; or Beanie Baby
BBC	Bottom of Back Cover
BC	Back Cover; Blister Card
BCE	Book Club Edition
BIM	Blown in Mold
BIN	Buy It Now
BIO	Biography
BJ	Ball Jointed Body (dolls)
BK	Bent Knee (dolls)
BKL	Booklet (stamps)
BLB	Big Little Book
BLK	Block (stamps)
BOMC	Book of the Month Club Edition
BP	Blister Pack; Stamps in a Booklet Pane
BU	Brilliant Uncirculated (top grade of coins)
BW	Black and White
C	Cartridge Only (video game); Cover (stamps or books)
C & S	Cup & Saucer
CART	Cartridge (video game)

Abbreviation	Definition
CB	Club Book (stamps)
CC	Carbon Copy
CCA	Comics Code Authority
CCG	Collectible Card Game
CDF	Customs Declaration Form (stamps)
CF	Centerfold (magazines)
CFO	Center Fold Out (magazines)
CI	Cartridge & Instructions (video games, computer equipment)
CIB	Cartridge, Instructions, Box (video games, computer equipment)
CIBO	Cartridge, Instruction, Box, Overlay (video games, computer equipment)
CLA	Cleaned, Lubricated, Adjusted (cameras)
CM	Customized
COA	Certificate of Authenticity
COL	Collection
CONUS	Continental United States Shipping
CPN	Coupon
CPP	Color Picture Postcard; Color Postcard
CS	Cup and Saucer
CTB	Coffee Table Book
CU	Crisp Uncirculated (currency)
D	Denver Mint (coins)
DB	Divided Back (postcards)
DBL	Double (2-in-1: paperbacks)
DG	Depression Glass
DJ	Dust Jacket, Disk Jockey Copy (records)
DOA	Dead on Arrival (item was not working when received by buyer)
DUTCH	Dutch Auction (multiple quantities available)
EAPG	Early American Pattern Glass
EC	Excellent Condition
EF	Extra Fine Condition, Extremely Fine (coins)
EG	Elegant Glass (Depression era)
EP	Extended Play (records, video tapes)
ERR	Error
EX	Excellent (condition)

B

Abbreviation	Definition
EXLIB	Ex-Library Book
EXT	Extended
FAQ	Frequently Asked Questions
FB	Feedback
FC	Fine Condition; Front Cover
FDC	First Day Cover (stamps)
FE	First Edition (books)
F/E	First Edition (books)
FFC	First Flight Cover (stamps)
FFEP	Free Front End Page/Paper
FFL	Federally Licensed Firearms (dealer)
FN	Fine Condition
FOR	Forgery
FPLP	Fisher Price Little People
FS	Factory Sealed
FT	Flat Top (beer cans)
FTLO	From the library of
FVF	Final Value Fee (fee charged by listing site based on the final price of auction)
G	Good Condition
GA	Golden Age
GD	Good Condition
GF	Gold Filled
GGA	Good Girl Art (paperback book covers)
GP	Gold Plate; Gutter Pair (stamps)
GSP	Gold Sterling Plate
GU	Gently Used
GW	Gently Worn (clothes)
GWTW	Gone With the Wind
HB	Hard Back or Hard Bound (book)
HB/DJ	Hardback (book) with Dust Jacket
HC	Hand Colored (maps/engravings); Hard Cover (book)
HIC	Hole in Cover
HIL	Hole in Label
HIST	Historical (books)
HM	Happy Meal (McDonald's)

Abbreviation	Definition
HOF	Hall of Famer (baseball memorabilia/autograph/trading cards)
HP	Hard Plastic; Hand Painted; Hewlett Packard computers
HS	Hand Stamp (stamps)
HTF	Hard to Find
HTML	Hypertext Markup Language
IBC	Inside Back Cover
IE	Internet Explorer
IFC	Inside Front Cover
ILLO	Illustration
ILLUS	Illustration; Illustrated
INIT	Initial; Initials; Initial Issue
IRAN	Inspect and Repair as Necessary
ISH	Issue
ISP	Internet Service Provider
JPG	eBay preferred file format for pictures
JUVIE	Juvenile Delinquency Theme
L	Large
LBBP	Large Bean Bag Plush (Disney)
LBC	Lower Back Cover
LCD	Liquid Crystal Display
LE	Limited Edition
LED	Light Emitting Diode
LFC	Lower Front Cover
LFT	Left
LLBC	Lower Left of Back Cover
LLFC	Lower Left of Front Cover
LP	Long Playing Record
LRBC	Lower Right on Back Cover
LRFC	Lower Right on Front Cover
LSE	Loose
LSW	Label Shows Wear (records)
LTBX	Letterbox (video that re-creates a widescreen image)
LTD	Limited Edition
LWOL	Lot of Writing on Label
M	Medium, Mint, Mono (refers to audio quality)

B

Abbreviation	Definition
MA	Madame Alexander (dolls)
MAP	Map Back (paperback books)
MC	Miscut
MCU	Might Clean Up
MEDIC	Medical Genre (paperbacks)
MIB	Mint in Box
MIBP	Mint in Blister Pack
MIJ	Made in Japan
MIMB	Mint in Mint Box
MIMP	Mint in Mint Package
MIOJ	Made in Occupied Japan
MIOP	Mint in Opened Package
MIP	Mint in Package
MIU	Made in USA
MM	Merry Miniatures (Hallmark)
MMA	Metropolitan Museum of Art
MNB	Mint—No Box
MNH	Mint Never Hinged (stamps)
MOC	Mint on Card
MOMA	Museum of Modern Art
MOMC	Mint on Mint Card
MONMC	Mint on Near Mint Card
MONO	Monophonic (again, refers to audio quality)
MOP	Mother of Pearl
MOTU	Masters of the Universe
MP	Military Post (stamps)
MS	Miniature Sheet (stamps); Mint State (coins in mint condition)
MWBMT	Mint With Both Mint Tags
MWBT	Mint With Both Tags
MWBTM	Mint With Both Tags Mint
MYS	Mystery (books/movies)
MWMT	Mint With Mint Tags
NAP	Not Affected Play (records)
NARU	Not a Registered User (eBay)
NASB	Nancy Ann Story Book

Abbreviation	Definition
NBC	Nightmare Before Christmas (Disney)
NBU	Never Been Used
NBW	Never Been Worn/Wrecked
NC	No Cover
ND	No Date; No Dog (RCA record labels)
NDSR	No Dents, Scratches, or Rust
NIB	New in Box
NIP	New In Package
NL	Number Line (books)—a means of telling the edition; occurs on copyright page and reads "*1234567890*"; lowest number indicates the edition
NM	Near Mint
NORES	No Reserve
NOS	New Old Stock
NP	Not Packaged
NPB	Non-Paying Bidder/Buyer
NR	No Reserve
N/R	No Reserve
NRFB	Never Removed From Box
NRFSB	Never Removed From Sealed Box
NRMNT	Near Mint
NW	Never Worn (clothes)
NWOT	New Without Tags
NWT	New With Tags
O	New Orleans Mint
OB	Original Box
OC	Off Center; Off Cut; On Canvas
O/C	On Canvas (paintings)
OEM	Original Equipment Manufacturer
OF	Original Finish
OJ	Occupied Japan
OOAK	One of A Kind
OOP	Out of Package; Out of Print
OP	Out of Print
OS	Operating System (computers)
OST	Original Soundtrack

B

Abbreviation	Definition
P	Poor Condition
PB	Paperback or paperbound (books)
PBO	Paperback Original
PC	Picture Postcard; Postcard; Poor Condition
PD	Picture Disk (the record itself has a photo or images on it)
PF	Proof Coin
PIC	Picture
Pink/Pinkliner	eBay staff member who posts a message on a discussion board
PM	Post Mark; Postal Marking; Priority Mail
P/O	Punch-Out (inventory that has been "declassified" with a hole punch)
POC	Pencil On Cover
POPS	Promo Only Picture Sleeve
POTF	Power of the Force (*Star Wars*)
PP	Parcel Post
PPD	Post Paid
PR	Poor Condition
PROOF	Proof Coin
PS	Power Supply, Picture Sleeve (records)
P/S	Picture Sleeve (records)
R	Reprint
RBC	Right Side of Back Cover
RC	Reader Copy (books)—a copy of a book in good condition, not mint
RET	Retired
RETRD	Retired
RFC	Right Side of Front Cover
RFDO	Removed For Display Only
RI	Reissue (records)
RMA	Return Merchandise Authorization Number
ROM	Romantic (books)
ROTJ	Return Of The Jedi (*Star Wars*)
RP	Real Photo Postcard
RPPC	Real Photo Postcard
RRH	Remade/Repainted/Haired (dolls)
RS	Rhinestones; Rubber Stamped on label (records)
RSP	Rhodium Sterling Plate

Abbreviation	Definition
RT	Right
S	Small; Stereo (records)
SA	Silver Age
SB	Soft Bound or Soft Back (referring to large softbound books)
SC	Slight Crease (hang tags, books, magazines); Sawcut (slice cut off record album jacket)
SCI	Science (books)
SCR	Scratch
SCU	Scuff (records)
SF	Science Fiction
SFBC	Science Fiction Book Club
SH	Shipping and Handling
S/H	Shipping and Handling
SHI	Shipping, Handling, and Insurance
S/H/I	Shipping, Handling, and Insurance
SIG	Signature
SLD	Sealed
SLT	Slight
SLW	Straight Leg Walker (dolls)
Snail Mail	USPS delivery
SO	Sold Out
S/O	Sold Out
SOL	Sticker on Label (records)
SP	Sticker Pull (books)—discoloration or actual removal of cover color caused by pulling off a sticker price
S/P	Salt and Pepper (shakers); Silverplate; Silver Plated
SPAM	Unwanted or unrequested e-mail
SR	Slight Ring Wear; Shrink Wrapped
SS	Stainless Steel; Still Sealed
S/S	Still Sealed
ST	Sound Track (records, CDs); *Star Trek*; Sterling
STCCG	*Star Trek* Collectable Card Game
STER	Sterling; Sterling Silver
STNG	*Star Trek: The Next Generation*
SUSP	Suspended, Suspense (books)
SW	Slight Wear; *Star Wars*; Shrink Wrapped

B

Abbreviation	Definition
SWCCG	*Star Wars* Collectable Card Game
SWCS	*Star Wars* Collector Series (toys)
SYI	Sell Your Item Form
TBB	Teenie Beanie Babies
TC	True Crime (books)
TE	Trade Edition (books)—standard paperback edition of a book
TM	Trademark
TMOL	Tape Mark on Label (records)
TNG	The Next Generation (*Star Trek*)
TOBC	Top of Back Cover
TOFC	Top of Front Cover
TOL	Tear on Label (records)
TOONS	Cartoon Art (paperbacks)
TOS	Tape on Spine; Terms of Service; The Original Series (*Star Trek*)
TOUGH	Tough Guy Genre (paperbacks)
TRPQ	Tall, Round, Pyroglaze Quart (milk bottles)
U	Used
UB	Undivided Back (postcards)
UDV	Undivided Back (postcards)
ULBC	Upper Left (corner) Back Cover (books, magazines)
ULRC	Upper Right (corner) Back Cover (books, magazines)
UNC	Uncirculated (coins)
UPS	United Parcel Service
URL	Uniform Resource Locator (web address)
URFC	Upper Right Corner of Front Cover
USPS	United States Postal Service
VERM	Vermeil—gold plating on sterling silver, bronze, or copper
VF	Very Fine Condition
VFD	Vacuum Fluorescent Display
VFU	Very Fine, Used (stamps)
VG	Very Good Condition
VHTF	Very Hard to Find
V/M/D	Visa/MasterCard/Discover Card
W	West Point Mint/Depository (coins)

Abbreviation	Definition
WB	White Border (postcards)
WC	Watercolor (paintings, maps)
W/C	Watercolor (paintings, maps)
WD	White Dog (RCA record labels)
WLP	White Label Promo
WOB	Writing on Back
WOC	Writing on Cover
WOF	Writing on Front
WOR	Writing on Record
WRP	Warp (records)
WS	Widescreen (same as letterbox)
WSOL	Water Stain on Label (records)
XL	Extra Large

Appendix C

eBay Business Marketplace Categories

Your eBay experience shouldn't be limited to the business section of the eBay site. Based on the type of business you run and the access to different inventory, especially the unusual, one-of-a-kind, or experience-related inventory you could offer, your auctions could span multiple main categories.

Entire eBay Site of Categories

Whether you're selling your company cars on eBay Motors, company-sponsored event tickets on the Tickets category, or excess uniforms on the Apparel category, eBay has a category for you. Just take a look at the main categories and subcategories that eBay has to offer. This snapshot was taken on a day in March 2004, and the numbers in parentheses represent the current number of auctions in that one category at that given moment.

What the snapshots will not show you are the thousands of "sub-subcategories" that allow collectors to group very specific auctions into one place, so people can find that 1967 GI Joe figure or that 1895 Indian penny. What the snapshot demonstrates is that the main categories and hundreds of primary subcategories cover an extensive range of merchandise you could offer for sale. If you don't believe us, take a look:

Antiques (230,865)

Antiquities (Classical, Amer.) (10,366)	Architectural & Garden (10,056)
Asian Antiques (46,847)	Books, Manuscripts (4353)
Decorative Arts (29,810)	Ethnographic (3746)
Furniture (11,267)	Maps, Atlases, Globes (10,357)
Maritime (3829)	Musical Instruments (835)
Primitives (11,291)	Rugs, Carpets (20,397)
Science & Medicine (1848)	Silver (37,358)
Textiles, Linens (16,226)	Other Antiques (12,279)

Art (223,679)

Digital Art (939)	Drawings (3975)
Folk Art (7595)	Mixed Media (2036)
Paintings (49,633)	Photographic Images (14,062)
Posters (22,863)	Prints (91,244)
Sculpture, Carvings (8958)	Self-Representing Artists (10,414)
Wholesale Lots (3136)	Other Art (8824)

Books (732,009)

Accessories (2548)	Antiquarian & Collectible (64,921)
Audio (25,999)	Children (68,053)
Education & Textbooks (40,394)	Fiction & Literature (137,522)
Magazines & Catalogs (99,221)	Nonfiction (281,993)
Wholesale, Bulk Lots (3064)	Other (8294)

Business & Industrial (229,631)

Construction (18,351)	Electronic Components (16,011)
Farm (14,796)	Healthcare, Medical (7167)
Industrial Supply, MRO (31,448)	Laboratory & Life Science (9417)
Metalworking (30,375)	Office Products (35,087)
Plastics Equipment & Materials (681)	Printing & Graphic Arts (6062)
Process Equipment (1307)	Restaurant (14,569)
Retail Equipment & Supplies (14,917)	Semiconductor, PCB Equipment (864)
Test Equipment (13,468)	Textile, Apparel Manufacturing (812)
Websites & Businesses for Sale (8310)	Woodworking (2385)
Other Industries (3604)	

Cameras & Photo (175,447)

Camcorder Accessories (11,955)	Camcorders (8722)
Digital Camera Accessories (33,366)	Digital Cameras (28,049)
Film (2021)	Film Camera Accessories (13,340)
Film Cameras (24,099)	Film Processing & Darkroom (3271)
Lenses (12,906)	Lighting & Studio Equipment (6193)
Manuals, Guides & Books (3379)	Photo Albums & Archive Items (1600)
Printers, Scanners & Supplies (2173)	Professional Video Equipment (5329)
Projection Equipment (3438)	Stock Photography & Footage (311)
Telescopes & Binoculars (3606)	Tripods, Monopods (2473)
Vintage (8861)	Wholesale Lots (355)

Clothing, Shoes & Accessories (1,636,134)

Boys (52,664)	Girls (117,401)
Infants & Toddlers (178,170)	Men's Accessories (67,120)
Men's Clothing (217,871)	Men's Shoes (56,323)
Uniforms (9041)	Wedding Apparel (29,262)
Women's Accessories, Handbags (143,715)	Women's Clothing (570,361)
Women's Shoes (115,136)	Vintage (68,876)
Wholesale, Large & Small Lots (10,194)	

Coins (209,974)

Bullion (11,219)	Coins: Ancient (8227)
Coins: US (109,237)	Coins: World (44,762)
Exonumia (9825)	Paper Money: US (9626)
Paper Money: World (14,112)	Scripophily (2966)

Collectibles (2,032,577)

Advertising (139,995)	Animals (126,399)
Animation Art, Characters (58,161)	Autographs (11,575)
Barware (14,572)	Bottles & Insulators (18,926)
Breweriana, Beer (46,131)	Clocks (12,470)
Coin-Op, Banks & Casino (34,468)	Comics (147,575)
Cultures, Ethnicities (59,939)	Decorative Collectibles (192,906)
Disneyana (64,262)	Fantasy, Mythical & Magic (22,734)
Furniture, Appliances & Fans (1449)	Historical Memorabilia (102,855)
Holiday, Seasonal (36,365)	Housewares & Kitchenware (79,102)
Knives, Swords & Blades (48,106)	Lamps, Lighting (16,554)
Linens, Fabric & Textiles (30,363)	Metalware (17,807)
Militaria (109,976)	Pens & Writing Instruments (16,422)
Pez, Keychains, Promo Glasses (8824)	Photographic Images (38,639)
Pinbacks, Nodders, Lunchboxes (16,353)	Postcards & Paper (189,909)
Radio, Phonograph, TV, Phone (16,499)	Religions, Spirituality (30,518)
Rocks, Fossils, Minerals (24,049)	Science Fiction (20,621)
Science, Medical (11,671)	Tobacciana (45,930)
Tools, Hardware & Locks (13,953)	Trading Cards (46,315)

Transportation (117,242)

Vintage Sewing (20,976)

Vanity, Perfume & Shaving (19,051)

Wholesale Lots (2915)

Computers & Networking (405,963)

Apple, Macintosh Computers (10,581)

Desktop PCs (11,058)

Input Devices (10,918)

Laptops (19,292)

Networking (56,405)

Printer Supplies & Accessories (47,959)

Software (68,263)

Video & Multimedia (15,772)

Desktop PC Components (48,548)

Drives & Controllers (29,365)

Laptop Parts & Accessories (42,774)

Monitors (6210)

Printers (20,164)

Scanners (2388)

Technology Books (7537)

Other Hardware & Services (8729)

Consumer Electronics (427,655)

Car Electronics (45,245)

DVD Players & Recorders (6899)

Gadgets & Other Electronics (23,843)

Home Theater Systems (2697)

PDAs/Handheld PCs (35,827)

Satellite, Cable TV (12,492)

Televisions (10,349)

Wholesale Lots (2122)

Cell Phones & Plans (186,377)

Digital Video Recorders, PVR (686)

Home Audio (43,847)

MP3, Portable Audio (22,724)

Radios: CB, Ham & Shortwave (19,917)

Telephones & Pagers (12,812)

VCRs (1818)

Crafts (296,362)

Basketry (491)

Bear Making Supplies (364)

Candle & Soap Making (7513)

Crocheting (9189)

Decorative, Tole Painting (6425)

Dolls (136,913)

Embroidery (9712)

Fabric Embellishments (5857)

Framing, Matting (891)

Bead Art (5377)

Bears (35,030)

Ceramics, Pottery (7312)

Cross Stitch (26,035)

Dollhouse Miniatures (17,127)

Dolls & Bears (192,851)

Fabric (38,512)

Floral Supplies (2743)

General Art & Craft Supplies (4114)

C

Glass Art Supplies (1074)

Handcrafted Items (4180)

Kids Crafts (1683)

Knitting (6816)

Lacemaking, Tatting (420)

Latch, Rug Hooking (1308)

Leathercraft (3426)

Macramé (403)

Metalworking (222)

Mosaic (3729)

Needlepoint (6344)

Painting & Drawing (6344)

Paper Crafts, Origami (834)

Paper Dolls (2728)

Quilting (10,151)

Scrapbooking (50,638)

Sewing (23,552)

Shellcraft (282)

Spinning (1240)

Stamping (21,702)

Weaving (753)

Woodworking (7535)

Yarn (11,475)

Other Arts & Crafts (8080)

Wholesale Lots (689)

DVDs & Movies (413,687)

DVD (220,489)

Film (2742)

Laserdisc (6503)

VHS (176,186)

VHS Non-US (PAL) (2237)

Other Formats (2318)

Wholesale Lots (3212)

Entertainment Memorabilia (332,040)

Autographs (33,681)

Movie Memorabilia (114,302)

Music Memorabilia (134,032)

Television Memorabilia (29,135)

Theater Memorabilia (4964)

Video Game Memorabilia (706)

Other Memorabilia (15,220)

Health & Beauty (244,533)

Body Art, Tattoos (2932)

Body Care, Personal Hygiene (34,676)

Coupons (380)

Face Care (28,484)

Fragrances (45,364)

Hair Care (13,044)

Makeup (59,731)

Manicure, Pedicure (7409)

Medical, Special Needs (10,393)

Nutrition & Wellness (29,710)

Vision Care (2925)

Wholesale Lots (3051)

Other Health & Beauty Items (6434)

Home & Garden (700,955)

Baby Gear & Furnishings (44,661)	Bath (17,806)
Bedding (45,593)	Building & Repair Materials (24,379)
Food & Wine (19,587)	Furniture (35,588)
Home Decor (164,341)	Housekeeping & Organizing (15,642)
Kitchen, Dining & Bar (89,581)	Lamps, Lighting, Ceiling Fans (21,048)
Lawn & Garden (80,806)	Major Appliances (4746)
Outdoor Living (10,004)	Pet Supplies (42,099)
Rugs & Carpets (11,540)	Tools (56,685)
Window Treatments (9260)	Wholesale Lots (7589)

Jewelry & Watches (893,320)

Anklets (3392)	Authenticator Pre-Certified (46)
Bracelets (36,967)	Cameos (2341)
Charms & Charm Bracelets (14,426)	Designer, Artisan Jewelry (17,370)
Earrings (56,760)	Ethnic, Tribal Jewelry (22,529)
Fashion Jewelry (70,097)	Hair Jewelry (2730)
Jewelry Boxes (5947)	Jewelry Supplies (19,835)
Loose Beads (71,652)	Loose Gemstones (44,648)
Men's (20,611)	Necklaces (46,717)
Pendants & Lockets (44,188)	Pins, Brooches (11,654)
Rings (99,812)	Sets (4185)
Vintage, Antique (62,015)	Watches (87,231)
Other Items (4638)	Wholesale Lots (13,695)

Music (465,257)

Accessories (2751)	Cassettes (10,647)
CDs (275,454)	DVD Audio (1021)
Records (166,896)	Super Audio CDs (307)
Other Formats (6447)	Wholesale Lots (1734)
Musical Instruments (143,743)	Electronic (3236)
Brass (4683)	Guitar (47,586)
Equipment (1810)	Keyboard, Piano (7416)
Harmonica (1276)	Pro Audio (25,869)

C

Percussion (11,123)

String (10,376)

Sheet Music, Song Books (20,686)

Wholesale Lots (454)

Woodwind (7881)

Other Instruments (1347)

Pottery & Glass (384,526)

Glass (133,095)

Pottery & China (251,431)

Real Estate (3471)

Commercial (349)

Land (1015)

Residential (901)

Timeshares for Sale (998)

Other Real Estate (208)

Specialty Services (9196)

Advice & Instruction (456)

Artistic Services (417)

Custom Clothing & Jewelry (414)

eBay Auction Services (81)

Graphic & Logo Design (242)

Media Editing & Duplication (86)

Printing & Personalization (5609)

Restoration & Repair (155)

Web & Computer Services (894)

Other Services (842)

Sporting Goods & Fan Shop (697,289)

Airsoft (6016)

Archery (7304)

Baseball & Softball (15,171)

Basketball (6014)

Billiards (6538)

Bowling (4614)

Boxing (1493)

Camping, Hiking, Backpacking (15,665)

Canoes, Kayaks, Rafts (1990)

Climbing (1584)

Cycling (29,653)

Equestrian (34,724)

Exercise & Fitness (12,338)

Fan Shop (251,151)

Fishing (60,313)

Football (6734)

Go-Karts, Recreational (990)

Golf (75,304)

Hunting (57,601)

Hockey—Ice & Roller (6203)

Ice Skating (1461)

Indoor Games (3088)

Inline, Roller Skating (2602)	Lacrosse (767)
Martial Arts (5404)	Paintball (12,686)
Racquetball & Squash (584)	Running (1432)
Scooters (4297)	Scuba, Snorkeling (6997)
Skateboarding (6467)	Skiing & Snowboarding (11,002)
Snowmobiling (3825)	Soccer (12,024)
Tennis (4149)	Triathlon (409)
Water Sports (7302)	Other Sports (9701)
Wholesale Lots (1692)	

Sports Cards & Memorabilia (524,592)

Cards (419,678)	Memorabilia (104,914)

Stamps (176,705)

United States (53,875)	Australia (4323)
Canada (8041)	Br. Comm. Other (13,361)
UK (Great Britain) (13,574)	Africa (1903)
Asia (7429)	Europe (33,079)
Latin America (4542)	Middle East (3589)
Publications & Supplies (2608)	Topical & Specialty (15,909)
Worldwide (14,472)	

Tickets (51,859)

Event Tickets (49,268)	Experiences (1535)
Other Items (1056)	

Toys & Hobbies (875,974)

Action Figures (111,737)	Baby Toys (3774)
Beanbag Plush, Beanie Babies (39,608)	Building Toys (14,157)
Classic Toys (9797)	Diecast, Toy Vehicles (182,579)
Educational (7411)	Electronic, Battery, Wind-Up (8427)

C

Fast Food, Cereal Premiums (7286)

Games (83,414)

Model RR, Trains (67,415)

Models, Kits (48,092)

Outdoor Toys, Structures (4036)

Pretend Play, Preschool (23,472)

Puzzles (11,816)

Radio Control (37,778)

Robots, Monsters, Space Toys (4861)

Slot Cars (9665)

Stuffed Animals (12,638)

Toy Soldiers (8464)

Trading Card Games (70,492)

TV, Movie, Character Toys (84,840)

Vintage, Antique Toys (20,386)

Wholesale Lots (3829)

Travel (12,862)

Airline (185)

Cruises (224)

Lodging (1257)

Luggage (7936)

Vacation Packages (478)

Other Travel (2782)

Video Games (190,654)

Accessories (36,499)

Games (116,039)

Internet Games (17,354)

Systems (11,644)

Vintage Games (5494)

Other (2566)

Wholesale Lots (1058)

Everything Else (208,120)

eBay User Tools (1549)

Education & Learning (10,398)

Genealogy (7172)

Gifts & Occasions (52,599)

Information Products (5695)

Mature Audiences (83,644)

Memberships (326)

Metaphysical (15,847)

Personal Security (4247)

Religious Products & Supplies (3232)

Reward Pts, Incentive Programs (1230)

Test Auctions (641)

Weird Stuff (21,540)

Index

INTERNATIONAL CONTACT INFORMATION

AUSTRALIA
McGraw-Hill Book Company
Australia Pty. Ltd.
TEL +61-2-9900-1800
FAX +61-2-9878-8881
http://www.mcgraw-hill.com.au
books-it_sydney@mcgraw-hill.com

CANADA
McGraw-Hill Ryerson Ltd.
TEL +905-430-5000
FAX +905-430-5020
http://www.mcgraw-hill.ca

GREECE, MIDDLE EAST, & AFRICA (Excluding South Africa)
McGraw-Hill Hellas
TEL +30-210-6560-990
TEL +30-210-6560-993
TEL +30-210-6560-994
FAX +30-210-6545-525

MEXICO (Also serving Latin America)
McGraw-Hill Interamericana Editores
S.A. de C.V.
TEL +525-1500-5108
FAX +525-117-1589
http://www.mcgraw-hill.com.mx
carlos_ruiz@mcgraw-hill.com

SINGAPORE (Serving Asia)
McGraw-Hill Book Company
TEL +65-6863-1580
FAX +65-6862-3354
http://www.mcgraw-hill.com.sg
mghasia@mcgraw-hill.com

SOUTH AFRICA
McGraw-Hill South Africa
TEL +27-11-622-7512
FAX +27-11-622-9045
robyn_swanepoel@mcgraw-hill.com

SPAIN
McGraw-Hill/
Interamericana de España, S.A.U.
TEL +34-91-180-3000
FAX +34-91-372-8513
http://www.mcgraw-hill.es
professional@mcgraw-hill.es

UNITED KINGDOM, NORTHERN, EASTERN, & CENTRAL EUROPE
McGraw-Hill Education Europe
TEL +44-1-628-502500
FAX +44-1-628-770224
http://www.mcgraw-hill.co.uk
emea_queries@mcgraw-hill.com

ALL OTHER INQUIRIES Contact:
McGraw-Hill/Osborne
TEL +1-510-420-7700
FAX +1-510-420-7703
http://www.osborne.com
omg_international@mcgraw-hill.com

Sound Off!

Visit us at **www.osborne.com/bookregistration** and let us know what you thought of this book. While you're online you'll have the opportunity to register for newsletters and special offers from McGraw-Hill/Osborne.

We want to hear from you!

Sneak Peek

Visit us today at **www.betabooks.com** and see what's coming from McGraw-Hill/Osborne tomorrow!

Based on the successful software paradigm, Bet@Books™ allows computing professionals to view partial and sometimes complete text versions of selected titles online. Bet@Books™ viewing is free, invites comments and feedback, and allows you to "test drive" books in progress on the subjects that interest you the most.

eBay Your Way to Success

eBay Your Business:
Maximize Profits and
Get Results
0072257113

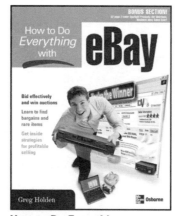

How to Do Everything
with eBay
0072254262

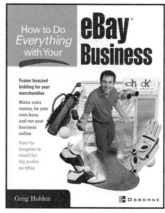

How to Do Everything
with Your eBay Business
007222948-9

eBay PowerSeller Secrets
0072258691

Available at bookstores everywhere